# The Sikhs

# The Sikhs

in relation to Hindus, Moslems, Christians, and Ahmadiyyas. A Study in Comparative Religion, by

John Clark Archer

NEW YORK
RUSSELL & RUSSELL

REISSUED, 1971, BY RUSSELL & RUSSELL
A DIVISION OF ATHENEUM PUBLISHERS, INC.
BY ARRANGEMENT WITH PRINCETON UNIVERSITY PRESS
L. C. CATALOG NO: 76-139895
PRINTED IN THE UNITED STATES OF AMERICA

# Preface

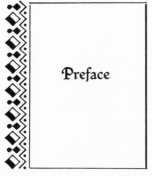

THE Sikhs of India, together with at least ten per cent of their numbers in service or in residence abroad, preserve among themselves a hardy tradition of religious and political activity and enjoy among Hindus, Moslems, Christians and other peoples an extraordinary prestige. Their movement, which can be accounted for within the compass of the last five centuries, originated actually in an earnest, hopeful effort toward the reconciliation, within India at least, of Hindu and Islamic orders and ideas. Their subsequent development provided them in India with opportunities of association with Christianity also. And all the while their religion and their institutions developed somewhat at variance from initial purposes, and Sikhism became an independent and conspicuous order of its own, with a character worthy of comparison at last with that of Hinduism and Islam, and with Christianity in particular. Although Sikhism may have developed separately out of its very failure to accomplish its initial purpose, the failure may be called to some extent successful. The five centuries of Sikh history provide many lessons in human thought and action which are of more than passing value—often bearing quite directly, for example, upon the major problems of comparative religion.

This volume is essentially a study in comparative religion, while devoting prolonged attention to the Sikhs and their religion in themselves. It essays a dual role, therefore, not altogether easy of accomplishment, but one which can be wholly justified by the Indian circumstances and the exigencies of comparison, if all readers will keep the dual role in mind. On the one hand, Sikhs in their homeland and Sikh history confront us with the need of some recital of pertinent events in their proper sequence. On the other hand, this recital provides materials in illustration of the principles which operate—or at least seem to operate—during the interactions of any and all contiguous religions. At all events, the liberty is taken now and then as the story of the Sikhs unfolds of inquiring into the story's meaning for the whole field of comparative religion.

Studies of the Sikhs are already numerous and the materials for study are increasingly accessible. Perhaps the fullest bibliography yet published in a book is that consisting of one hundred and thirty-two titles of Persian, Urdu, Gurmukhi, Hindi and English works included in Ganda Singh's *Banda Singh Bahadur*, Amritsar, April 1935. Among the sixty-five English titles are the notable volumes of M. A. Macauliffe on *The Sikh Religion*, of Khazan Singh on *The History and Philosophy of the Sikh Religion*, and J. D. Cunningham's *History of the Sikhs*—although reference should be made to the new and revised edition of Cunningham edited extensively by H. L. O. Garrett and published in 1918. Since Ganda Singh's primary concern was Banda Singh, he made no mention of many of the works which Cunningham relied on and listed in his *History*. Nor does he mention Dr. Ernest Trumpp's monumental translation of the *Adi Granth*, the Sikh holy scriptures. L. R. Krishna's *Les Sikhs*, N. K. Sinha's *Rise of Sikh Power*, and many another title might be added to these lists, including Ganda Singh's own *History of the Gurdwara Shahidganj*, Bhai Jodh Singh's *Gurmati Nirnay* and Teja Singh's *The Psalm of Peace*. But all these works either deal exclusively with Sikh history and religion, or else provide the general setting for the same. They do not undertake comparative appraisal; they are *not*, strictly speaking, studies in comparative religion, whether with respect to the relation of religion to other disciplines of life or with reference to Sikhism in comparison with other faiths. The volume which this preface introduces now is by contrast with the others a study in comparative religion based upon a study of the Sikhs.

The first two chapters of the present work depict the Sikhs of today in their north Indian habitat, primarily, and indicate many of the most influential factors in their history. This contemporary entrance into their midst is intended to be realistic, to give a picture of the living Sikh community. The still more definitely historical portion of the volume begins with Chapter III and concludes with Chapter XI, except that Chapter VI is devoted to the teachings of the founder Nanak and to his peculiar book of psalms. Chapter XII includes a comparative view of many things in prospect, with some reference to the Sikhs' own prospective role in Indian reconstruction. The twelve pictorial illustrations come from negatives exposed by the author. The glossary, immediately preceding the index, includes brief definitions and explanations of relatively unfamiliar words used in the book. The index will introduce, or else recall, to any reader the specific contents of the volume.

The expression Disciples of Timeless Truth (Akal Sat ke Sikhen, as in the Urdu on the title page and elsewhere) is derived immediately from Sikh history, but is used to serve a wider purpose in the process of comparison among the many faiths. Sikhs are themselves, as their very name implies, "disciples." They have been in quest of "truth," and profess to have discovered in their quest the "timeless." They are devotees of God, but have worshiped him as Sat Nam, "True Name," their own chosen designation, being themselves disinclined to use more specific names such as the devotees of other faiths so often use, lest such a name might unduly qualify for them the timeless truth.

Exact markings are not generally included in the transliterations of foreign words, nor are these words italicized—

they are treated typographically as they are intellectually, as part of the regular texture of the book.

Sikhs in general have not denied that truth may have its temporal expressions, although they have not explicitly affirmed that truth's own disciples anywhere in any faithful household may achieve its essence and share its immortality. They have indeed acknowledged the mortality of all men with themselves as seekers of the truth *in time*. Sikhs may stand, therefore, as symbols and examples of all who search for God and truth, in whatever measure these are to be found, and this volume appeals to Sikhs and their career for insight and instruction in historical and comparative religion. The author stands in the guest's debt to many of them, but to Bhai Jodh Singh and the Khalsa College of Amritsar, its staff, students and resources, as of 1937, in particular. Acknowledgment of further obligation, including much unspecified, is made here and there in some detail throughout the book. The ample footnotes mention many special sources and often comment on their value. Perhaps the author's greatest obligation, after all, is to the Trustees and staff of Princeton University Press for the publication of the work, and he records with peculiar gratitude his indebtedness to his wife for her pertinent comments on the form and content of the manuscript during composition. Of course, India itself is ever in the author's mind and he would here acknowledge his lasting debt to the people of the land who have produced so much for the world's good, of whom the Sikhs themselves are noble and prominent examples who have suggested progress for humanity through their own peculiar discipline. He would toast them in the figure if not the substance of their own resistless *amrita*.

JOHN CLARK ARCHER

*Yale University*
*New Haven, Connecticut*
*January 1, 1945*

# Contents

# List of Illustrations

# The Sikhs

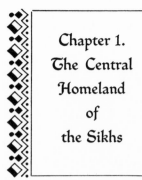

# Chapter 1. The Central Homeland of the Sikhs

THE outward forms of Sikhism—if this religion may be thus designated for the present—are often most attractive. Several of its houses of worship are impressive and unique in a land of many famous shrines and monuments. The most notable are in the Panjab, in Amritsar, Tarn Taran and Lahore. But even the unpretentious gurdwaras of the Sikhs in the villages reflect the faith itself and preserve the essential meaning of all Sikhs' common worship. Sikhism has its own peculiar scriptures, also, in use in public and in private worship. These are known in general as The Book. The religion has its treasury of relics and its own peculiar symbols. And Sikhs as worthy sons and daughters of the Indian motherland have furnished many leaders of real consequence in Indian affairs, among whom stand Nanak, Arjun, Gobindji and Ranjit Singh.

The inner values of the faith may not be immediately apparent, but they are no less real than the more visible forms themselves. Sikhism is a variety of Indian religion and it reveals even in its variation something of essential India. Indeed Sikhism in itself reveals something of what in the last analysis *religion* is. The Sikh movement is comparatively modern in a land of ancient precedents. Nanak was the very first Sikh or "disciple" in the special sense.[1] Coming late upon the scene and finding so much conflict in religion, he proposed hopefully that hostilities should cease, that the warring factions adjust their differences and be reconciled through a method which he offered. But we may

[1] The term has a history of its own, of course, and there are other designations, also, applied to certain Sikhs, as we shall see, by some who would disparage them.

ask what were the conflicts of the day, and out of what had they arisen? And we may appropriately inquire if Nanak really understood the issues and what it was that he proposed by way of solving them? We must go deeper still and ask if religions then *could* be reconciled and, if so, by what means? What prompted Nanak? Could he, did he, point to any antecedent instance of reconciliation in religion?

Whatever he knew, hoped for or proposed, upwards of six millions of his followers remember him devotedly, and among the multitudes who know about him and his order are 265 millions of Hindus and 85 or 90 millions of Moslems in India alone. The Indian Moslems do not hold the Sikhs in high esteem, and Sikhs count Moslems enemies. Most Hindus, however, are tolerant toward Sikhs, and perhaps one-half of the Sikh community is not readily to be distinguished by ordinary outward signs from their Hindu kinsfolk. Both halves are friendly with the Hindus, but one-half bears distinctive marks representing an enduring order which is at once non-Moslem and non-Hindu. This half is the Khalsa or "nation" of Gobind Singh, which came into existence a century and a quarter after Nanak's death and gave the Sikh community a new identity which, although precarious at first, laid later a sure claim to fame. But all Sikhs share more or less a communal consciousness, and have been dealt with in India for some time on such a basis.

Our chief concern, under the circumstances, must be with Sikhs who are distinctive. Our approach to the whole community must be undertaken through them, if we are to understand Sikhism most readily in relation to the total Indian setting. This does not necessarily mean that the Sikh movement is best judged exclusively by Indian standards. There may be universal criteria and general rules of judgment to which the values of Sikhism in the end must yield. We might indeed appropriately remind ourselves for the moment that Sikhism, by being essentially Indian, comes

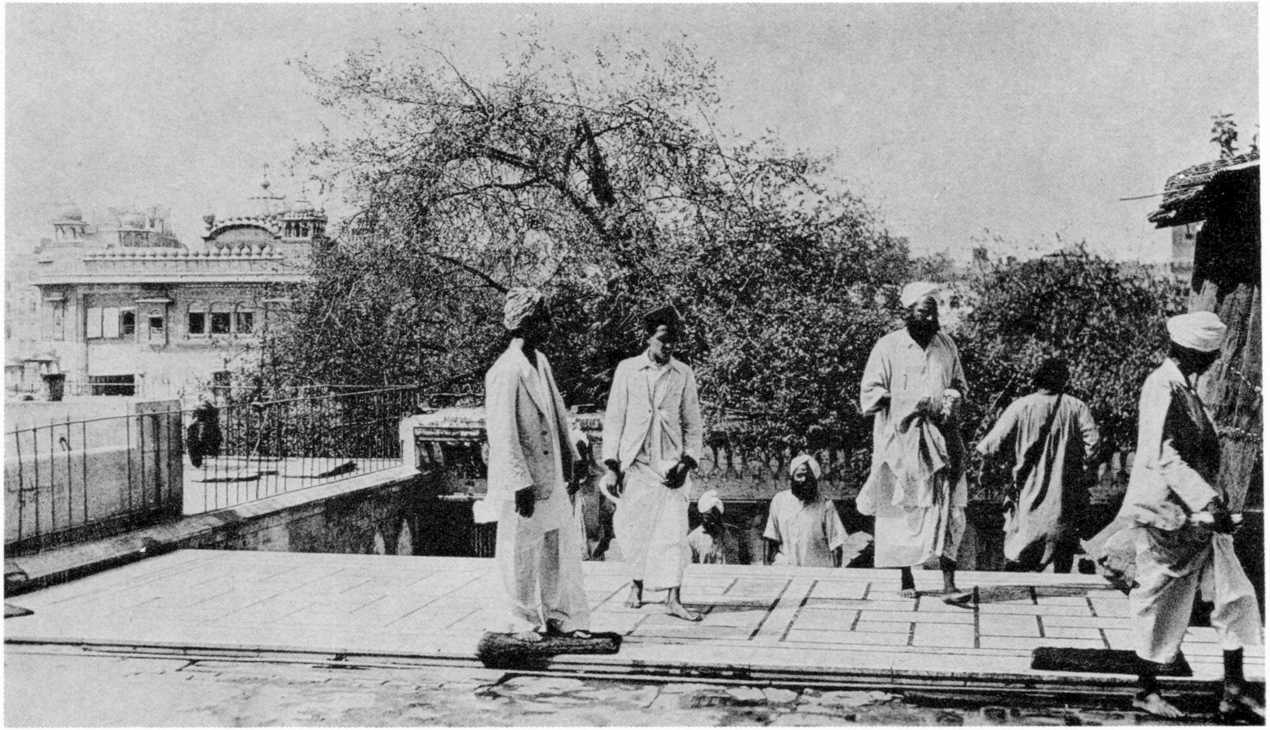

THE GOLDEN TEMPLE OF AMRITSAR, THE BABA BUDDHA TREE AND DEVOTEES MOSTLY BEARDED SINGHS —A SCENE AT THE NORTHERN ENTRANCE

THE DARBAR SAHIB (GOLDEN TEMPLE) IN THE POOL OF IMMORTALITY (AMRITSAR),
SEEN FROM THE LOWER PAVEMENT ALONG THE NORTHERN EDGE

within the scope of culture which includes much of the West, also. This study, therefore, need not take the westerner too far afield, but may rather serve to acquaint him further with elements of an extensive Indo-European cultural tradition. While Sikhism has thrived almost wholly in a foreign sphere—foreign to the West, that is—Sikhs have been for long familiar figures in police and military service in Durban, Aden, Penang, Singapore, Hong Kong and Shanghai, posts of passage for many western travelers. Moreover, Sikhism has run a course parallel in time with the modern Christian era of social, religious and political reconstruction.

The fact that Sikhs and Sikhism have played a prominent and influential part in British imperial affairs need not dispose us to a partisan political appraisal of their movement, even though circumstances lately have linked Britain and America by peculiar ties of fellowship. Politics, of course, cannot be excluded from the picture. Perhaps it was politics, primarily, which after a while gave Sikhism a much altered character in relation with the Mughals and the British. Nanak himself seemed to give no thought to politics, unless to reject it. Was he in this regard more truly Indian—or less? Can a religion be altogether other-worldly, can a religion endure abstraction and yet live? Or does the role of a religion vary with the times? We are seeking in this present study some answers to such questions. Man's world, we know, is one of change, in which the essential and the circumstantial make insistent and compromising demands on one another.

An illustration might be immediately in order to indicate a way in which politics operated in the movement's later history, thus supplementing the founder's (Nanak's) otherworldliness and showing how the temporal and the spiritual competed: in the latter days of the Sikh Khalsa Moslem pilgrims bound for Mecca from interior India by way of Persia avoided the convenient route which ran through Sikh territory along the Sutlej river in the Panjab.[2] The English wife[3] of an Indian Moslem, herself contemporary with the situation she describes, says there seemed to be "always a disposition to fear the Sikhs, who are become a powerful nation." She does not indicate the ground of fear, unless, as she says, it lay in the circumstance that Indian Moslem pilgrims "could scarcely expect the same courtesy from [Sikh] peoples" that they received from others, whether Hindus or fellow Moslems of India and Persia. According to some other sources, even sectarian Shiite Persian Moslems allowed free and undisturbed passage to Meccan pilgrims, who usually were mostly orthodox Sunnis. But Sikhs, for good and sufficient reason, both religious and political, were hostile then toward *all* Moslems. The two communities had fought each other frequently and the Sikhs—the time was that of Ranjit Singh—had won the supremacy of the Panjab. It was obvious[4] that Sikhism under Ranjit was not a "pure and undefiled" religion. Even before Ranjit's day Sikh politics had established many precedents. For one thing, there had been a line of Gurus, personal guides and counselors, from Nanak down to Gobind Singh—ten in all—some of whom had had recourse to political expediency in their perpetuation of the faith.

While we shall take account of many factors in the story of the Sikhs, we are not intent upon a history in the sense of *all* the major facts, whether these be persons, events or institutions. Our concern is a review of a minimum of materials

[2] This name, when properly pronounced, sounds like the English *pun* and *job*.

[3] Mrs. Meer Hasan Ali. See her *Observations on the Mussulmauns*, 1832 (2nd edition, London, 1917), p. 114. *Note:* Indian Moslems, or, more exactly, Muslims, have been commonly called by the variant title Musalman or otherwise, a form derived from a Persian plural equivalent to the Arabic *muslim*, or *muslimin*.

[4] Mrs. Hasan Ali and others were aware of this.

which may explain Sikhism as a venture in the reconciliation of religions, which issued ultimately in a distinct religious order and a separate political community. If now we undertake for a brief space to scan the present order we call Sikh,[5] we shall find the bulk of it still within the broad stretches of the level, alluvial region along the borders of the Sutlej river. The Sutlej is a major tributary to the extensive Indus river system whose waters run finally into the Arabian Sea. It is the traditional southern boundary of the Panjab, this famous land of the "five rivers" all tributary to the Indus, and it figured critically in territorial arrangements between the British and the Sikhs.

We may with prudence as well as convenience visit first the important Panjabi city of Amritsar. It bears the name the Sikhs themselves have given it. It is a Sikh foundation and is their premier city, although they usually make up only about ten per cent of the city's total population of over two hundred thousand persons. The ninety per cent is made up of Musalmans (*cf.* note 3, above) and Hindus in somewhat equal numbers. It is the site of the Sikhs' central shrine which they call the Darbar Sahib or, in several English equivalents, the Lordly House, the Court of Honor, or the Hall of Audience. Westerners know it better by the name of Golden Temple.

This lordly, honorable house of worship,[6] the principal place of visitation for all varieties of Sikhs, is in itself a symbol and expression of the comparatively minor role which Sikhs have played in Indian affairs. And yet the temple's setting of a sacred pool of *a-mrits-ar*, or "un-dying-waters" frequently renewed, is also symbolic of some refreshment

[5] In this name we have been using, the *i* is rather short than long, having a sound somewhere between the *i* of the English *sick* and the *ee* of the English *seek*. Sikh actually means a "seeker, a learner, a disciple" of Truth and True Name.

[6] See illustration No. 2.

which Sikhism has furnished India. Amritsar is not in itself one of the attractive cities of the earth, although it is a thriving seat of trade and commerce next in wealth in all north India to the ancient and at present federation capital of Delhi. Lahore, some thirty miles away, is a larger city than Amritsar, more amply laid out, and has been for many centuries the leading seat of culture in northwestern India. It was the Sikhs' own capital while their Khalsa flourished and their shrines are still conspicuous there. And Sikhs are much in evidence in Lahore, on memorial occasions, especially, which they celebrate.

By mentioning Amritsar and Lahore we do not mean to indicate that Sikhs are an urban people. They are rural—pastoral and agricultural—in origin, and are still predominantly agricultural. Their chief crops have been wheat, sugar-cane and pulses. Many of them have engaged in trade—including trade in horses, in particular—and have had a share in the general north Indian trade in livestock, implements of agriculture, precious metals, ivory and merchandise, and in the manufacture and sale of carpets, shawls and textiles. Rural Sikhs have had much experience of the cities, nevertheless, through visitation in ordinary course and on days of special celebration.

These folk called Sikhs were at first a converted people, and those who throng the shrine surroundings on occasion still represent the major stocks from which the early converts came. Sikhism may be viewed, therefore, as typical of a certain stage of culture among people of a somewhat restricted racial heritage. There is still among Sikhs some persistent and potent distinction of "race and clan." That is, there are Jats and some Rajputs, for example, among them. These terms indicate in general not only racial but also social character and have some psychological significance—Rajput is superior to Jat. The Rajput stock, in a broad sense, is ancient Indian (Hindu) aristocracy which has maintained itself somewhat apart during the many centuries which have witnessed the gradual Indianization of all immigrant peoples. The Rajputs brought their own women with them when they entered India, and have thus been able to preserve a purer racial strain. Rajputs are Hindus by tradition and being of "warrior" stock they have likewise a tradition of hostility toward Moslems. Had Nanak been of Rajput lineage he might not have begun his mission as he did, or held high hopes of reconciliation with Islam.

The Jats, on the whole, are the most important people of the Panjab. In sheer bulk they make up at least a quarter of the total population. Jats have "married out" more freely than Rajputs have, and in general they represent fairly evenly both Hinduism and Islam throughout their ranks. Sikhs who have a Jat inheritance have nevertheless some pride of race. For a while, at least, there was little if any desire on a Sikh's part to be considered Rajput, even though Rajputs stood higher in the social scale. In the India census of 1881, for example, only one tribe in the Sikh area returned itself as "Rajput." Some change of mind developed afterwards, with noticeable results observed in 1941. A heightened social consciousness has long been noticeable among the Sikhs, and many of them would now choose to pass for Rajputs, although many of them in outlying districts, among the foothills of the Himalayas, for example, could not hope to share in such prestige. There has been, however, in one section of the Panjab an explicit unwillingness on the part of Jats to be called Rajputs. But the ranking princes of the Sikhs, the Maharajas of Patiala and of Nabha, claim and are accorded Rajput lineage. Their dominions lie within the region of "protected" states at the edge of Rajputana and they have had peculiar benefits from English rule.

The Jats are uniformly sturdy, manly, industrious and honest folk, even though they pride themselves on doing "what is right in their own eyes." They are peasants, husbandmen, cattle-dealers, traders, revenue-payers and moneylenders, mainly villagers ordinarily peaceably inclined and yet independent to a degree of impatience over too immediate government control. Many of them have expressed their virile character through enlistment in military service —in the British Indian Army or in the corps of native states. Some have gone into other branches of the public service.

Now the Sikhs, in particular, have come largely from this Jat stock. Half, at least, of their number, are Jat by inheritance and disposition. The other half? Well, they have come of various and sometimes indefinite caste and tribal origin. They were Jat Sikhs, however, who organized the Khalsa and once ruled the Panjab. And Jat Sikhs have given Sikhism most of its stolid and compelling substance, whatever random spark of Rajput aristocratic militancy may sometimes have kindled unusual enthusiasm among them and led them irresistibly.

The Sikh homeland which they still occupy is principally the region around Amritsar, Jalandhar and Ludhiana. More extensively, their sphere of operation and influence has included an area of between fifteen and twenty thousand square miles, with its teeming population and its vast resources. This larger sphere extends from Dera Baba Nanak, a town above Lahore, southeastward toward Ambala, a town well to the south of the oft-disputed Sutlej river boundary— a stretch of one hundred and seventy-five miles, whose width may be nearer a hundred. Is it to be wondered at that Sikhs cherish the memory of their control of this wealthy region? Their sense of nationality has several times of late been stirred by political events. They share today a widespread restlessness whose most evident expression is antipathy toward Britain. The Sikhs, however, have had many opportunities to weigh themselves in the balance of circumstance. They are conscious of some rivalry with the Hindu Mahasabha, or "Great Assembly," the Indian National Congress and the Moslem League (all three are purely voluntary organizations) as well as with the rule of Britain operating[7] now under the India Act of 1935. The Congress has become a radical independence party, while the Mahasabha continues to be more conservative, and the Moslems have proposed an independent state called Pakistan. Meanwhile the Sikhs cherish their own ideal of the Khalsa! And while, in the words of a saying of theirs, they are "born with a plow-handle for a plaything," they may still rather fight than plough. Half of them, the *bearded* Sikhs, especially, are ever martially inclined, and have had long, intimate acquaintance with the dagger and the sword.

We have spoken of Amritsar and its Golden Temple, the Darbar Sahib, as symbolic. They, the city and the temple, reflect and echo the many aspects of Sikhism *after* it became a separate movement, while the simpler, original elements of the faith must be sought elsewhere, also. In one sense, therefore, the Darbar Sahib for the Sikhs is something less than what the Meccan Ka'bah is for Moslems, the latter representing in its way the *entire* history of Islam. But the Sikh shrine represents at least something similar to what the second temple in Jerusalem represented to the ancient Hebrews. It may not rightly be likened, however, to one of the holiest Hindu shrines, the Golden Temple in Benares, for example, because there is no such emphasis on miracle with the Sikhs as may be found among the Hindus. It is less an agency of magic and more an atmosphere of spirit. And, moreover, images are absent from it—it is as bare of images as is a Moslem mosque. In a high religious sense, it is a place of "court" (darbar) where deity gives audience to

[7] In theory only, both on account of passive rejection by most of the native Indian leaders and the circumstance of war. If any-one would review the constitutional problem in India, he should read R. Coupland, *The Indian Problem* (Oxford, 1944).

his worshipers in some such manner as that in which from times immemorial Indian rulers have made themselves publicly accessible to their subjects, for instance at times of coronation. But in the Sikh darbar the divine Sovereign presides invisibly, and the shrine is a special "doorway," or gurdwara, to his presence. In fact, the common name of any house of worship among the Sikhs is gurdwara—a dwara, or "doorway" to the Guru or head of their religion. Guru is itself an ancient and common Hindu term for guide and teacher, as distinguished from various types of priests concerned with sacred ritual. While the Sikhs have adopted it, they have given it a special meaning, as we shall see, and have had their special uses for it. The Sikh shrines in the scattered villages and towns are always called gurdwaras and are thus to be readily distinguished from Hindu temples, Moslem mosques, Christian churches or any non-Sikh place of worship. They are all pale copies of a grand original and parts of a consistent whole.

But the Darbar Sahib is unique—except for some duplication of it at Tarn Taran, a town not very far away. It is at once a sign of Sikhism historical, ideological, practical and comparative. There is a central structure (cf. illustration No. 2) topped with glinting gold, rising from a five-acre, quadrangular pool of water—this amritsar, or "water of immortality." Along the four sides of the pool run ample, tesselated marble pavements, and beyond the pavements at unequal distances from the pool stand chapels, hostels (dormitories), schools and public kitchens. The temple area amounts in all to about thirty acres in the very heart of Amritsar "City"—by "city" is designated in Indian usage the main, compact native settlement in contradistinction to the neighboring "cantonments" or military quarters and the "civil lines" bounding the spacious foreign residential section. All approaches to the temple are narrow lanes leading through the midst of huddled houses and densely packed bazaars. The temple area itself is roomy and well-kept—conspicuously clean, for there is usually a daily washing of the pavements.

The temple faces, roughly, westward—cardinal directions have no special significance in Sikh architecture, nor is there any "prayer direction" (qiblah) as in Islam. You reach the temple by a marble causeway from a spacious plaza at the western side of the pool of water. Behind this open plaza stands a building called the Akal Takht, or "Throne of the Timeless," the special shrine of the Akalis, a famous and influential sect of Sikhs. And over the head of the causeway stands a marble arch supporting what is called the Treasury, or place of deposit of certain precious objects yet to be described. The temple proper is not really imposing, although built elaborately of marble and partly covered with embossed and gilded copper plates. There are nobler buildings nearby in Agra, Delhi and Lahore. The Sikh may say that the Agra Taj is not *imposing*. Truly, it is not large, but what structure can be compared with it, if the standard be beauty of situation, harmony of proportions and exquisiteness of form and finish! And most of the imperial Mughal buildings, whether small or large, represent usually the skill and scope of master builders. The style of the Darbar Sahib tends to puzzle the critical observer at first glance. It seems to follow a pattern all its own. It reflects obviously some Mughal influence in the roof design,—but *not* in the prominent gilding of the upper portion of its walls. There are domes, cupolas and pinnacles, and arch-indented parapets about them. The gilded copper plates on the upper walls are pressed into figurative designs of vines and flowers. There are marble panels with flower designs about the doorways (somewhat in the fashion of the Taj, perhaps). Many of the flowery panels are chiselled with inscriptions—texts from the *Granth Sahib*, the Sikh's Bible.

Whatever its style and whatever its origin, Sikhs themselves built it (whereas the Taj is scarcely altogether *Indian;* Italian hands molded its perfection). While it may be small and unimposing, it has, nevertheless, a character of its own —it is a temple of the *Sikhs.* Sikhs have been comparatively unskilled in architecture and the arts, but they have had some skill of imitation in the use of purloined stocks for building. The present Darbar Sahib is, in fact, a reconstruction. The original, which had stood two centuries, suffered demolition in 1761. It had been built during the reign of the tolerant Mughal Akbar. But when the Persian Moslem Ahmad Shah invaded India it was in his eyes a rock of offense, because of what it represented of the religious and political importance which Sikhism had acquired. Ahmad's visit is called by Sikhs themselves the Great Disaster, or Ghulu Ghara. He not only demolished the temple buildings; he slew Sikh devotees and piled their heads amidst the ruins; and he despoiled the waters of the lake with the blood of slaughtered cattle—he may have thought the cow as sacred to the Sikhs as to the Hindus whom he would also outrage.

The present structure and situation are the work of the Sikh Maharaja Ranjit Singh who came to power in northwest India in the early nineteenth century. He repaired the "great disaster." He gained ascendancy over various elements among the Sikhs themselves and over many of their neighbors. He welded the Sikhs into a strong confederacy and made their central shrine pre-eminent. He restored it in enlarged and handsomer proportions by means of the spoils of conquest. He took materials from famous Moslem buildings in and near Lahore—from the tomb of the Great Mughal Jahangir, for instance, in the Shahdara Gardens five miles outside Lahore. If Ranjit's temple has about it even more of a martial atmosphere than that which typified the first, it is because Sikhism itself had become meanwhile more militant. The present Darbar Sahib is a dignified memorial and a genuine expression of what the predominant form of Sikhism has become. Yet this "borrowed" reconstruction houses modestly Sikhism's original simplicity of unadorned ritual and plain scripture. It lacks the idols of a Hindu fane, together with the Hindu temple's fetid odors, and something has saved it from the bleak austerity of the Moslem mosque. It is on the whole a house of simple faith.

It has its "treasures," as has been said already, and there may be more to Sikhism than meets the eye at once in the Darbar Sahib's precincts. For one thing, the Sikh calendar includes many special days, and the Treasury[8] may yield up its store of relics for special celebrations and processions. It is worth noting that among the treasures are: eight gold doors which are sometimes substituted for the four pairs of silver doors which usually hang at the four temple doorways; the curved sword of Maharaja Ranjit Singh, its handle and its blue plush-covered scabbard adorned with costly jewels; five gold spades which were once used—at least ceremonially —in an enlargement of the pool; a fan designed somewhat in the fashion of a horse-tail with fine threads of sandalwood, which is kept usually in its teak wood cabinet, but is used occasionally in a temple ceremony for fanning the sacred *Granth;* a costly wedding-veil of numerous strings of fine pearls attached to the lower edge of a gold, forehead plate which is itself inlaid with precious gems; several smaller, symbolic, golden swords, each set in its circle of gold; many tassels made of cords of gold and silver intertwined; sixteen large, tall, silver candlesticks which are sometimes used ornamentally along the railings of the temple causeway; and—by no means the least important item in the storehouse—a hemispherical shell of gold, an inverted bowl about twenty pounds in weight, surmounted by a jeweled, ornamental peacock, and having attached to one-half of its circular rim many short strings of pearls—one hundred and eight large

[8] See illustration No. 3.

pearls, in all, a number which, whether by design or some chance, is precisely that of the beads in a rosary of the Shivite Hindu devotee. These treasures are generally used in public five times yearly—on each of five prescribed memorial occasions, including the birthday of the first Sikh, the Guru Nanak. At such times some are placed for decoration in the temple and some are carried in procession. They are merely stored away the rest of the year and play then no part in the common, public worship. This fact is worthy of more than passing notice and may be alluded to again, with implications, in a later chapter.

The Akal Takht has been already mentioned (p. 11, above). It has its peculiar significance in the temple compound. This Throne of the Timeless, sanctuary of the "eternal" God, Akal, stands three stories high beside the plaza opposite the Treasury, facing eastward toward the causeway leading to the temple. There is some unintentional significance in the fact that the Akal Takht and the Darbar Sahib stand vis-à-vis, for the first takht was erected by the fifth Guru, Arjun (A.D. 1581-1606), was later reconstructed and enlarged (*cf.* illustration No. 6), and was specially dedicated by the tenth and last Guru, Gobind Singh (d. 1708), who founded the national Khalsa. When it was reconstructed, it was at last topped with a pavilion roofed with a gilded dome, and—as if the builders were oblivious of, or unconcerned over, possible implications—two *minarets* were added! And yet these minarets might represent to the loyal Sikh not Islam, or merely the persecution of his compatriots by the Moslem Mughal Aurangzeb, but also the Khalsa's own later triumph over Moslems in the Panjab. And to be reminded of persecution in a former day might add some zest to living in the present.

While the Darbar Sahib is dear to all Sikhs, the Akal Takht is especially dear to Sikh Akalis (devotees of the *warlike* deity, Akal), who hold the bitterest memories of Moslem persecution, have scant respect for Allah and little love for Allah's religion of Islam. There are treasures of its own in the Akal Takht, including Gobind's sword, a four-foot-long falchion whose blade widens gradually from the handle toward the tip until the edges break abruptly and taper to a sudden point. There are also some initiation vessels used in admitting members to the Khalsa; and a mace once used by a Guru who was possibly Har Rai. *Two* sets of treasures! Nevertheless, in both the Darbar Sahib and the Akal Takht the place of supreme importance, reverence and honor is held by the *Granth Sahib* itself—or, more explicitly, by the Adi or "original" *Granth Sahib.*

One other item and we are done with a bare description of the sacred premises in Amritsar: a short distance from the northeast corner of the pool stands the Baba Atal tower seven stories high. Baba Atal Rai was a son of the sixth Guru, Har Gobind, who once, contrary to sound Sikh doctrine and proper practice, wrought a miracle of healing at the temple. Since this was for any Sikh, whether Guru, Guru's son, or any other, a display of false piety and devotion—for God alone works miracles!—the *baba* suffered appropriately afterwards and was duly penitent. The tower stands, therefore, commemorative of his penitence and a warning to any who would encroach on God's prerogative of miracle. Such, to be sure, is the legend, but there may be later some just reason to qualify its meaning, unless indeed Sikh miracles have all been wrought by God.

## Chapter 2. A Company of Pilgrims

We should not undertake this early in our study to follow Sikh pilgrims with too minute intent. Nanak himself deprecated pilgrimage, reproved his people for any practice of it. The twenty-first stanza of the Japji has these four opening lines on this very theme:

> Tirthu tap daia dat danu
> Jeko pavai til ka manu
> Sunia mania mani kita bhau
> Antaragati tirathi mali nau,

or, freely rendered into English, without rhythm or rhyme,

> One gains but a seed's weight of merit
> Through pilgrimages, austerities and benevolence;
> One might rather mind God's bidding and cleanse himself
> By the love he bears within his heart.

There are similar sayings among other Indians with reference to the pilgrimage, for example,

> Tirth gae tin jan, Kashi Prayag ko daur
> Ekhu pap na katiyan, das man lade aur,

or,

> Three men went on pilgrimage to Benares and Allahabad,
> But instead of their losing a single sin, they acquired near a half-ton more.

Other deprecatory sayings include these:

> If bathing in the Ganges affords salvation, how fortunate are fishes and frogs.
>
> Going on pilgrimage, you may indeed gain some reverence for water, but
>
> All places of pilgrimage are valueless, even though the pilgrim drown himself at Kashi (Benares).

Without prejudice, therefore, and merely for a glimpse of Sikhs at their common round of worship, we shall follow several pilgrims on a tour of visitation in the habitual manner of the Indian. Many types of Sikhs may be encountered. In fact, some people called Satnamis may also come upon the scene. Their very name is derived from the Sikhs' own name for God, Sat Nam, but their connection with the Sikhs is by no means altogether clear. These Satnamis are, in general, a low caste stock and are to be found mainly in central parts of India, but their scriptures and their simple worship are those of Sikhism. The Satnamis are especially numerous in the villages north and east of Jabalpur, Central Provinces. They may have been first organized from among Hindu outcastes. Hindus, at any rate, have considered them not only ceremonially unclean, but otherwise filthy and immoral. Moslems, also, have sometimes despised them, and they have been at times oppressed and persecuted by Moslem rulers. The Satnami movement originally took hold among chamars, or leather-workers, in particular, and actually offered them some hope and demonstration of improvement. When, for example, they adopted the worship of Sat Nam, the formless and eternal God, they ceased using flesh of animals and certain "bloody" vegetables for food, and they gave up their idols. While Sikhs, on the other hand, in the stricter meaning of the word, have kept themselves separate from their Satnami co-religionists, these latter have not been excluded from the Sikh gurdwaras—and they are welcome at the Darbar Sahib, although very few of them, we may suppose, have ever visited this shrine.

One of the pilgrim band, whose movements now engage us, came from Jabalpur where he was a member of the sabha or association whose gurdwara stands beside a small lake known as Mara Tal. The site was once occupied by Udasi Sikhs—a special type with whom we shall get better acquainted in Amritsar—who had taken it over about 1880 from a Hindu sect. The regular Sikh association, the Guru Singh Sabha, took possession of it about 1907. In the small compound near the gate of entrance are still some Udasi graves on whose flat cover-stones[1] are inscribed the "feet" (footprints) of the *Hindu* deity Vishnu. While these markings are unorthodox, the regular Sikhs have not disturbed these graves—any graves are commonly respected by all Indians—nor is there any other burial ground connected with this gurdwara. Sikhs, who usually follow the practice of cremation, do not even make provision for common places of deposit of the ashes of their dead. Nor do they ordinarily mark the spot where ashes rest, but only in the case of famous men for whom samadhs or tombs are reared. Cremation is, of course, the common practice of the Hindus, while burial is the practice of the Moslems. It might possibly be said with reason, in the case of the samadh, that Sikhs both cremate and bury.

The Jabalpur gurdwara is in most particulars an up-to-date establishment. It welcomes to its worship adherents of any faith, if only they observe the general custom of leaving off their footwear in the outer court. For Sikhs themselves—and for any others, also—there is a water-tank at the gurdwara doorway, which supplies water by a spigot for ablutions. Non-Sikhs need not there observe ablution, if they are not so inclined. This is primarily a shrine of Guru Nanak, let it be remembered, although its congregation is composed mostly of the bearded type—the pilgrim himself was a bearded Sikh. Above it hangs a nishan sahib, a symbolic flag of the order—a new flag yearly, installed on Nanak's birthday. A memorial library of a modest sort is being gathered and housed nearby—in itself a symbol of increasing literacy among the Sikhs.

Within[2] the covered sanctuary stand two desks, side by

[1] The Christian visitor might be reminded by these level stones of a Moravian graveyard.

[2] See illustration No. 12.

side, each with its copy of the *Granth Sahib.* A square cloth canopy is stretched high above them, from which festoons of paper flowers hang, while more immediately above them stands a double arch whose supporting pillars rest upon the floor, and on whose façade is an inscription in Gurmukhi, the Sikh's own sacred language, which reads "Nanak Nirankari," or the "revered or formless Nanak" (what then has happened finally to Nanak's person?). High on the rear wall above the level of the arches hangs a painted likeness of Guru Nanak, with the face of the minstrel Mardana at one side and the face of the disciple Bala at the other. On the side walls of the sanctuary appear the likenesses of still other Gurus, including that of Gobind Singh in the midst of the five "martyrs" who offered themselves to death (but were not slain) at the foundation of the Khalsa. And there is a startling representation of Baba Dip Singh, a legendary figure. This Baba was once in conflict, as the story goes, with the Mughals several miles from Amritsar, and the picture tells what happened: although his head was severed from his body, the eyes fell out upon his shoulders and the devoted warrior made his way to Amritsar and to the Darbar Sahib, bearing his head in his left hand and waving his sword defiantly in his right!

In this setting the Jabalpuri Sikh was by habit a faithful worshiper. He was an official, in fact, of the gurdwara. Religious exercises were held every Sunday morning from six to nine and at special times in the annual calendar of worship (we shall observe elsewhere something of the common ritual). But the "paths" (the Hindi "path" sounds, if properly pronounced, like English "pott") or lessons, which the *granthi* (reader of the *Granth*) offered on behalf of certain Sikhs, were often quite irregular. They smacked of magic, in spite of orthodoxy. These lessons might be recited on behalf of a Sikh who wanted to give thanks for especially good fortune or on behalf of someone who would escape danger or distress. A single Sikh might arrange for such a lesson to be completed for his benefit in fifteen days, an hour a day. Two or more Sikhs might combine and provide for the completion of the lesson in two days of continuous recital. The Jabalpuri pilgrim was to learn that no such practices were tolerated at Amritsar! However, the Jabalpur association was, in general, regular and its membership had been increasing both by individual conversion and by natural propagation, with the keshdari or bearded type of Sikhs predominating.

One member of the pilgrim party was an ex-soldier (the Jabalpuri member was in government service as an exciseman, or agent of the liquor administration). He had been in a "Rajput" regiment which served in Iraq (Mesopotamia) during the First World War. He had been there as far afield as Khanikan in the country of the Kurds, rude and hardy hillmen, of whose stock had come the famous "Saljuq" Saladin.[3] The pilgrim had been, of course, in Baghdad and had been particularly impressed with the fact that in this famous Moslem city the Jewish merchants dominated trade. He had not known Jews in India, nor had he served in Aden or in other parts where Jews are active. He had had in India dealings aplenty with merchants, some Hindu, some Moslem, some of his own religion, and had made some acquaintance with Indian money-lenders, but he had had occasion to observe that the Iraqi Jew was still more clever and exacting. More recently, since his discharge from the Indian Army, he had been living quietly as a farmer in a village near the foothills of the Himalayas.

Another member of the little band was himself a merchant in a simple way. He dealt in horses and had occasionally furnished mounts for the Indian Army. He was a villager from up in the northwestern part of India. He and the ex-soldier and the Jabalpuri were all keshdaris, or the

[3] Saladin (Salah ad-din), often referred to as a "Turkoman," was Sultan of Egypt and Syria A.D. 1174-1193.

bearded type. There was another bearded member of the party, but he was also an Akali. There was some suggestion that he had, at least, a special point of view, politically, and that he claimed to be of Rajput lineage. The ex-soldier and the merchant were manifestly Jats. And the Jabalpuri—well, he seemed by his features to be neither Jat nor Rajput, but of some down-country stock equivalent to Jat. His features were slightly finer than Jat features. Jats are dark-skinned, slightly yellowish, men of heavy countenance and stolid mien, in contrast to men of so-called "Aryan" lineaments and of sprightlier deportment. If, then, these three brands of heritage were represented in the group, there was still no sign of tension, for all were members of the Khalsa, and Guru Gobind's gospel of equality and fraternity prevailed among them. Nationalistic sentiment, also, has lately taught Sikhs further solidarity, and even the Jat constituents of the Khalsa often do not make, as they once did, the *Hindu* Rajputs peculiar objects of their hatred and contempt. The ex-soldier himself had once, in fact, belonged to a "Rajput" regiment, even though he laid no claim to actual Rajput blood.

There were two other members of the pilgrim group, making six in all. These two were "easy-going" Sikhs of the sahajdari type, devotees of Nanak, in particular. They were residents of Dera Baba Nanak, where all had met at first. The sahajdaris sometimes are scarcely to be distinguished at first glance from Hindus, but these two, as well as many others of their order, were truly Sikh. They may not have held Guru Gobind Singh in equal regard with Guru Nanak, whereas the keshdaris gave Gobind at least equal rank with Nanak. But all together shared enthusiasm for the larger mission of the Sikhs, and their tour was undertaken in the confidence that Sikhism was still a living faith, an active principle, and, perhaps—who knows?—a nation in the making. The Khalsa might yet rise again!

Indeed the Akali pilgrim had such a point of view emphatically, and he intended on the tour to afford himself occasion for recollection of certain stirring incidents in Sikh history. He would see again the garden where Akalis had been "massacred" in 1919 by soldiery of the Raj, themselves Indians, including Sikhs. The Akali pilgrim knew that the responsibility for this incident had not been fully and finally assessed.

It was near the end of the hot season and just before the breaking of the rains when the little party arrived in Amritsar by train, the Panjab Mail, from Dera Baba Nanak. They alighted at the station in the Cantonments, and when the mail train had departed, they looked out across the open to the nearby Gobindgarh, or Fort of Gobind the tenth Guru, which Maharaja Ranjit Singh had built in 1809 with the assistance of French Army engineers. But it had been in British hands since 1857. It was usually garrisoned by a company of infantry and a battery of artillery. But a still more ominous reminder was encountered as the pilgrims made their way afoot from the station to the City—and it was the Akali who refreshed their memory. They soon found themselves, in other words, on the very bridge where military pickets in 1919 had stopped the mob surging out of the City toward the "foreign" quarters, that is, into the Cantonments. Having been turned back, the mob ran amuck within the City, committed many acts of violence and outrage, and gathered one time in the Jallianwala Garden where the "massacre" then took place. As the pilgrims stood awhile upon this bridge, a student of the local Khalsa College joined them (this college is the imposing and extensive institution of the Sikhs, in the western environs of Amritsar on the Grand Trunk Road; see illustration No. 11). He accompanied them a little farther, giving them guidance through the Hall Gateway and the Hall Bazaar. He himself was on his way home from college to his father's house inside the City beyond the Darbar Sahib. His family, we may say, were grain merchants of some prominence.

From the Hall Bazaar their route lay through the Kaisarbagh, or royal gardens, beyond the quarters of a government military guard—barracks of the King-Emperor George VI. In the gardens stands an originally white marble statue of the Queen-Empress Victoria, which has now and then been disfigured by unruly hands. The general setting and the circumstance of current war suggested some unusual caution on the pilgrims' part, although no such prohibition of "assembly" was in force as the Rowlatt Acts demanded in the First World War—acts which had given rise to very serious "unrest." But the pilgrims took the precaution to walk singly now and then, sometimes incommunicado, sometimes, while together, exchanging merely casual and commonplace remarks. Their mission itself was inoffensive. They, nevertheless, decided not to visit at this time the Jallianwala gardens, but to go on directly to the temple. Instead, therefore, of going straight into the gardens from the Kaisarbagh, they turned to the right through the narrow street of shops leading southward to the plaza on which the great Clock Tower stands at the north side of the Golden Temple grounds. The Khalsa College student left them by the tower and went on home, after having told them some details of their surroundings. He had pointed out, among other things, the headquarters of the Udasi Sikhs, across the street from the tower, mostly hidden from view amidst the thick cluster of buildings and accessible by a narrow alleyway.

One of the "easygoing" pilgrims excused himself immediately, asking leave to act on the student's information and to visit the Udasi guru. The others of the party prepared to go at once to the Darbar Sahib—not that they would have been unwelcome among Udasis. There were public kitchens to serve them food at the temple, and quarters where they might spend the night—in a lesser degree the

Udasi headquarters made the same sort of provision for their own visitors. Perhaps the "easygoer" who spent the first night with the old Udasi guru knew more the next day about the temple itself than the others whose first acquaintance was merely with the present normal facilities and routine; for the guru had had long acquaintance with events.

The Darbar Sahib is always a lively place, during the day especially. Visitors are everywhere, and their movement is impressive. Sikhs find here something peculiarly satisfying, something which custom has seemed for centuries to demand for Indians. Sikhs would surely have found it difficult, if not impossible, to obey strictly and literally Nanak's own injunction against pilgrimage and the pilgrim center. Moslems go about, visiting their own saints' tombs and monuments. Some of them get beyond India to Meshed in Persia, where the bones of Ali rest, and to Karbala in Iraq where the tomb is of Husayn, Ali's martyr son who was also the grandson of the Prophet; and some get as far as Madinah where the Prophet's relics are and on to Mecca and the sacred Ka'bah, Allah's own peculiar shrine. There is distinction for the Moslem who has made the pilgrimage even by proxy and who thereafter is entitled to be known as hajji, pilgrim.

Hindus visit various sacred waters and the special seats of their many gods. Certain places are unusually sacred to Shiva Mahadeva and to his wifely "powers" (shakti), Durga, Kali, Parbati, and many more. Some sites are very dear to one or another of the two Krishnas of the Vishnu sect; some others are revered in the name of Vishnuite Rama and his pure bride Sita. Even the comparatively small Jain community—not many more than a million members—furnishes many pilgrims to their holy places on Mt. Abu, or at Girnar, Shatrunjaya or Parasnath. There is little that is more impressive to a visitor to India than the constant movement of the crowds of pilgrims to the many centers of the several faiths. Some devotees are more ardent than others; some seek spiritual satisfaction, while some seek but an outing and a change of scene. For womenfolk and children an annual pilgrimage breaks the heavy, often dreary, monotony of the daily village round. For all alike, men, women and children, there is indispensable value in these journeys, whatever else they may entail.

There is nothing necessarily surprising, therefore, in similar movement among the Sikhs. Perhaps they do not often have as far to go as do Moslems, Jains and many Hindus. Perhaps their practice is indeed for them something *less* than the traditional pilgrimage observed by those of other faiths. But Sikhs have been known to visit Hindu and other sacred places, as well as their own. Visiting *polytheistic* centers? Yes! Do they visit Moslem shrines? No, their monotheism never made them friends of Moslems! There may be some exception in the attitude of a few Sikhs now and then toward sufi Moslem shrines, but to none other. In so far as Sufism has been ascetic it has, in fact, attracted many Indians of different faiths, Hindus and Jains, especially. And the mystical Moslem Ahmadiyya movement of Qadian (*q.v.* below) has appealed sometimes to Hindus, Jains and Sikhs—to Sikhs who may be somewhat aimlessly inclined toward the formlessness and the timelessness of True Name. For most Sikhs, however, there is an intense world-consciousness, with its own due political implications. They are among those Indians who nowadays give more thought than ever to activity whose interests combine education, finance and government with spiritual objectives. All of which tends, to be sure, to modify considerably some common, traditionally Indian beliefs and habits. Sikhs, among others, for example, have believed in transmigration, but what of such a doctrine in *new* India?

The pilgrims made ready in the shadow of the Clock Tower to enter the temple grounds for worship—by custom they were to go in unencumbered. It may be needless to remark that any use of liquor or tobacco is forbidden on the grounds. Tobacco, of course, is always taboo among good Sikhs—the bearded, in particular (*cf.* p. 326, note 24). Sikh abstinence in this regard is in marked contrast with the almost inordinate use of tobacco by Hindus and Mohammedans. But Sikhs sometimes do indulge in liquor, have often indulged most freely, whereas indulgence in liquor is *doctrinally* taboo to Moslems. The worshipers, to be unencumbered, left their parcels and their shoes at a lodge beside the entrance on the north—there were three other means of access to the grounds, but the pilgrims had arrived at this. And they bathed their feet at the water-tap nearby. Steps then lead them down to the pavement which surrounds the pool.[4]

The reader has already become acquainted with the general setting of the shrine, but there is much detail to see. There is the famous Baba Buddha tree that grows beside the pool—the tree's name has, of course, nothing to do with Gotama *the* ancient Buddha; "buddha" has long been a common title of respect in general use in India. The tree is a memorial to the saint who shared in laying out the grounds originally. To some devotees its properties are magical. For that matter, the waters of the pool, also, are possessed of magic in the view of some. Does not legend have it that the waters of the lake bubbled forth first at a Guru's bidding? And has not the water sometimes wrought a cure, they say, on a single bathing in it? And does it not confer something of "immortality" on all who worship there! And, also, there is a marble block in the pavement over in the causeway near the temple door, which keeps miraculously cool even in the hot season when all the other pavement stones would scorch the pilgrims' feet with the sun's rays'

[4] This northern entrance is shown in illustration No. 1. Notice the Baba Buddha tree at the foot of the steps, with a partial view of the Temple beyond.

stored-up fire, except that they are covered with strips of carpet for the walker's comfort. The author can testify to this to this extent, at least: he stood on the block in his stockings (stockings, by special permission) and a passing Sikh observed that the coolness was that of the eternal snows of the Himalayas whence this block first came!

And there are a few peculiar "soldiers"[5] in the crowd. Whereas the worshipers, in general, are clad in white, the devotee who bears the name of "soldier" in an exclusively religious "warfare" is mostly clad in blue. He wears a dark blue gown, a turban of blue cloth wound around an inner, yellow, conical headpiece whose tasseled tip protrudes above the blue. A yellow shawl is worn about his shoulders and at his side is slung a dark red plush scabbard containing a gilt-handled sword. These devotees give themselves entirely to religion, whereas the usual worshiper is just a layman taking time off from business or other normal occupation. They are within Sikhism what the faqir is to Islam, and what the sannyasi and the sadhu are to Hindus.

The round of worship for Sikh laymen is quite simple. Each is there in his individual capacity and worships as he will. He may read from his own book of prayers and scripture, if he can, or he may recite from memory certain "morning" or "evening" lessons, or thus repeat certain rags or hymns. He may have brought his own copy of the *Japji*, Nanak's little book of psalms. Or, he may have at hand selections from the psalms of Gobind Singh (it is very probable that the Akali pilgrim had some of the psalms of Gobind with him). There is at the Darbar Sahib little truly congregational worship—although congregations do gather at the various gurdwaras here and there. At the temple there are granthis, relays of them in succession, who carry on throughout the day continuous ritual and recitation. There are, also,

[5] See illustration No. 5.

singers and instruments to accompany them in an alternation of responses.

There actually is not room inside the temple for a congregation. The worshipers must keep moving, or at least no one may tarry long in the central sanctuary. At the rear of this central room is an altar on which the canonical scriptures rest, and from which the granthis perform their recitation. A sheet is spread on the floor before the altar to receive the coins which the faithful bestow as they pass by, or pause to listen to the reading. There is little else on ordinary occasions. A worshiper may lave himself at the waterside beyond, from steps which lead down at the temple's rear. He may wander about the building to the second floor and balcony or to the third floor roof with its central kiosk and corner cupolas. Everything is orderly and reverent—and the "easy-goer" who had spent his first night with the Udasi guru was prompted to comment on what he had then learned of less orderly times at this very temple site. A son of the Khalsa College principal, who dropped in on the guru that evening had himself given most of the details.

It was before the days of the Gurdwara Reform Movement, and that was not so long ago. This movement had aimed at "purifying all the Sikh shrines of un-Sikhlike deviations and practices and at protecting their endowed properties from the misappropriations of their self-aggrandizing custodians," says Ganda Singh in his *History of the Gurdwara Shahidganj*. Politics, patronage and even graft had previously been rife in temple and gurdwara management. Mahants, religious "superiors" or elders, had been in control, and, being often of uncertain, undependable character, they had indulged in many irregularities. But in 1925 the Panjab government enacted the Sikh Gurdwara Act, under whose provisions a sort of episcopal oversight and control was established—but without bishops or any such high dignitaries as would defy the fundamental Sikh democracy.

Instead of the merely local control by mahants, a central board of management was instituted, with branches throughout the whole region of the Sikhs. Gurdwara endowments were thenceforth cared for by responsible trustees—and, be it said, many gurdwaras had been richly endowed, with investments representing shops, mills and a host of private houses. The Darbar Sahib itself had much endowment, and its funds had often been abused. This was no longer the case, and the reformation had heightened Sikh religious self-respect considerably. Moreover, it heightened Sikh prestige not only in the Panjab but throughout the whole of India. Additional honor thus accrued to Nanak and to Gobind, to the *Granth*, the ritual, the saints and martyrs, and to the festivals of Sikhism—to that of Arjun, in particular, annually celebrated in Lahore. The pilgrims whom we are following were themselves heirs of this heightened self-respect and prestige for their people.

The Jabalpuri Sikh, coming from so great a distance, was especially eager to attend the Arjun festival while he was in northern India. Meanwhile—the festival of Arjun was not yet due—he and the other bearded members of the party went on to the village of Tarn Taran, while the two "easy-goers" stayed behind with the Udasi guru in an atmosphere more nearly like what they knew at Dera Baba Nanak. The four, on their part, found Tarn Taran very interesting. Its temple is only second in importance to the Darbar Sahib itself. The town it occupies a dozen miles below Amritsar is humble and the temple, in contrast, is most conspicuous. It is a costly shrine built by Maharaja Ranjit Singh on the site first occupied by the gurdwara built by Guru Arjun (d. 1606). Guru Arjun had lived in Tarn Taran during a time when Sikh fortunes were at low ebb.

There is at Tarn Taran a large reservoir of water which may have come at first from springs, but which is now supplied from an irrigation, public works canal. The story goes that leprosy had once afflicted Arjun and that he had been cured in the waters of Tarn Taran. Lepers visit the lake even yet, hoping for a cure—but mere canal water seems ineffectual! There is better prospect for them at the leper-asylum on the outskirts of the town. The temple itself stands not in the midst of the pool but at one side facing eastward—we have said the Darbar Sahib faces *west*, and that mere direction is nothing to the Sikhs. These two shrines are by no means duplicates, except with reference to their simple properties and ritual—unless it be noticed that the temple at Tarn Taran also is built throughout of marble and with a second story covered with gilded bronze.

But the student of religion may well be greatly interested in some special features of the temple at Tarn Taran.[6] It seems at once to be pre-eminently Sikh; its visitors are mostly Sikhs. On the eaves at the edge of the roof in front stand panels bearing in the sacred Sikh Gurmukhi character the legends "Satinamu" (True Name) and "Wahiguru" (Hail, Guru). While the temple walls themselves bear plain panelling or bronze work embossed only with flower and vine designs, there are other surfaces within the temple area which display painted designs of gods and goddesses! The pilgrims, however, saw nothing incongruous in that—at least, they made no comment on the matter. If one were really very critical, he might not only wonder at these deities. He might call the title Wahiguru into question, as in itself an elevation of the Guru to the level of the God and, in consequence, a confusion of God and the Guru—unless, indeed, the intention was to indicate that God himself is actually the Guru! On the altar in the temple is the *Granth* which to many itself is the Guru. Here is, in any case, a phenomenon of interest in the history of religion. There may be in Tarn Taran something not altogether unlike the confusion of

[6] See illustrations Nos. 7 and 8.

Krishna the "avatara" and Vishnu the God in Hinduism, or the qualification of Allah in Islam by Husayn's atoning martyrdom, or yet the confusing association in Christianity of the Logos and Hail Mary.

The pilgrims found Tarn Taran in a quiet mood—quieter, if anything, than usual. No Army men were there at this time and many other Sikhs had "joined up" for military service and were in camps far off. No continuous ritual is there performed as is the case at the temple in Amritsar. A granthi merely sat beside the Book, not reading from it, but lifting the cover now and then and sometimes turning over several pages while wishful devotees caught glimpses of the, to them, sacred writing. No musical instruments were in action. A mat lay on the floor before the altar to catch the gifts the worshipers tossed down. There was a vessel containing the precious, sweet amrit confection, which the worshiper might taste after he had made his offering. There were treasure-jars nearby, each with its own three padlocks, each lock responding to a different key, in which the offerings were deposited every now and then by an attendant present for such a service (the jars were opened in due time and their contents reckoned by three officials of the local sabha).

Some visitors were bathing in the lake beyond the temple. Small groups of visitors at rest were gathered here and there about the plaza and along the pavements by the lakeside. In one group, for example, sat a sickly, suffering, moaning woman, too feeble to sit alone, and, of course, too feeble to bathe in the lake for the cure for which she came. Nor did her attendants seem inclined to carry and dip her in the water—indeed, she seemed very near to death. Was this not, after all, a proper place to die! If she did actually die there soon thereafter, her body, we may suppose, was immediately cremated and her ashes were scattered on the lake or similarly disposed of somewhere else. It was altogether a quiet scene, but would be livelier soon, for Tarn Taran itself was especially dear to Guru Arjun and his coming festival would be appropriately celebrated there.

But for the Arjun celebration the pilgrims, rather, were bound for Lahore. They had come out to Tarn Taran by third class passage on a local train. They returned by the same route, but in an Intermediate compartment. There were other passengers, also, in the "Inter," several other Sikhs, two Hindus, a young Moslem inspector for the railway, and a family group including children—no question of caste or "touchability" was involved in merely railway travel. One of the Sikhs was a PP, or Public Prosecutor, of the city of Faridkot. And the route lay through fertile country where, as the passengers could see, stolid, efficient Jats were working the wells and ploughing the fields with buffaloes and oxen. The down-country Jabalpuri Sikh remarked often the fertility and prosperity of the Panjab.

Back in Amritsar for a day, the Akali chose to go at last alone to the Jallianwala Garden. There he saw the bullet-marks on the walls of the surrounding buildings, and in imagination he made some reconstruction of the tragic episode of April 1919. Many bullet-marks were high up on the walls, but *all* the shots, he mused, were not fired "over the heads" of those assembled in the garden. Several hundred of the assembled persons lay dead and many hundreds were wounded in this Amritsar shooting. But the episode had faded somewhat from the people's minds, leaving only a vague impression of a "massacre." "Independence" partisans, in particular, of all camps, besides the Sikhs, used "Jallianwala" as a watchword and a battlecry. The Akali pilgrim mused awhile on this impression, weighing something of the intimate connection of politics and religion, but could not see the final outcome. Nor did he discuss these matters with the other members of the party after he rejoined them. It were better, anyway, he thought, *not* to discuss such matters along the public ways. Then, too, the Jabalpuri was himself a government official, and he and others of the party might have a different view of things. After all, he thought, they were brothers in a common faith, and as pilgrims were bent upon religion.

The "easygoers" would again have tarried in Amritsar, while the bearded members started for Lahore with the intention of pausing along the way in Wanieke and Atari. But along came "Kaka" (a nickname), son of the Khalsa College principal, to the Udasi guru's quarters once again, where the "easygoers" were. The young lad was devoted to the old, blind guru and called him father. He believed in him as both a holy man and a physician. He claimed to have been cured of colic by him and was ever ready to cite other cures through herbs—and common sense—which the venerable guru had employed. Kaka suggested to the "easygoers" that they, too, along with the bearded pilgrims, visit Atari —of whose stock he came, said he, characterizing the Atari family as "the most important in the Panjab." The bearded pilgrims, of course, were interested not only in Atari, but also in Ranjit Singh's connection with Wanieke, a village quite close by. They all, accordingly, decided on the trip.

They *bargained* for their fares by bus—the driver and the fare-collector were probably themselves the licensed owners of the vehicle. This bargaining is common practice, we may say, whether for personal passage or the transport of merchandise. The competition once was keener among the buses on this route until the war brought scarcity of gasoline. It was but a short run to Atari, sixteen miles or so, and the pilgrims found the village picturesque and interesting, and very reminiscent of somewhat better days among the Sikhs.

Atari today holds about two thousand citizens, more than half of whom are Moslems. There are five hundred Hindus and four hundred Sikhs. Someone, in an aside, accounted in this wise for the preponderance of Moslems: in the days of Sikh ascendancy Moslems were the menials, and there was need of many of them! But it was apparent to the visitors that Moslems and Hindus were nowadays among the leading citizens of this historic Sikh community. Females of all faiths move freely about the town, although several prominent Moslem families still remain "in pardah." One-third of the five hundred children in the schools were girls.

The headmaster of the high school at that time was Sikh, a graduate of the Khalsa College in Amritsar. He took much pride in his post and in the whole community. The sardar, or "proprietor," of the town was himself a Khalsa College matriculate and ex-student who, in reply to a query as to what he was now doing, said, "Oh, nothing much, only living as a gentleman at large." He lived, in fact, in the "high" (atari) buildings on Atari's central hill. He and his family owned 4,000 acres round about the town and 6,000 acres more elsewhere in the Panjab. There were still other imposing quarters in the town where now a Hindu priest presided over pupils in training for the Hindu priesthood. A Moslem faqir had until recently occupied the building. There was also the samadh or tomb of Sham Singh, a general under Ranjit Singh, which contained along with Sham Singh's ashes those also of the builders of the town and of some of their descendants. This samadh had become the local Sikh gurdwara—partly to prevent saint-worship, someone said. The pilgrims, once inside the shrine, bowed there before the *Granth*, made a formal offering, and paid their homage to the memory of Sham Singh.

Wanieke proved to be within easy walking distance of Atari and the party, accordingly, made its way across the fields afoot. The villagers there are mostly Moslems and Hindus, with only several families of Sikhs. The chief house of worship is the Moslem mosque. The Hindus have a shrine or two, one an altar with its idols underneath a sacred tree, but the Sikhs have no gurdwara; they have only the strong fort of Ranjit Singh to keep Sikh memories alive. Ranjit himself had sometimes occupied this fort, and it stands as a memorial to him, although until quite recently it had been used by a cooperative agricultural association as a storehouse for tools, implements and grain, under the auspices of the Panjab government. The party paused a while in token of respect and recollection and went back to Atari.

And then on to Lahore! This meant a further journey westward on the Grand Trunk Road. Yes, the ex-soldier knew the road and also the swing at least of Kipling's "Route Marchin' " on it. But the pilgrims "got along" again by bus and not by foot, having bargained once again for passage. And as they rode along, they passed through the season's first light fall of rain—the Rains (barsat) had come at last with their annual relief from drought and dust, if not from heat. It was the month of June. It was time for the Arjundeva mela, and, except for the tragedy it commemorated, the breaking of the rains would in itself insure a happier occasion.

The pilgrims found accommodation near the Roshni Gate, Lahore, and agreed at once that each would go his own way thereafter. The crowds were fast assembling from every quarter—mostly Sikhs, to be sure, but there were Hindus and Moslems everywhere, also. Hindu merchants had set up their stalls already to sell their various goods. Venders of many sorts of wares moved about in readiness to serve the gathering crowds. Several side-shows made ready for display. The whole of the lowland between the Fort and the Ravi riverside filled gradually with what makes up a mela. There were tents erected, also, for conferences and lectures on religion, and Sikhs would dominate the situation for many days to come. No war restrictions, as it happened, were imposed upon the mela. Government itself had no wish to handicap religious gatherings, so long as order was consistently preserved.

This mela is the most important of the annual occasions of Panjabi Sikhs. The grounds allotted to it are within and just outside the gardens of the once imperial Mughals. The chief gurdwara of Lahore is just beside the Mughal Fort itself, with the samadh of Ranjit Singh quite near it. The Hall of Audience which Ranjit built stands in the very gardens between the Fort and the badashahi or "royal" mosque. This inner area is reserved by Sikhs for the womenfolk and children, of whom there are great numbers. It matters little for the moment to the Sikhs that the great Mughal mosque overshadows all, although those assembled are not forgetful of the vanished Mughals. Indeed the primary motive of the mela is recollection of the martyrdom of Guru Arjun at Moslem Mughal hands—and of many other tragedies in Sikh history. In the large tent of meeting (a shamiana) addresses and discussions would rehearse Arjun's career and sacrifice, and emphasize likewise the leading tenets of the Sikh religion. In the gurdwara, exercises of worship would be continuously in process, and visitors might worship as they would. A Sikh Sewa, or "service" association, would provide any necessary attention and assistance for all those in attendance on the mela.

There and then the pilgrims shared in an occasion properly to be compared with any other known in India—with the Indian Moslem muharram, for example, as well as with some major Hindu festivals, all of which we must observe in some detail before our study ends. All Sikhs who shared the mela celebration experienced much worth cherishing thereafter, something which at least augmented their own communal consciousness and increased their faith and hope. The "easygoers" witnessed, incidentally, some such scenes as had never been enacted in their quiet town of Dera Baba Nanak, some scenes, perhaps, that the simple Nanak in his day would not have tolerated! The bearded Sikhs reacted with heartier approbation, for the memory of Guru Arjun was especially dear to them.

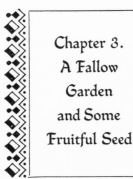

## Chapter 3. A Fallow Garden and Some Fruitful Seed

THE homeland of the Sikhs, despite particular localities, is more or less indefinite, and it has belonged to a larger and more complex whole. Boundaries have always been numerous but generally indistinct in northwest India. The political history of the region has been kaleidoscopic and even the topography has varied greatly. The rivers of the Panjab, for example, have changed their courses often and at random. It is of the very nature of all things Indian that boundary lines of any sort in any realm are faint and soon get blurred by circumstance or wiped out by force. Sikhism arose in a vague and very general setting, but its initial elements are not at all beyond precise discernment.

The movement—call it merely such to indicate some vagueness—which gave rise to it appeared about A.D. 1500. In northwest India then were many kinds of Hindus and many sects of Moslems, and, also, we might say, some "lesser breeds without the law." The accumulations of three thousand years, at least, were strewn around—and some debris of far more ancient institutions had long been covered out of sight by shifting sands and meandering rivers (along the Indus river valley, in particular). Obliterated also were many earlier human strains, and many popular ideals were no more than memories. But much, also, that was tangible was present in the congestion and confusion of the scene—certainty enough to work on in attempting an analysis of Sikh origins.

We have two persons, in particular, to start with, Nanak and Kabir—and, for that matter, the whole history of Sikhism is predominantly personal. Both were typically Indian within the compass of their experience and heritage, and this defines them somewhat at the outset. Perhaps they knew each other, although usually they lived many miles apart. Kabir moved and taught in and near Maghar, a village near Benares (Kashi), in which he died about 1518. He said with some unusual significance that he considered Maghar to be "the same as Benares" which is the holiest of all Hindu cities. Nanak, on the other hand, spent most of his life up in the Panjab, in the neighborhood of Lahore, where he died at Kartarpur in 1539 or 1540. If *location* has anything to do with it, Kabir would have been more Hindu than Nanak was.

Kabir himself made some effort toward the reconciliation of Islam and Hinduism, and Nanak may have known about it, but Kabir achieved no great success in this—which is not to say at once that Nanak did! But Kabir, nevertheless, may be considered an excellent example of those who have sought harmony between Moslems and Hindus—may be viewed as a personal embodiment, in fact, of the qualities and the culture which in solution might be the very medium of accord. But perhaps the culture of the day which Kabir embodied was too eclectic. Perhaps Nanak, also, had been affected by a similar condition. From Benares to Lahore, throughout the Ganges and Jumna valleys and beyond, this eclecticism was prevalent at the time. It was a theory of many and the practice of a few, and some of those who practiced it attained the rank of saints. Kabir may be considered the first conspicuous and widely influential saint of modern India whose *teachings* represent a reconciliation of the major doctrines of Islam and Hinduism, however few were the Moslems and the Hindus who were reconciled by them. The household of Islam itself was not inclined to yield to them.

Long before Kabir's own time, Moslem missions and political activity had begun in India. In fact, Islam had been affecting India for five centuries with increasing power, sometimes winning its way at the sword's point, but often extending itself by peaceful, persuasive means. India had been, as usual, wide open to military conquest, and again the Moslems had found, as others before them had, that India could be conquered with comparative ease and speed. And once inside India in force, they found that conversion to Islam soon brought great numbers to them. India has ever been comparatively disorganized and a fertile field for political intrigue. And Hinduism's utter lack of *creedal* solidarity allowed Islamic dogma ample opportunity of penetration, with freedom to become the state religion within the bounds of Moslem imperial prestige. Some Moslems who had themselves been converts to Islam *outside* India, including many Turki, Afghan and Pathan stocks (the *th* in Pathan is an aspirated *t* and not equivalent to the *th* in the English *this*), had come into the Panjab wave by wave and had established ruling houses among the subjugated Hindus. In those days Rajputs, Jats and other "native" stocks were no match for the hardy, well-trained and martial-minded Moslems. And the process of Moslem conquest, infiltration and accommodation seemed often to parallel that of the much earlier entry of the "Aryans" into India—when the Rajputs, for example, were indeed the *lords* of passage.

A convert to Islam, to Sunni or orthodox Islam, the Afghan Mahmud of Ghazni was the first invader of modern times to use force freely and destructively. He was the real trail-blazer at the dawn of the eleventh century, and he made annual incursions for many years in the name of jihad or "striving" (holy war?) for the faith. Was it indeed jihad? Moslem canon lawyers themselves have not always been unanimous in a definition of jihad. That there were other than religious factors in Mahmud's aggression may, however, be acknowledged by us all. But Moslems themselves count him one of their greatest champions of the faith. Unsuri, his contemporary and a poet of distinction, said of him,

> You are that monarch whom, in both East and West,
> Moslems, Christians, Jews and Parsis name,
> When they count their beads and utter praise of Allah,
> Saying, "O Allah, grant us what in the end is *mahmud*."[1]

Mahmud went as far in 1024 as the town of Somnath (from soma-natha, or "lord of soma," whose shrine was there) in Kathiawar in western India, where in the storming of the town he slew fifty thousand Hindus, because they would not "be converted." He destroyed the famous idol there and carried off booty in the amount, they say, of two million dinars (perhaps four or five million dollars). A poet of his own court, Asjudi by name, composed and offered the following lines in a kasidah in praise of the sack of Somnath,

> When the zealous-minded Sultan made his expedition to Somnath,
> He sealed his own exploits as the standard guage of miracle.[2]

It is not at all clear what opportunities Mahmud gave the Hindus for conversion—unless indeed he gave them none! His methods of warfare, at least, were not conducive to conversion. And yet—amazing though it be—he enlisted and employed Hindu troops, without their turning Moslem. There may actually have been mixed motives on the part of all. But if Mahmud had *religious* zeal in his campaigning, it was inspired in him by the "wooden-minded literalist" Ibn Karram whose convert to Islam he was.

Ibn Karram was himself a fanatic of little or no education who had recoiled from the theological subtleties then widely current in the Moslem world, and he fell into the crassest anthropomorphisms in his views of the Koran: Allah sat like any monarch on his throne; he had made a primal covenant with the seed of Abraham and administered this

[1] From Khondamir's *Habibu's-Siyar*. *Cf.* H. Elliot, *History of India*, IV, p. 189. *Note:* the last word of the quotation—a pun on Mahmud's name, means "very praiseworthy."

[2] *Cf.* Elliot, *op. cit.*, p. 189.

covenant from his seat in heaven. Hindus were apostates, having lapsed from the covenant. They were actually mushriks, unbelievers, or "those who associate" other gods with God. Thus Ibn Karram. It is not clear, however, to what extent Ibn Karram and those of his persuasion had had opportunity to observe that Hindus might justly come within the range of Moslem tolerance, being in the Koranic phrase ahlu'l-kitab, "people of the book," as were Christians, Jews and Sabians, whom Mohammed and Moslems tolerated on that account—these tolerated peoples were allowed to pay tribute and were not forced to adopt Islam on pain of death. But the Koran does not mention Hindus. They, therefore, may be mushriks—such, in truth, they were in Ibn Karram's eyes, and also in Mahmud's. Karramites were altogether literal fundamentalists and gave no place to such liberal theories as that of "analogy," for instance. By analogy, if not by direct citation, Hindus might legitimately have been tolerated. Yet even to liberal Moslems they were such manifest idolaters! And to Moslems of all sorts idolatry was a monstrous, insufferable form of "shirk" (association). Mahmud the Karramite is therefore particularly famous as "the idol-smasher."

But again a contradiction! Mahmud was the patron of many learned and *liberal* Moslems, including the Persian poet Firdawsi who composed the epic *Shahnama*, and the Khwarizmi historian al-Biruni, whose knowledge of the sciences, antiquities and customs of India surpassed that of other Moslems of the time, and also Ibn Sina (Avicenna), the Persian philosopher and scientist. Mahmud's madness was thus better instructed in Ghazni than in India. His inconsistency, however, was more than the common weakness of human nature, and he may serve in striking illustration of the complexity of the contemporary scene. The same holds true of succeeding generations, during which various types of Moslems mingled with various types of Hindus. Such was the state of things throughout the four centuries between Mahmud and Kabir. To most Moslems the time was one of testing true faith from false. The Persian poet Sa'di of Shiraz who died in A.D. 1291 looked back on Mahmud's mission as one of such a testing and made a long poem to commemorate it. And while many Hindus were all along converted to Islam, there were certain Hindu writers who kept denouncing the Moslem's missionary zeal.

The last of the Moslem dynasties which preceded the coming of the Mughals several centuries after Mahmud was that of Lodi (1451-1526), whose capital was Delhi, two hundred and fifty miles below Lahore. One of its sultans, Sikandar, earned for himself, also, as Mahmud had done, the title But Shikan, or "idol-smasher." Since his rule extended from northwest India down the Ganges valley through Jaunpur to Bengal, he had far more opportunity for idol-smashing than Mahmud had. But time, at least, was telling. It seemed to be the Moslem policy of state to destroy all but-khanas, "idol houses," every now and then. And there were Moslem missionaries and theologians aplenty who kept urging such activity. Yet there were nice problems of common and of Moslem canon law. And there were Moslem saints in growing number who advocated and practiced toleration under conditional circumstances which many Hindus seemed willing to fulfill. There were many Moslem "heretics" who could themselves be tolerant, and there were many mystics with an India-bred indifference to mere dogmatic creed.

However, despite any softening by time and circumstance, the official Moslem attitude was hostile, ready to take advantage of the Hindu. Take an illustration of Moslem tactics in Sikandar's day: a brahman down Bengal way was asserting in typical, consistent Hindu fashion, that "Islam and Hinduism were both true religions, were effectual but different roads to God." This at last aroused the indignation of certain orthodox Moslems who persuaded the authorities to arrest the brahman and take him to Delhi for trial, to be questioned by Moslem canon lawyers and the Sultan. The lawyers (qadis), who may have been of the rigid school of Ibn Hanbal, a Koranic literalist, had recourse to a stratagem. They proved that the brahman had proclaimed Islam to be a "true religion" and contended that since there can be only *one* true religion the brahman had proclaimed Islam to be *the* true religion. The brahman, accordingly, was called upon to give the "witness" (tashdid, public testimony) to Islam. The brahman saw the trap and declined, as may have been anticipated (the tashdid is "I testify that there is no God but Allah . . . that Muhammad is the prophet of Allah"). Nevertheless, his refusal was judged to be renunciation of Islam, for which in the Moslem state the penalty is death. He was put to death.

Hindus of all kinds were always under pressure, whether overt or subtle. The tests were not all theological. There was often an economic test, the jizyah, a toleration tax upon non-Moslems—all because the status of the Indians was professedly obscure, or alterable. Technically, jizyah could not be levied upon or accepted from mushriks and apostates. It was not accepted at the outset from Arabian infidels. But the tax-collectors in India employed their own devices, in spite of precedent—and they acted sometimes at variance from official proclamations. Many of the poorer folk among the lower classes of the Hindus embraced Islam to escape the frequent and often heavy taxes. Their own stake in Hinduism was not too high and their faith was quite undisciplined. But it was not so with the upper classes. There were proud warrior-castemen, the Rajputs, for example; and there were prouder brahmans. These were not only the heirs of ancient, ruling houses; they were patrons and conservators of theories, rites and institutions in an old, indispensable tradition. Moreover, many of them held posts of dignity and honor, were valued servants of the state. These all protested and held out firmly against the imposition. And, in consequence, many of them suffered cruel persecution and great disaster. Their fiefs and offices were seized, their womenfolk abused, their sacred shrines were razed, and many of them lost their lives.

Hinduism had itself enduring qualities. Even its idolatry could not be "broken" by sheer force. Nor could Hindus of the better type, especially, be forcefully converted. And when mass conversion did occur, as it did occasionally, it was rather a submission to mere enrolment than a subscription to Islamic doctrine. This in itself meant some deterioration for Islam, some dilution of its faith and rending of its fabric.

Then, too, a change of attitude occurred in many learned Moslems as they came to know and took account of Indian realities, as they became better acquainted, for example, with ancient Hindu culture, learned in more detail about its sacred scriptures, and observed here and there sometimes the purer sort of Hindu worship. They learned to detect the Hindu's own distinction between ideas and practices, between doctrine and social regulations—a distinction which Islam in and for itself had been disinclined to make. Perhaps this distinction had its faults, but, at any rate, Moslems might welcome the experiment. All this tended somewhat to relieve the pressure and to qualify in Islam a too prevalent, blind intolerance. Some Moslems began at last to think that Hindus might properly be classed as dhimmis instead of mushriks, meaning that Moslems might enter legitimately into some sort of "treaty" with them. While dhimmi had a political connotation, mainly, it had implications also for religion. It comes from dhimmatun, a good, Koranic term (cf. *Koran* 9:7-10), meaning "covenant or treaty." So, Mohammed himself had made provision for understandings with non-Moslems—for treaties, in fact, with kitabis, or "book-people"! Why, then, might not Hindus come to enjoy under Moslem rule, as dhimmis and kitabis, security of life and limb and property!

Other factors, also, tended to modify the strained situation. One was increasing intermarriage between Moslem men and Hindu women, especially in areas where Islam was sovereign. In Kipling's version of Hafiz,

> If She be pleasant to look on, what does the Young Man say?
> "Lo! She is pleasant to look on. Give Her to me today!"

Whether the Hindu woman joined the Moslem household by gift or otherwise, she took into it some strange ideas and customs. Some Hindu widows, for example, became Moslem wives or concubines with no change at all of faith. While reliable figures are few in evidence of the extent of intermarriage during these early centuries, the general records of the period give incidental witness to a steady increase in the practice.

Now we must understand that Islam throughout these centuries did not in itself present a solid front. We have referred to Moslem "orthodoxy" already, and have hinted now and then at "heresy." Many Moslem heresies persisted, with active sects to further them. Many sectarians had fled from time to time to India from Iraq, Arabia and Egypt to escape the pressure or the persecution of the orthodox. Some of them had heard that India was hospitable to all creeds, that she had even welcomed Zoroastrian Parsi "fire-worshipers" (so-called). Some of these fugitives, however, suffered further persecution later on in India at the hands of Sunni Moslems (the so-called orthodox) after they had come. Mahmud of Ghazni, for example, was a sunni. Most of the rulers, of course, were sunnis. While Baghdad was the leading Moslem capital (until it fell to the Mongols in A.D. 1258) and the Abbasid khilafat (caliphate) of Baghdad was more or less intact, orthodoxy reigned, although intrigue and heresy wrestled violently with it. After the fall of

Baghdad, heresy played in India an even stronger role—not only in the Panjab, but also in the Doab (the region of the "two rivers," the Ganges and the Jumna). Heresy, together with political intrigue, may indeed have been strongest in the Lucknow region between Moslem Agra and Hindu Benares. In this region the Shiites were the most active and influential of the many heretics.

These Shiites have gone by many names, as we should know: they are Alids, if descended from the fourth khalifah Ali by his first wife Fatimah (the Prophet's daughter) and from the families of their sons, Hasan and Husayn. They are Imamis, if of the line of Imams, which includes Ali, Husayn and their direct descendants who as pretenders to, or rivals of, the Khilafat established an Imamat. Or, there might be Ismailians of the family of Ismail, a rival imami line, which includes the Indian Bohrahs and Khojahs. And there were Mahdawis, those who looked for a mahdi or "coming leader" who would be instead of, or in addition to, the imam—or yet a special type of imam. And there were Qarmatians, also, followers of a certain Ibn Qarmat who had established his claim of "prophet" with them.

These all were Shiites representing in general adherence to a line of blood-descent rather than one of electoral succession—and, at that, a line of restricted kinship as near as possible to the Prophet's own blood-line. Otherwise, they were in general liberals in theology, for their blood had mingled with a liberalizing strain. At least, they adhered to a theocracy of their own within the larger house of Islam. Their essential theory is really comparatively simple, but its demonstration has been confusion—and this includes its ultimate theology (*q.v.*, below). In the regular Moslem view Shiism is quite schismatic. Its most insistent form is Persian rather than Arabian—it gained *complete* control in Persia—but it has played a leading part in India, also. In 1490, the Shah of Bijapur, in the Indian Deccan, proclaimed Shiism the religion of his state. In 1512 Shiism was introduced still further south in territory which became "The Nizam's Dominions," the modern state of Hydarabad, Deccan. Moslem strife with Hinduism was continual, sometimes violent, and violence would sometimes occur also between Shiites and Sunnis. The great annual celebration of the Shiites was often the occasion of such strife. This, known as the Muharram, commemorated the martyrdom of Husayn at Karbala, near Baghdad, and stirred Shiite sentiment to fever pitch.

There was still another type of Islam, one that was more or less "orthodox," which played a widely influential part in Indian religious life. It seemed sometimes, indeed, to make terms with Hinduism or even to yield peaceably to it. Or, possibly, it yielded somewhat to the environment which in a longer space of time had also molded Hinduism. The reference just now is to what we may call Sufism. Sufism is a pervasion, something eclectic and mystical, rather than in itself a sect. It was not a sect like Shi'a, for example, and, moreover, had little if any thought of politics. It was, in fact, ascetic. The Sufi emphasized peculiar, personal habit, such as the wearing of the coarse garb, suf, rather than putting stress on anything institutional, although in time certain Sufi orders were established.

Sufism was in germ, at least, something in Mohammed's own experience (cf. below) and something, also, in the atmosphere of religion in other lands where Islam spread. It was a vague way (safar) of life and thought. Sufis were and generally remained true Moslems, although many of the stricter Moslems considered them irregular, heretical. Perhaps the Sufis disregarded public prayers (salawat) and overdid their dhikrs, or periods of devotional "remembrance." But the general theory of the more thoughtful of them had long since become orthodox through the life and work of the distinguished al-Ghazali (d. A.D. 1111), the eminent

Moslem doctor who added kashf, mysticism, to traditional practice (naql) and rational interpretation ('aql). At least, he emphasized acceptably the way of kashf as separable from these other two.

Sufism was widely current in India by 1500, before the coming of the Mughals. It had developed a doctrine of the essential, mystical unity (tawhid) of Allah, beyond the crass anthropomorphism (*cf.* Ibn Karram) of the *solitary*, the high, the great, deity who sits aloft upholding both the heavens and the earth (*cf.* the "throne verse," *Koran* 2:256). And by their dhikrs they made progress on the "path" toward final, mystic tasawwuf, or "abnegation." But they stopped short of giving up entirely the theory of persistent personality—Sufis never deemed the "person" of either man or God a mere mental construct or spiritual idea. Hindus of many kinds, nevertheless, could welcome Sufis, or recognize in them familiar habits, attitudes and theories. The yogi already practiced self-disciplinary exercises which he might at least suspect the Sufis also practiced. The Sadhu and the sannyasi usually saw nothing strange in sufis. Even the vedanti sometimes thought he saw in Sufism something of his own "non-dualistic" pantheism, and was inclined to identify as one the Moslem sufi Unity and the Hindu universal Brahman. And some Hindu bhaktas, following the way of personal devotion (bhakti) to this or that god (Krishna, Rama, or any other avatara or "descent" of God) could sense their kinship with certain Shiites if not with Sufis, who looked to Ali or to Husayn as a pattern and a guide.

Saints, indeed, of all sorts were common sights in India, Hindu sadhus, Moslem pirs, and many such examples of loosened ties with any particular religion. But of Sufi saints alone, on the eve of the establishment of the Great Mughal empire, there were many well-known by name and widely respected; for example, in Lahore, Kaku Shah of the Chishti order; in Delhi, the Chishtis Hasan Tahir and Muhammad

Hasan; and in Jaunpur, the Chishtis Muhammad Isa and Mawlana Allah Dad. There were also several prominent members of the Qadirite and Shuhrawardi Sufi brotherhoods.

All this immediately foregoing is background and setting for Kabir, in whom many of these elements mingle more or less distinctly, although he himself seems to have belonged to no closed order, whether theological or philosophical, neither to any given sect, nor yet to any one religious household. He was something of a Sufi and something of a bhakta. Hindus have revered him as a guru and Moslems as a pir. There are, however, today six or eight millions of Indians, including Sikhs, who count themselves his heirs. And many single individuals are especially "devoted" to him. A dozen sects, in all, share Kabir's inheritance, but the Sikhs have been the most conspicuous, alert and virile of them all.

Kabir may have been dead by 1449, as a recent biographer[3] asserts, but the dates usually assigned him are 1440-1518. Whether Nanak the Sikh knew him in person or only knew about him, Kabir is a proper symbol of the very heritage of Nanak and the Sikhs, and they have explicitly acknowledged him. He was born near Benares, the very heart of Hinduism, and ended his days there. His father was possibly a Moslem and was certainly a julaha or weaver. His name at any rate is Moslem—"kabir" is Arabic for "great." The designation "al-Kabir" occurs in the Koran as one of Allah's ninety-nine "most excellent names" or titles (qualities, some would say; see *Koran* 7:179 and 34:22). Weavers, if Hindu, were actually low caste. Since most weavers then, as evidence seems to indicate, were Moslems, these may have changed their original religion for the sake of some slight relief by the

[3] Mohan Singh, *Kabir and the Bhagti Movement* (Lahore, 1934).

operation of Islamic "brotherhood." Kabir's father may himself have been a convert to Islam. His mother, however, was a Hindu, possibly of brahman caste, who first or last may have suffered social ostracism for some reason; but we cannot say whether her marriage to a low-caste weaver was the result or the occasion of her degradation. Weavers' women, whether Hindu or Moslem, did not in any case observe the veil, "seclusion" (pardah).

Kabir himself has said, "I am a julaha of Kashi" (*i.e.*, of Benares), and we may accept this evidence. This saying, also, is ascribed to him, namely, "Musalman is my jati, how can I wear the mala!" (*i.e.*, I was "born" a Moslem, how then can I wear a "rosary"!)—but we may hesitate to accept this latter evidence. Why? There was nothing to prevent either a Hindu or a Moslem from wearing the rosary—the holy men of both jatis or "births" wore them. There is yet stronger evidence in a shabd, or saying, of the poet Ravidas, in the Sikh *Granth Sahib*, that Kabir's family slew cows at the Moslem festivals of 'Id and Baqr 'Id, and revered Moslem shaykhs, shahids and pirs. The Moslem connotations are clear enough, but it is equally clear that the neighborhood of his birth was pre-eminently Hindu. Benares, dear especially to Shiva, was an active center of the Hindu bhaktas, of the Ramaites, especially. Pronounced traditions, also, lingered there of the twelfth century Vaihnava vedanti Ramanuja, whose follower was the bhakta Ramananda of whom Kabir himself was a disciple. Benares was the headquarters of this same Ramananda who worshiped the Hindu avatara Rama and Rama's bride Sita, and taught a doctrine of salvation for *all* men through "devotion" to Rama. Ramananda was himself a brahman, his gospel loosely Hindu, and among his followers were a Moslem, a Jat, a shudra, a woman and an outcaste. And there were very many rigid brahmans, also, in Benares. It was a center to which Hindu pilgrims, high and low, of any sect or origin, had recourse.[4]

The *real* clue to Kabir is, after all, not his birth or his associations, but his critical, almost completely hostile, attitude toward all formalism in religion. It is not altogether clear, however, that this came of his own initiative. Perhaps, he was not at all original, except in his unique means of transmission of selected elements in his family and social situation. He made no effort to invent ideas, to offer any which had not been previously expressed. Nor did he advocate a revolution of any sort, thus making of himself an object of partisan attack. If he denounced idolatry as "foolish, false and wrong," he was no more than a theoretical, passive idolbreaker. He questioned the validity of the Koran, and that also of the Hindu Vedas. And he denied that pilgrimage anywhere had any value.

He was a guru, not a deva (god), he called himself "a pir of both religions," *i.e.*, of Hinduism and Islam, and a "novice" of the "true Guru," *i.e*, God. He held fast by the One Name, he said, which in itself covered such names as Rama, Khuda, Shakti, Shiva, or others which applied to God. He sometimes called on God as Rama, but qualified this title—by excluding Sita or any other consort or companion, and by denying that Rama was himself an avatara of God. By "Rama" he meant not the epic hero but the True Guru, the One God, the True Name. In this sense, he advocated personal devotion (bhakta) to Rama, and was himself, therefore, a theistic devotee. But he adhered to karma and transmigration (metempsychosis), and if he spoke of his own

[4] Devotees of Kabir recite this doha, "couplet,"

Kashi taji Maghar gaya, Kabir bharose Ram,
Saindehi Sain milyo, Dadu pure kam,

(Kabir trusting in Ram forsook Benares [Kashi] and went to Maghar [nearby];
O Dadu, that Lord who meets our wants may readily be found).

jati, birth, he meant one of many births. He would have granted that he might have belonged to different sects or faiths at different births. His career, he doubtless thought, was "capable of every form," as the Moslem poet Ibnu'l-'Arabi might have put it. Indeed many Moslems—for example, the thirteenth century Rumi—accepted and expounded the theory of transmigration, as did also some Moslems of India.

Kabir, then, used words and voiced ideas which represented his evaluation of the times he lived in. He recognized philosophy, we know, because he once remarked that such-and-such was "the preaching of the Upanishads." The Vedantic "tat tvam asi" (that thou art), meaning that the individual soul of man, the *atman*, is really one with the Absolute, the *Brahman*, and other abstract phrases were current in the neighborhood about him. But he himself was no philosopher, but only an extraordinary saint among the common people. He was the "teacher" in the sense of transmitting what he had himself selected. He was the "preacher" in a blunt, unpolished Hindi, his own vernacular. He was a "theist" and a "mystic." Although he may have left no record of himself in his own handwriting,[5] or any manuscript of his teachings, there is sufficient record for some thorough reconstruction of it all. There is the *Bijak of Kabir* which the Kabirpanthis cherish, in which occurs the saying, for example, "I touch not ink or paper, or take a pen in hand . . . Kabir has given his instruction with his lips." And there are the "Kabir portions" of the *Granth Sahib*. Someone has claimed that these "portions," sometimes in bulk and some-

[5] A Kabirpanthi doha puts it this way,

Masi kagad chhuyo nahin qalam gahi nahi hath,
Charon jug mahatam jehi, Kabira janayo Nath.

(Without touching ink or paper,
without taking pen in hand,
Kabir praises the Lord who is the
glory of all four eras.)

times in scattered fragments, make up in reality "two-thirds of the *Granth*."

Here is a possible gist of Kabir's teachings in words ascribed to him:

> God is one; there is no second. The One is everywhere.
> Search in thy heart; there is His abode.
> O men and women, seek the sanctuary of the One.
> He pervadeth thy body and the universe as well. . . .
>
> Sacrifice, the rosary, pilgrimage, fasting and alms are cloaks of falsehood.
> Why perform so many ceremonies! Of what avail to Hindus to bathe, and to Moslems to pray at the mosque?
>
> Some pride themselves on the practice of yoga.
> Put away suspension of the breath and all the attitudinal in devotion. . . .
>
> Worship God, thou fool!
> Renounce family, caste and lineage, lest thou think the Maker thus distinguished men. . . .
>
> Birth is in accordance with penalties for deeds;
> Through wanderings and error man keeps coming to his house [*i.e.*, the body].
> If attention be fixed on God, the dread of and the fact of rebirth are at an end. . . .
>
> I have met God who dwells within the heart. . . .
>
> Renounce honors, renounce boasting.
> They who crave for liquor and incline to drunkenness nowhere find content. . . .
>
> When thy stewardship is ended, thou must render an account. . . .
>
> Repeat the name of Ram, thou madman!
> The ocean of existence is difficult to cross;
> The name of God savest him who has tasted of its savour. . . .

I take no thought of sin or virtue; neither go I to a heaven
or a hell;
I shall not die as the rest of the world of men.
The soul that is joined with Him is indestructible. . . .

Although Kabir himself was scarcely more than a feeble voice in the murmuring crowd, his gospel, nevertheless, proved to be a leaven in the total lump. He gathered to himself during his own lifetime of seventy-five or eighty years several thousand devoted followers who stored away his teachings in their minds and perpetuated the fluid order he had formed. He met some opposition while he lived, was censured sometimes by the common people who could not understand his ideas and who thought his habits careless, and was especially opposed by brahmans on account of his lower caste and his own condemnation of them. He freely denounced their pride of race and office, their formalism and their inefficiency—he denied that they were wholesome guides. Some Moslems, also, expressed their disapproval of him, and charges were once brought against him that he was a disturber of the peace!

Now Hinduism, especially when Islam held the civil power, could deal with a reformer only through some priestly agency, or some social regulation which religion authorized. Hinduism thus had ways of ostracizing those who resorted to irregularities in religious ritual and social habit. But Kabir, and others, could defy all this. Moslems could not only bring social pressure to bear on a reformer; they could appeal to the Moslem *state* whose civil law was virtually Islamic canon law. There is evidence that Kabir was brought to judgment in 1495, on the occasion of a visit of the Delhi emperor, Sikandar Lodi, to Benares. No conviction, however, was won by the complainants, nor any penalty imposed—Kabir had not *treasonably* disturbed the peace! Nor was Kabir ever defiant of the state. His sole interest was religion, and he maintained that he had found the very essence of both Hinduism and Islam. On his demise, his memory was, accordingly, preserved by devotees from both households, even though he had not in his own lifetime accomplished the union of these faiths!

> Gyan ratn ka yatn karu, mati ka singar
> Aya Kabira phir gaya, phika hai sansar,

> Kabir came and went back again, having found the world insipid;
> Effort to find the jewel of knowledge is effort to adorn the dust.[6]

[6] For one version of these dohas see W. F. Johnson, *Dharmm Dohawali* (Ludhiana, 1909). *Cf.* F. E. Keay, *Kabir*, and Mohan Singh, *Kabir*.

# Chapter 4. Nanak: the Factual and the Formless

KABIR came and went, as the doha says, his career spent at the chief center of Hindu pilgrimage and reverence, where his memory might have faded into the dim light of the common Hindu day. It escaped that fate, however, due not altogether but mainly to the fact that Nanak the Sikh, also, came and inaugurated a more virile movement nourished partly by Kabir, which gathered Kabir's teachings to itself and included them in its own sacred scriptures. The "Kabir portions" of the Sikh *Granth Sahib* are in themselves sufficient evidence that Sikhism is not only a product of the times in general, but intimately connected also with Kabir's reformation, in particular. There is even the linguistic connection between Kabir and Nanak (cf. below)—they shared something of a common vernacular.

But Nanak and Kabir were, after all, distinct phenomena, differing one from the other. There was between them a distance of many miles, if not some cultural distinction, also. The ripe times in the Panjab brought forth up there a movement of their own. It may one day be concluded that there was even a distinguishable middle ground between Benarasi Kabir and Panjabi Nanak. That is, the Satnamis whom we have mentioned already (cf., p. 17 above) may stand somewhere in between, not merely geographically, as the fact is, but also in matters of religious theory and practice. Or we may find some very close connection between Kabir's own peculiar followers, the Kabirpanthis, and a major portion of the Sikhs, namely the "easygoing" sahajdaris who are most intimately linked with Nanak. And yet something more than miles and cultural variation may enter casually into the final explanation of differences among Kabirpanthis, Satnamis and the two main types of Sikhs, namely, the fact of Moslem overlordship with its variations of administrative policy and, in consequence, varied reactions on the Hindu subjects' part.

Furthermore, there have been *two* Nanaks, the factual and the "formless." This may be recognized at once as something common in the history of religions. He was an historical person; he is also a theological construction. He is what India and the world in general think he is; he is also what Sikhs think of him—he is historico-theological to them, a real person and also a creature of religious fancy. He is emphatically the latter where and when he is the most revered. He is then Nanak Nirankari (nir, "without" and akar, "form"), or Nanak who is not only spiritual but incomparable as well. The reader may recall the inscription to this effect above the altar in the Jabalpur gurdwara (above, p. 19). And yet the two Nanaks are not always to be distinguished from each other. They are two in one, both in practice and in theory.

Sikhs themselves do not usually ascribe divinity to Nanak —he is not "incomparably" divine. He has been called by some of them Nanakdeva, with a faint implication of divinity in such a title, since deva has done duty frequently for "god." But the term itself has its own peculiar history and a varied usage among Indians. In general there is some mortality ascribed to gods, for their divinity is not independent of the common, transmigratory round. The numerous devas of the common people were themselves subject to transmigration, even as men also were, although the gods, nevertheless, were on a higher plane of life. Even "God" among the Indian theists has not been the final Absolute. Nanak was himself a theist, but in such measure that he could not have associated himself in divine intimacy with the one God whom he exalted. Nanak himself made no claim to divinity. Nor do Sikhs think of the *historical* Nanak as "incomparable." They know him as one of many reformers of his day, some of whom they deliberately associate with him in their regard and recollection. This does not make impossible, nor does it even unduly qualify, his life and gospel as their chief concern. We might say that Nanak is *practically* incomparable, that he is unique instrumentally if not in essence, that he was the founder of an enduring order for which his gospel has become unique. But our comparative concern with Nanak and his order requires us to make whatever distinctions are reasonably possible between the factual Nanak of the northwest Indian setting and the legendary, "formless" Nanak, even though the two be mingled in the one account as the Sikhs' own tradition offers it.

The factual Nanak is the more important with special reference to Hindu-Moslem intercourse, although the records of the factual Nanak are comparatively meager. The formless Nanak is the more important as a typical phenomenon in the total history of religion, and the records of him in this role are ample. It was faith in him which made him a compelling figure, the general situation in his day having taken little notice of him. Believers filled to overflowing the small cup of his life, drank deeply of it and endured in the strength of the draught, often laying the cup aside and sometimes quite forgetful of it. But we must find the cup and what its simple contents may have been, and appraise them within their general situation. We must appraise the records, those especially which the Sikhs themselves have made.

An early, western historian of Sikhism, Lt. Col. John Malcolm, who freely acknowledged that his volume was "defective," while we find it very entertaining, gave this expression to the problem of interpretation and reconstruction:

There is no part of oriental biography in which it is more difficult to separate truth from falsehood than that which relates to the history of religious impostors [*sic!*]. The account of their lives is generally recorded, either by devoted disciples and warm adherents, or by violent enemies and bigotted persecutors. The former, from enthusiastic admiration, decorate them with every quality and accomplishment that can adorn men; the latter misrepresent ehri characters, and detract from all their merits and pretensions. This general remark I have found to apply with peculiar force to the varying accounts given, by Sikh and by Muhammedan authors, of Nanac and his successors (*Sketch of the Sikhs*, pp. 4, 5. London, 1812).

Although Malcolm, somewhat in the manner of his nation at the time, thought of Sikhism as religious "imposition," he gave, he said, "a preference, on almost all occasions, to the original Sikh writers," because

In every research into the general history of mankind, it is of the most essential importance to hear what a nation has to say of itself; and the knowledge obtained from such sources has a value independent of its historical utility. It aids the promotion of social intercourse, and leads to the establishment of friendship between nations (*ibid.*, p. 5).

Sikhism was a "nation" at the time, as well as a religion, and was to give an even more impressive account of itself. Malcolm's words about it are those of a statesman as well as of an historian. Though he may have considered Sikhs impostors, he did not class their nation among "savage states." He thought of savage states as "those who have most prejudices, and who are consequently most easily conciliated or offended" (p. 5). If his preference for Sikh writers was valid for his day, ours has yet further ground of confidence in the fruits of Sikhs' own investigation of their history. Sikhism has begun to produce scholars of its own who are competent to deal not only with Sikhism as religion but to interpret its relation to Sikh politics which came into the expanding scene, whatever the founder Nanak may have planned.

There was something in Nanak—or was it circumstantial?—which made possible a religion and a state. Perhaps he perceived more truly than did other reformers of the time the effectual principles of reformation and laid surer foundations of reform. He may, indeed, have had much in common with Kabir and with several lesser predecessors and contemporaries, but his own mission yielded more positive and lasting fruits. The *equality* of faiths had been preached by Gorakhnath, also, a thirteenth century north Indian, a noted Shivite yogi from whom the so-called "split-eared yogis" sprang. And the Vishnuite Ramananda of Benares and Kabir himself had preached this doctrine, although in a somewhat limited degree. Many other voices also had been raised against images and idolatry in worship—Nanak's was not the first, nor has it been the last. Some fraternities had been formed which practiced seva or "service" among the common people, linking it in the daily round with bhakti, or personal devotion. A south Indian Telugu brahman, Vallabha, who died in 1531, preached "service" in the name of Krishna, an avatara of Vishnu. Chaitanya of Bengal and north India, who died in 1533, himself aroused many Indians to devotional excitement over the idea of the equality of *men*. He preached in the name of Radha-Krishna (she was Krishna's spouse, or at least his favorite mistress, who became by a higher kind of interpretation the type and symbol of the human soul which was drawn at last to the ineffable God, having been purified by divine love of the sensuality to which the fickle, human lover is devoted). And, to mention yet another item in the changing scene, Kabir also had set an example of appeal to the common people through their own vernaculars—Nanak, again, was not the first with such an emphasis.

But Nanak's accomplishments were greater for some reason. Was he more constructive, while the others seemed to be, for the most part, dissenters? Kabir was more critical than constructive. He and others seem to have been impressed by life's futilities. Some sought escape from priestcraft, and some, alienation from the world of sense and form. Most of them were quietistic Hindus, even though they had felt something of the force and pressure of activistic Islam. They had all yielded to this extent, at least, to the pressure of Islam, namely, that they would escape from polytheism, from idolatry and from caste—or else from the earthly realm where these prevailed and subsequently find a realm quite free of them. The very service which some of them preached was usually a means of other-worldliness for those who served, rather than a program of reconstruction of the worldly order. While Nanak himself was critical of the world and had much to say of life-negation, there was something positive and realistic in his life—something which the Panjab, at any rate, could utilize and make permanent in religious and political reconstruction. And what it was may be gleaned from many records, including what the Sikhs themselves composed. We shall prefer Sikh sources to the extent of examining them first of all, together with the manner of their origin.

There was, of course, no Sikh literature of prediction which *preceded* Nanak, for there was no prior expectation of his "coming." Later on, however, Sikhs "saw" in certain Hindu and Islamic sources references to Nanak's coming. His advent could be made to fit into the Shiite Moslem theory of the invisible imam or that of the prophetic mahdi, and into the Hindu theory of the avatara, the "descent" or incarnation of divinity. The Sikh "birth records" (janampatris) and "birth stories" (janamsakhis) make much of such prophecy and expectation. On the whole, they embody more of portent and the miraculous than of substantial, historical fact—as is the case, likewise, with birth stories which are so common in accounts of all the Indian religions. The ancient Buddhist Jatakas, for instance, rehearse the many wonderful "births" of Gotama the Buddha—although there seems to be no good evidence that the early Sikhs knew about them. Sikhs must have known, however, something similar among the Jains, and without doubt they knew the reputedly "old" but comparatively modern *Puranas* of the Hindus, which recount in fantastic detail the origins and repeated births of gods and men.

One Sikh janamsakhi may properly be singled out from all the rest of them, that which bears the name of a certain Sewa Das and a date equivalent to A.D. 1588. The date and the authorship may justly be questioned, in view of the fact that it contains thus early an exceptionally full account of Nanak, including some details which are not to be found in the original Sikh scripture itself, the *Adi Granth*, which was composed by Bhai Gur Das at the dictation of Arjun, the fifth Guru (1581-1606). This Gur Das who died in 1629, through whom much of the "life" of Nanak has come down to us, does not mention this Sewa Das's janamsakhi. Gur Das may indeed not have known of it. But whatever the age and authorship of this document, it enjoyed the good fortune to escape the destruction which befell numerous Sikh manuscripts at the hands of Moslems. It escaped—not because it had not been written! It actually constitutes the fullest "life" of Nanak and is on the whole as trustworthy as any other single, purely Sikh source. We may assume that it was written about fifty years after Nanak's death, thus affording evidence of what Nanak had become so soon in the minds of his own faithful.

The *Granth Sahib*, that is, the *Adi Granth*, or the "first" book, is the earliest *official* record. That Guru Arjun should have ordered its composition is in itself some evidence that there had begun to be some need of an accepted canon. We have no means of knowing, however, whether this canon was altogether original, or was an extract or a condensation of writings previously in circulation. It may represent Guru Arjun's own estimate—or even Bhai Gur Das's—of Nanak's life and teachings. Arjun seems to have been the first Sikh clearly to comprehend the master's meaning. In any event this record is authentic within the Sikhs' own tradition, and its biographical details constitute the basis of the complete *Life of Nanak* which Bhai Mani Singh, a granthi ("reader" of the *Granth*) of Amritsar, composed after the death in 1708 of Gobind Singh, the tenth and last Guru.

An excellent biography entitled *Nanak Parkash* (making "manifest" the "famous" Nanak-parkash has a host of meanings) was written in 1823 by a certain Santokh Singh, but it also relied mostly on the *Granth* for facts, while drawing freely on the "birth" stories for legend. Pamphlets have frequently appeared rehearsing incidents in Nanak's life. In 1936 Bhai Jodh Singh of the Khalsa College, Amritsar, considered in his *Gurmati Nirnay* Nanak's contribution to Indian religion. But no Sikh has yet examined the career of Nanak by the full means of modern, critical technique. Historical criticism has yet to measure him. He is still, therefore, in general, nirankari, "formless." A writer who deems himself a Sikh "with limited credulity," Mohan Singh, of the staff of the Oriental College of the Panjab University, has applied to the life of Kabir the critically historical method. Some Sikh must do the same one day for Nanak.

Mohan Singh professes to find in the Indian setting itself conclusive evidence of the very normal process by which a creature of legend is made, such as a bhagat, or a saint. Kabir, the subject of his sketch, was deemed a bhagat, one possessed of at least a measure of divinity. Nanak called himself, it seems, sachiar, a "man of truth," an imam or "guide," a pir or "saint" and claimed some extraordinary character—and Sikhs have called him deva, "god." By some process deification qualified and completed Sikh reverence toward him. Has Mohan Singh described the process in terms of his legendary bhagat? This, according to his reckoning,[1] is the bhagat's usual career:

1. He is lowly-born, the re-incarnation of one of the vague and numerous host of the "immortals,"
2. Miracle attends his birth,
3. In his early years he questions, through that divinity which is manifest in him, the current rites and ceremonies, and composes and sings songs in expectation of a reformation,
4. In his second stage, as a householder (the 2nd ashrama), he meets either his own guru or else the Lord himself, and sees more clearly the vision of the new ideal about which he sings,
5. He experiences some displeasure in his own household from his and his wife's children and from human kindred of his own station, and yet, nevertheless, wins the favor of some through his exercise of virtue,
6. He is challenged by many associates and neighbors, but meets their tests, proving his capacity by miracles,
7. He enjoys special interviews with his Lord,
8. He acquires a special following from among whom he designates intimate disciples,
9. His life is miraculously prolonged, sometimes to a hundred and twenty or even to three hundred years,
10. He makes at last an ascent to heaven from the midst of his disciples who, upon his departure, fall into disputation over his true teachings and over the legitimate succession to him in the leadership of the new order which he founded,
11. He re-appears to one or more of the original disciples, giving specific indication of sound doctrine and of the true succession!
12. He operates thereafter as a free, invisible yet potent spirit giving guidance to anyone who needs it, inspiring and transforming willing men and ultimately saving them.

And the saint's career by the legendary process reaches possibly half the bhagat's distance:

1. The saint is born, according to all, even brahmanical, accounts, of low-caste,
2. He lives normally, according to his station and the usual stages, although giving meanwhile some evidence of unusual longing,

[1] The eighteen items following are the author's own formulation of Mohan Singh's somewhat incoherent exposition.

3. He turns in time altogether to religion and its ways in obedience to a special "call,"

4. In retirement he finds his guru or his Lord, and practices devotion to him,

5. He follows actively the religious way, relying for support upon the fellowship of saints,

6. He has recourse, whenever necessary, to miracle in demonstration of his saintly life and of the perfect doctrine which he preaches.

Was Nanak saint or bhagat, according to these recipes? The records (sakhis, etc.) do not draw one line between the two; he is both: there was miracle at his birth, he enjoyed special interviews with his Lord, he chose some intimate disciples, and since his death some followers have known him as free spirit. Let us look awhile at his whole career, the fabric woven of fact and fancy—with each quite obvious almost always.

Nanak (1470-1540) was born in the neighborhood of Lahore in a village on the bank of the Ravi river, which was then called Talwandi and later known as Rayapur. Lahore was the old capital of the Moslems of the Panjab, but the village had been founded by a Hindu raja, and the villagers were mostly Hindus. It had been sacked several times by Moslems who were engaged primarily in civil war, with incidental reference to the Hindu populace, and was at last assigned by the Moslem king of Delhi to one of his retainers, Rai Bular by name, whose family, of Rajput ancestry, had been converted to Islam. Rai Bular was himself a Moslem convert. The village was thus in itself typical of Panjabi Hinduism under Moslem rule. The Moslems of upper India about A.D. 1500 were, on the whole, a small proportion—ten or fifteen per cent, perhaps—of the total population. Some of them were of alien stock, but most of them were already of native Indian parentage.

Nanak himself came of stock which was predominantly if not altogether Hindu. Mohsan (or Moshan) Fani, a Persian resident in India, who was born "not later than 1615," according to Professor A. V. W. Jackson, identified Nanak in his *Dabistan,*[2] or "School of Manners," as having been born of "the tribe of Bedians, who are Kshatriyas" (p. 284 of Jackson's edition, New York, 1901). The Bedi or Vedi folk were a clan of the Bunjahi tribe which claimed descent from Raja Kalpat Rai of Kasur, who had studied the Hindu Vedas (whence the designation "Vedi") under priestly instructors in Benares. Being "warrior" (*kshatriya*) stock, however, it was most unusual for them to have any claim to Vedic wisdom, for learning was not incumbent upon warriors. They took special pride, nonetheless, in the title, and in their connection with Benares, holy city of the Hindus and seat of Hindu culture. The Bedis' own headquarters have long been in the village of Dera Baba Nanak, above Lahore, from which the pilgrims (*cf.* p. 22 above) set out for Amritsar. Within Sikh tradition, therefore, the Sikh holy city of Amritsar and the Hindu holy city of Benares are much closer to each other than the interval of seven hundred geographic miles might indicate. Nanak's own father's mother in Talwandi was known as the Banarasi or "woman from Benares," having come to the Panjab in a migrant family. And his father's father, named Shiv Ram (Shiva Rama), was not only Hindu, but one who, if his name has any special meaning, held a theological point of view in which Shivite and Vishnuite (Ramaite) elements mingled indiscriminately. There is, of course, nothing curiously extraordinary in this, for while Benares was Shiva's seat pre-eminently, Vishnu shared it with him, without objection, through the incarnations (avataras) Rama and Krishna. A Hindu might appropriately wear the name or names of any deity within the Hindu pantheon.

Nanak's father was Kalu, a "khatri"—a designation which by its usage then would give him social standing above that

[2] Mohsan Fani, *Dabistan* (ed. Shea and Troyer, London, 1843; ed. Jackson, New York, 1901).

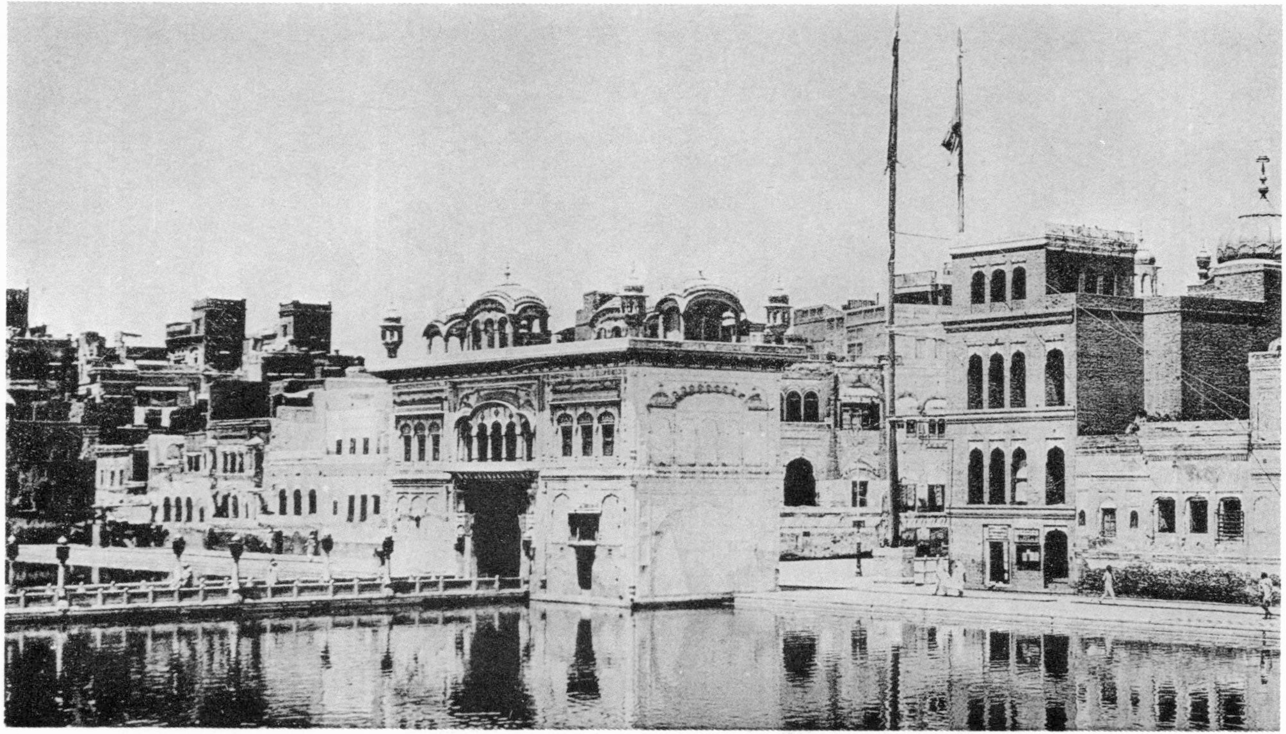

THE TREASURY GIVING ENTRANCE TO THE CAUSEWAY AT THE WESTERN EDGE OF THE POOL

THE DARBAR SAHIB VIEWED THROUGH THE ARCHWAY OF THE TREASURY

of the Jat, but lower than that of the Rajput of genuine kshatriya or "warrior" stock. There was nothing necessarily martial in the very designation. One record says that Kalu engaged in trade as a grain-merchant and also in agriculture. His wife, Nanak's mother, was Tripta, daughter of Rama, a native of the Manjha country south of Lahore between the Ravi and the Beas rivers. She was doubtless of humble origin. In accordance with the custom prevailing then among the humbler folk, she resorted to her parents' home for confinement and delivery. Nanak was born there—in Talwandi or Rayapur—as was his sister Nanki, also. The names Nanak and Nanki are related directly to nanke, one's *mother's* parents. All the personal names in Nanak's family and ancestry, moreover, tend to indicate his humble, Hindu origin.

His native village was not without distinction of a sort. Its Moslem zamindar, or "landlord," had provided some improvements in it and had built a qila, "fort," for its protection against ordinary dangers and assailants. Round about the village was ample acreage for cultivation, and there was "jungle" conveniently near with its supply of wood. It enjoyed a limitless supply of water from wells and the Ravi river for irrigation. And some provision for simple education was in force. Security, peace and prosperity were its lot in Nanak's boyhood. In all this there may have been no unique distinction, for there were dozens of such Panjabi villages, but its fame became a legend later on, because it was the place of Nanak's birth and childhood.

According to the legend, earthly signs and heavenly portents attended Nanak's advent. It was "the Lord" who came and at his coming "unbeaten sounds" were heard at the gateway of his mother's parents' home. The midwife Dawlatan said that the babe's voice was at once that of a wise man whose very laughter rang with wisdom. Among those who came to pay him homage and to bear witness that in him "a great saint had come to save the world" were "six ascetics," "nine naths," "fifty-two birs," "sixty-four yoginis," "eighty-four siddhs" and "three hundred and thirty million devas" (*i.e.*, thirty-three karors of gods)—every grade of being, that is, in the ideal round of life expressed appreciation and devotion. The family priest himself, Har Dyal, an astrologer, viewed the babe "hath jorna" (with clasped hands), and predicted that the child when it became a man would "carry the umbrella" (the chhatar, sign of dignity, authority and rule), would be highly regarded by Musalmans and Hindus, would enjoy the acclaim of the hosts of heaven and the men of earth—and would himself worship "none but God." From all these signs and portents, including his and the midwife's testimony, Har Dyal, the astrologer, composed a horoscope, as the custom was, charting auspicious seasons of the new-born babe's career and recording prophecy's fulfilments (but we detect therein this major contradiction and ask, Why a horoscope if Nanak's knowledge came by intuition, as the birth stories themselves declare?).

The plainer fact is, of course, that Nanak's round of life was from the first dictated largely by common custom. He received some formal education in the local pathshala or madrasa—an elementary school—and learned from specimens on the upper margin of a patti, or wooden "slate," to trace the nagari characters of the Hindi, and the Arabic and Persian alphabet of the Urdu—tongues representing different cultures on the whole. Some other lessons he learned by the memoriter method, sharing in their recitation in group concert. And he learned many things outside of school. A Moslem villager, Sayyid Hasan, himself childless, took a fancy to Kalu's son, having long been a neighbor and friend of Kalu, and, as we may suppose from the Persian record and Hasan's title of sayyid, introduced the lad to Shiite Moslem doctrine. Nanak learned many things from observation, including both mosque and temple ceremonial. Indeed he seems to have displayed early an unusual disposition toward religion. His piety was often more pronounced than his willingness to engage in manual labor on the family's behalf, and his father sometimes complained at this, even to the extent of rebuking the lad. The father, however, died in Nanak's youth, leaving the boy more than ever, perhaps, free to follow his own desires.

Nanak became acquainted in due course with portions of the Hindu shastras, sacred writings, with bits of Moslem lore, such as some of the hadith, or "sayings" of Mohammed, and with portions of the Koran which were in circulation. Although legend represents Nanak as talking spontaneously of these sacred writings and as understanding instinctively all that he heard recited, we may account for his "divine knowledge" by other means, also. He may have given expression to "inspired" sentiments, and may have amazed his teachers by his profound questions. But he was becoming a mouthpiece for what the environment provided. It is recorded that his curiosity was much aroused over the Arabic-Urdu letter *aliph* and the Hindu Indian numeral *ek* (*ikk*, *ekka*) for "one." In each instance the sign is a straight, perpendicular stroke which has been made to represent in theology the "oneness" and "unity" of God. He may have heard wandering teachers, Moslem and Hindu, discussing this very item.

Nanak was initiated at nine years of age by the family priest, Har Dyal, into the ranks of the dwijas, or "the twice-born," and received then the emblematic janeu, or "thread," to be worn thereafter always about his neck.[3] This initiation and assumption of the thread distinguishes members of the three upper castes from the fourth-caste shudras. These upper-castemen are subject to brahman codes, and enjoy

[3] Among Hindus, ascetics in the fourth "stage" of life—for example, sannyasis and sadhus—might discard the thread.

the ministry of brahman priests—whereas shudras have their own, different order. Legend tells us that Nanak caught the janeu in his hand during the initiation and questioned its real worth! Upon the priest's insistence that the thread was suggested by the ancient Vedas as a proper, indispensable symbol of religion, Nanak, as the story goes, uttered these lines spontaneously,

> Make mercy thy cotton, contentment the twisted thread
> and continence the knot,
> And thus make a janeu for thy soul. . . .
> A man dies, the thread is broken and his spirit departs
> without it. . . .
> By praise and adoration of The Name comes honor and
> the true janeu
> Which does not break, but lingers for man's entrance into
> the court of God.

Nanak's opportunities for a career in religion increased with the passing years—he breathed a lively atmosphere. Whatever may have come to him from formal schooling and his local contacts, far more, perhaps, came through association with faqirs, sadhus, yogis, sufis and the like, toward whom he had, it seems, a natural (or supernatural?) inclination. Some of these were Hindus of the third ashrama, or "stage," of the holy life, in retirement about Lahore, while others, of the fourth stage, moved about freely in the world with staff and alms-bowl. There were not only Hindus and Moslems, but also Parsis, Jews and, most likely, Christians among the "saints" in those parts of India. They had much in common, not only in the manner of their life, but in the phraseology, also, of their teachings—how much indeed there is in common, after all, among sentiments and phrases all the way from Damascus to Benares, whether recorded in the Bible, the Koran, the Avesta, or the Shastras! And the *Granth Sahib* was already in process of formation—if we recall Kabir. Nanak came under the influence of kindred expressions by various devotees. Nevertheless, it would be wrong to insist that he was merely acquiring the mind and the manner of imitation, and to say that if, later on, he expressed his teachings in any similar phraseology, he was exhibiting dependence and not initiative. He need not, for example, have been in debt to other sources for these teachings of his: "It is the man himself that soweth, and he himself that eateth" (*Japji* 20), and "Even as one sows, so also will he reap; as he earns, so let him eat" (*cf. Japji* 3, 25). These are very common sentiments. Job had said, "Men reap the evil that they plough, the trouble that they sow" (Job 4:8). An ancient Upanishad had said, "According as one acts, so does he become; the doer of good becomes good, the doer of evil, evil" (*Brihadaranyaka* 4.4.5). St. Paul had said, "Whatsoever a man soweth, that shall he also reap" (*Galatians* 6:7). And Mohammed had said that "He who presents himself bringing good, to him a tenfold reward; who comes with evil, he shall receive naught but the like" (*Koran* 6:161). There is some simple leaven of figure and idea throughout the whole human lump.

Although a certain piety was early evident in Nanak, he did not neglect altogether the method of the normal round of life. He observed the second, the grahasti, or "householder's," stage, and thus kept the family record "spotless." He was married—at nineteen? Or was he only fourteen? Marriage in India is never merely one event on a certain day; it begins with betrothal and concludes with the consummation. In any case, a bride named Sulakhari was found for him from among the Chona family of the village of—Pakho (or perhaps Batala?) near Sultanpur. Once married, he took service in Sultanpur with his brother-in-law, Jai Ram, a revenue-collector. He was, however, restless and unhappy during these days of married life. A janamsakhi says that he "showed little affection for his wife." Was his mind actually divided? Had he really wished to avoid the grahasti stage? Did he know, for instance, that the famous Vedanti Shankara had avoided it for himself by securing release from his marriage-contract and entering immediately into the sannyasi, or "separated" stage—in which the janeu thread also is dispensed with (and Shankara was a brahman). Whether the fault lay with Nanak or not, his wife went often to visit her parents—every time, of course, as the custom was, on the eve of her confinement; but her visits otherwise were frequently extended. The two families, furthermore, became embroiled in altercations. The wife's father, Mula, called Nanak "mad." And at last she and Nanak separated. She took her two sons, Sri Chand and Lakhmi Das, a babe "on the hip" (or "in arms," as we should say), and went to live in her parental home, while Nanak went his way. He quitted his post in the revenue-collector's service and took to wandering.

Nanak was then, possibly, in his early thirties—not too young to undertake ascetic ways, in accordance with ample precedent in India. But some distress of mind in connection with family and occupational affairs may have hastened his decision. He was bound, sooner or later, to take up an exclusively spiritual career. The record is not altogether clear. Perhaps Nanak had periods of separation, now at home and now abroad (he was not a brahman). Indeed, even after "final" separation, there were certain associations with his family—as in the case of Mr. Gandhi at a later time. Gandhi continued merely formal association with his wife after his renunciation, the two living together in continence. Also, Gandhi's "numerous bickerings" with his wife (of which he tells us in his autobiography) may match some of Nanak's, although in Gandhi's case, at least, they gave way in the end to peace.

There were forty years which Nanak devoted to his special mission, whatever may have prompted its beginning. The Moslem *Dabistan* declares in its own version of the story that Nanak renounced the "granary" and abandoned his wife and family in response to the plea of an ascetic darwish (himself a Moslem, probably). And it goes on to say that "at first he took little nourishment; afterward he allowed himself but to taste a little cow-milk; next, a little oil; then nothing but water; and at last took nothing but air, becoming what Hindus call a pavanahari, or 'consumer of air only.' "[4] Again, it is not clear that this reference is to more than some periodic fast, although it may refer to the final entrance of Nanak upon his prophetic mission. There may have been an interval between his first separation from his family and his final determination to follow the strict religious way. There was a period of fifteen or twenty years, which concluded his career. This is the time of most importance, for which the earlier years had been a preparation. In this period a definite following of disciples was established in response to a more clearly formulated gospel, including among them his own son, Sri Chand—who, after Nanak's death, founded an ascetic order of his own (that of the Udasis) whose headquarters have been near the Darbar Sahib in Amritsar (cf. pp. 18, 23 above).

Nanak may have been about fifty years of age when, in response to a special vision, he entered the final phase of his career, when God offered him the cup of amrit, "nectar," in token and pledge of divine favor and in promise of Nanak's ultimate success. God then commissioned him to "repeat the Name," to inspire others, also, to repeat it, and to teach all mankind the "true religion." It is said that Nanak under the inspiration of this experience uttered the mul mantra, or "basic text" of Sikhism, namely,

> Ik onkar satinamu
> Karta purakhu nirbhau nirvairu,

[4] A common expression in north India for having a stroll or taking a walk is "hawakhana" (eating the air).

Akalmurti ajuni saibhang gurprasadi;
Japu,
Adi sachu jugadi sachu hebhi sachu,
Nanak hosi bhi sachu,

or,

One, the essential Om, True Name,
Doer, pervader, fearless, without enmity,
Figure of timelessness, self-existent, the kindly guide,
Praise!
Primeval truth, ageless truth, the actual truth,
The truth, O Nanak, which can never fade.

There came to him in this experience the very sound of the True Name and the consciousness of his commission as the True Name's guru—Nanak, therefore, was henceforth gūru of the true religion. Sikhs have sometimes compared this "revelation" with the "This is my beloved Son, hear ye Him!" of the Christian tradition, with the Koranic "Say, He alone is God, the eternal One," and with the Vedanti thesis, "Thou art That" (which makes the Hindu devotee at last one with the infinite).

This crucial experience of Nanak consumed "three days," says Sikh tradition. He had gone into the jungle with his faithful minstrel Mardana. Normally this would have aroused no concern on the part of anyone, but in this instance some were worried over his long absence, and a searching party which included a Moslem mulla, or schoolmaster (who may have been in charge also of the village mosque), sought and found him—he had not been devoured by a jungle beast, nor had he strayed to the river Ravi and been drowned in it. But upon discovering him, the party was amazed at his appearance! The mulla thought him "mad" and made ready to exorcise the "demon" that had seized him—and devised an amulet to hang protectively about his neck. But Nanak assured them all that he was not mad—not mad, said he, unless beside himself in Sat Nam, "True

Name." He bade Mardana play the rebeck[5] in accompaniment, while he himself improvised and sang a chant in exposition of his wonderful experience and of his commission by Sat Nam. He may have recited then and there the mul mantra, as above. He did proclaim, as the legend puts it, that "there is no Hindu, nor is there a Musalman," but only brethren under God. Several of the party fell at the guru's feet and would have offered him gifts—which Nanak declined, bidding them give them to the poor, and affirming that he himself was faqir, or "poor," for God's sake and a darwish[6] of Sat Nam.

The full story of Nanak's mission is very varied—very full and varied as legend, especially, has shaped it. He wandered widely throughout India and beyond, if legend is to be believed, and the story includes some reference to every major aspect of the India of his time. But we may assume that even his actual wanderings were extensive. He may have traveled as far into the southeast of India as Puri in Orissa, seat of the famous, ancient shrine of Jagannath, "Lord of the Earth"; as far southward as Ceylon, where Tamil Hindus and Hinayana Buddhists flourished; as far into the northwest as the Khaibar Pass into Afghanistan—although we may indeed distrust the story that he made the pilgrimage to Mecca!; and as far to the southwest as Gujarat, around the Gulf of Cambay—although "Gujarat" in the records is sometimes specifically only a village of the Panjab. In any case, all of these journeys are at least symbolic, exhibiting the kinds and quality of culture and religion in Nanak's world. For example, Nanak may actually have interviewed the Moslem Mughal Babur. He had occasion, at least, to comment as an eyewitness on Babur's military conquest of the Panjab. He sought to reconcile the religions of his day, and even the

[5] A simple, stringed musical instrument.

[6] These two terms, "faqir" and "darwish" have a distinctly Moslem flavor.

costume that he wore in traveling was symbolic of his mission to the larger world.

Since garb was a means of identifying teachers of religion, his was usually composite. He wore on his head a qalandar, head-dress of a Persian Moslem order of faqirs or darwishes; on his forehead, the saffron tilak mark of the Hindu (its actual form uncertain, unless in imitation of the Shivite horizontal line; although it may have been a perpendicular, something of a compromise combination of the Vishnuite and Shivite marks); about his throat a necklace of bones; about his body a mango-colored jacket and a loosely draped white sheet; and in his hand a string of beads. And, it appears, he wore a beard, as did the minstrel Mardana, also, and other followers, according to the tradition, at least, of the "bearded" Sikhs. But evidently his hair was cropped under the qalandar. All this gave him an appearance emphasizing the composite character of his religious office. And many attended him as he went about, some choosing to become his regular companions and permanent disciples. Mardana, the minstrel, was soon his boon companion and sworn devotee who was skilful with the rebeck, which he played in accompaniment of his master's oral teaching. Among those of the inner circle were Lahna, a simple, sincere man who under the name of Angad later became at Nanak's death head of the Sikh movement; and Bala, a Sindhi Jat, and Ram Das who was affectionately called Buddha, meaning "old fellow." And there was Sri Chand, Nanak's own son, also. They were an informal band, much in the traditional manner of the Indian teacher of religion and his intimate disciples.

We have some special reason for deeming the band informal, for, after all, Nanak may not have labored consciously toward the establishment of a new order and a new religion. And the matter of teaching is in somewhat the same case—there is no reason to think that he had definitely in mind a new Scripture, for example, to bequeath to India and the world. The origins of institutions are seldom instantly specific, regardless of numerous details that enter specifically into view. Nanak indeed took account of various creeds and popular practices, and mentioned now and then religious leaders, but he seemed—somewhat vaguely, to be sure—in search for truth, the basic truth on which, or within which, the followers of various orders might unite. The two chief orders, incidentally, to be reconciled were Hinduism and Islam! Was this chief objective reflected not only in his thought and in his teaching, but also in his conduct? For one thing, his renunciation of his family had never been complete—he died at last at the ripe age of seventy years among his own kinsfolk in Kartarpur (forty miles above Lahore) where they had meanwhile gone to live. Does this reflect some compromise, at a casual venture, between a Hindu and a Moslem way? But what the motives and the fruits of Nanak's mission were is a matter to be studied later on.

Meanwhile we are concerned with many of the travels of Nanak and his followers. They kept on the move usually throughout the year. Although the rainy season sometimes hindered them, during which they would put up awhile in a "rain-retreat," they nevertheless moved about locally even then. This season from June to September afforded them occasion to review their work and sometimes to change their habits. The "rains" are often mentioned in the janamsakhis. They say that Nanak would designate a village, if ever Mardana would ask about a place to spend the rainy time, a village which they thought might offer unusual hospitality. But again, in this connection, also, we may observe that Nanak did not seem intent on establishing an *order*. He made no effort to leave in any village a definite group of followers, even though inevitably local, informal groups came into existence in loose, quasi-monastic bonds. There were many who came to realize that a new teaching was actually abroad. But this was true of other seasons, also. Even during the "touring" season, and especially in the hot weather (from March to May), the band would often stop a while along their way. There were dharmshalas, or "religious establishments," which offered temporary hospitality. And there were many banglahs, or "rest-houses," provided by the government or by private benefactors—forerunners of the more modern dak-khanas, "posthouses," or travelers' retreats, which the government has furnished.

Indeed, we may further qualify what has been said about the informal band before attempting to recount typical aspects of the mission. As the janamsakhis tell the tale, Nanak and Mardana are usually alone "on tour." This is especially true of any longer journey, whatever the number in any one locality. These two were truly *Sikhs* and boon companions extraordinary.

They came once upon a house over which a Moslem shaykh, Sajjan, presided. He had provided in it not only for Moslem but also for Hindu worship—it had its masjid, "mosque," and its but-khana, "image-altar." He seemed to welcome anyone for any form of worship. This was quite in keeping with one aspect of the times, and the hostelry offered weary travelers a place of rest. But the establishment was not altogether what it seemed to be. The keeper's piety was, in reality, a cloak for crime! He was a thag,[7] or something of that sort, accustomed to slay his sleeping guests, take possession of their goods and throw their bodies into a well. Next day the shaykh would take his rosary and staff to walk about, or spread his rug at the appointed hours and sit on it "at prayer"—doubtless prayer for new victims of his "piety." He was, accordingly, "at prayer" one evening when

[7] Meadows Taylor, *Confessions of a Thug*, ed. C. W. Stewart (New York, 1916), is a classic on the subject of the thags in India.

Nanak and Mardana arrived, and they waited respectfully until its end, until the shaykh could indicate the night's accommodations. Of course, the two had little goods in their possession, and might have gone unharmed throughout the night, with never an inkling of their host's true character. But to their great surprise they found themselves confessors to him, to this outlaw-in-disguise, because at bedtime they recited such a hymn to God, with such manifest devotion, that the shaykh "came to his senses" when he heard it, fell at Nanak's feet and kissed them, confessing his evil ways and seeking pardon. And Nanak promised pardon, on condition that his repentance be followed duly and confirmed by the restitution, wherever possible, of stolen goods and the transformation of the house into a gurdwara! The story says that all this was done, including the establishment of what, therefore, must have been the first truly Sikh gurdwara—although the time and place are both uncertain.

The incident is highly probable, and may be taken as reflecting something of the general state of things in those days. The thags were ostensibly religious devotees, a society devoted to a phase of the shakti, or "power" (really *female* energy) of the "great god Shiva." There were many names for this power, as there were many wives of Shiva. In particular, the goddess Durga, the "distant," and the goddess Kali, "the dark," were Shiva's chief shakti. The thags acted under such patronage, more especially in the name of Kali. But robbery, not religion, was their motive, and by it they made their livelihood in Kali's name. Often they would lie in wait along the highway for travelers of whose movements they had had some prior information. Some of them might have offered a traveler their services as guides and guards. Merchants, for example, were often in need of convoy and protection as they moved about the country with goods and money. In any case, whether accompanying the prospective victim or lying in wait for him, a pleasant evening was arranged somewhere along the way at a spot where they would pass the night. There would be the evening meal and the campfire circle (always the campfire, if in the cold season) and some entertaining conversation. But a grave had already been dug nearby for the probable accommodation of the victim's body, with heavy stones available to cover it against exposure by wild animals. And by prearrangement a thag within the circle would steal up casually behind the unsuspecting merchant and deftly, instantly, strangle him with a knotted cloth without an outcry. Nor was any sign of the tragedy left anywhere. And the merchant's goods were the thags' reward in Kali's name.

Nanak and Mardana encountered one evening in a jungly spot men whom Nanak recognized at once as thags—in fact, they said they were and demanded his "money." They would have set upon the wanderers immediately except for the effect on them of Nanak's "lustrous face." As they hesitated, Nanak said to them, "Very well, but first do one thing, and then do what you will with us. Let us all go yonder to where the smoke is rising from a fire." Did Nanak really know of thagi practice and imagine that he had stumbled into a camp already made ready for some unsuspecting traveler? But the fire was not the thags' own; it was a funeral pyre with the corpse already burning on it in the midst of mourning relatives of the deceased. The thags consented, however, and a most unusual scene was enacted about the pyre. Nanak professed to tell the awed company what he saw there: Yama, the god of the underworld was there with his attendant spirits contending with Rama, the savior god, for the dead man's soul; Rama was there with his angels ready to bear the soul to heaven, and Yama's demons were ready to take the soul to hell. The presence of Nanak with his "favorable glance" lent the balance of power, and Rama's angels at last bore the soul away. This impressed the thags especially, and they forthwith fell at Nanak's feet, begged his pardon for their sins and asked to be enrolled among his followers. Nanak was moved with compassion for them and granted them forgiveness on condition that they renounce their evil ways and take to—agriculture! They were to confirm their penitence by giving to the living poor what they had stolen from the departed rich and were to practice the utmost self-denial. Nanak assured them finally that their "life had been adjusted" and that they had attained janam savaria, or "saving birth."

On another occasion Nanak came near a village where a domestic celebration was in progress. A son had been born there to a grain merchant, and the farmers in their joy were gathered about his house throwing red powder and offering their congratulations. Nanak tarried a little way off, while Mardana went nearer to observe details and bring back a report. Nanak's comment on Mardana's report was somewhat enigmatic, to the effect that it was not really a "son" who had been born to the merchant, but a "creditor who had come to settle an account," and that this creditor would depart next morning after settlement. Since Nanak seemed in the mood for recitation, Mardana took up the rebeck to accompany him as he extemporized a hymn on the "watches" of the night, likening them to the "stages" through which a whole life passes. But for this creditor the night was the entire span of life—Nanak was, in fact, predicting death for the new-born son with the passage of the night. And, sure enough, next day the red powder of joy gave place to the ashes of mourning, the "settlement" was attended with lamentation, and the body of the little "creditor" was taken to the funeral pyre.

Nanak met at Panipat one day the chela, "pupil," of a Moslem pir, and astonished him by responding in the precise Moslem phrase to the chela's greeting. To the chela's salutation, "Peace be upon you" (salam alaykum), Nanak replied, "And on you be peace" (wa alaykum as-salam), by the use of which Nanak seemed to be acknowledging some debt to Islam. The pir and his chela may have taken Nanak, therefore, to be a fellow-Moslem, although the Sikh account may merely mean that these Moslems themselves admired Nanak. Nanak, however, was often asked if he were a Hindu or a Musalman? Neither his mixed garb nor his religious practices could be certainly interpreted by *all* observers.

Once at Hardwar (Hari-dwara, "Shiva's door-of-access," a sacred site of the Hindus on the upper Ganges, where the river comes out of the Himalayas through the foot-hills and flows on into the lower plain), the question of his real character arose. Crowds were bathing there in the magic waters and tossing handfuls toward the East in honoring their ancestors, as custom bade them. Nanak joined the bathers and took to throwing water toward—the West! In such a place this meant the Moslem prayer-direction—Mecca was off that way. The Hindus, therefore, criticized him, only to hear him respond, "And how far off are your ancestors whom you honor here?", while he went on tossing water westward. Still they pressed for an answer, and he said that he had sown a field at home (in the Panjab, westward) on the eve of his leaving for the pilgrimage to Hardwar, and that since there was no one at home to water it in his absence, he was tossing water on it from Hardwar. When his fellow-bathers jeered him on hearing this and called him pagal, "crazy," he reminded them calmly that his watering was doubtless as effective for his distant field as their's was on their ancestors' behalf. At which their jeering ceased, as if assenting to his wisdom, and, taking advantage of their silence, he warned them of their own false ideals and their ineffectual acts of worship. He bade them understand that rites and ceremonies were not the final tests of true religion!

Nanak's travels gave him opportunity, likewise, to talk of social problems. Once he visited Lalu, a low-caste carpenter, who lived in Sayyidpur. Lalu would have prepared a "clean" spot on his modest, otherwise "unclean" premises, where his two guests might eat their food without defilement. But Nanak prevented Lalu from doing this, declaring to his host that "the whole earth" is clean in God's own sight. And when, later on during Nanak's visit in the village, the zamindar himself, the village "proprietor," sent an invitation to Hindus "of all castes," as he said, to attend a public feast in Nanak's honor, Nanak declined the invitation, giving as his reason the fact that he did not belong to any "caste." This offended the zamindar who asked at once how Nanak could eat food with Lalu the low-caste and refuse the food of a man of higher caste? Nanak responded, according to the sakhi, by securing a morsel of the food of the zamindar to put with some of Lalu's food which he had taken with him (because he had not eaten all that was set before him), and by squeezing the two bits. From Lalu's food dropped milk, sign of the bread of honest toil, while from the zamindar's dropped blood, sign of gain by bribery and oppression. There are, to be sure, some inconsistent elements in such a tale, but the burden of it as a whole is evident.

Near Ambala, again on the broad plain of Panipat, Nanak visited a mela, "gathering." India's destiny has often been decided for several centuries at a time on the plain of Panipat where armed combat has occurred. It is the "field of honor" on which the Mughal Babur beat the Afghans in 1526. Later, in 1556, Akbar beat the Hindus there, and there in 1761 the Persian Ahmad Shah Abdali massacred the Marathas. In ancient times it was the scene of battle between the rival Hindu dynasties of Kurus and Pandvas, whose fortunes constitute the theme of the epic *Mahabharata*. Much has taken place within its broad expanse. This time it was a mela with special religious significance, in celebration of the sun's eclipse. Nanak went and preached his mission, and the common people heard him gladly. But the brahmans felt outraged when it was reported to them that Nanak had once eaten venison! No violence was done him, but their opposition continued into the capital itself (Delhi), while the Lodi Ibrahim was king, and where Nanak at someone's request restored a dead elephant to life! This to a Moslem was merely a praiseworthy miracle, but to Hindus, to brahmans, in particular, it was sacrilege, being an unworthy, unjustifiable interference with the law of karma and an interruption of the cycle of transmigration.

Nanak endured temptations as well as other trials, as the janamsakhis tell us now and then. And his own words, while cast as warnings to other men, may reflect his own experience. These words, for example, may contain some record of his own temptations:

> There is pleasure in gold, in silver and in women,
> Pleasure in the scent of sandalwood;
> There is pleasure in horses, in couches and in palaces,
> Pleasure in viands and in sweets, also.
> But these all are pleasures of the body;
> How then may Sat Nam reside within them!

It scarcely matters, however, whether the records represent fact or fancy, mental or physical temptation. There was an episode in the neighborhood of Kamrup. Is this a village name? Or is it a figure, a play on words? "Kama" is "love" of a sensual sort and "rupa" means "figure." Are we to understand that we are learning of Nanak's resistance to a kama-mood? He encountered at "Kamrup" a band of females under the leadership of Nur Shah (this is a Persian name which means "a light unto the king," the name of a royal courtesan, perhaps). These women were skilful as dancers and musicians, could practice incantation and give pleasure of all sorts. They performed for Nanak as if before some royal personage and tried their spells on him. On his own part, he recited hymns to counteract their wiles. And in the end they conceded his success. But Nur Shah herself was yet to try him out. She took up the contest with unusually alluring gestures and an extraordinary display of tempting charms. And Nanak sang a hymn to her, to Mardana's accompaniment. It was the hymn called "Kachchhaji" (the bad performer), whereat she left off her useless display and brought out gold, silver, diamonds, pearl, coral and fine raiment with which to tempt him. But he continued his resistance unabated—to Mardana's musical accompaniment. At the last, Nur Shah herself and all her women saw the folly of their ways, declared themselves the slaves of virtue, asked and secured Nanak's blessing, and swore allegiance to him.

Once the Devil himself, under the name of Kaliyuga, finding him in retirement in the wilderness, came to tempt him. Now "Kaliyuga" is a common designation of this current evil age of Indian things. This incident, therefore, may actually hint at something of the problem of good and evil in Sikh thought. It concedes the reality of the "devil," as Moslem, Parsi and Christian theology usually has conceded it. And the outcome of the incident may indicate the Sikhs' own lack of any expectation of an *immediate* end of evil. They may have held the view that the evil age itself must pass before the final good will come. The Devil, at any rate, offered Nanak the wealth of the world in payment for his adoration. He offered Nanak the sovereignty of East and West, the power to work miracles, and beautiful women for his enjoyment. But Nanak was then beyond the wiles of women, if ever he had been subject to them, and wealth had ceased to lure him. As for miracles, he already had the power to work them. Nor had he any desire for sovereignty, except over his own self—and he had acquired that, too, already. He had yielded himself to the sovereign Lord of all the worlds. He informed the Devil that he, the Devil, had no right to make his offers, nor any power to fulfil them. Kaliyuga, therefore, was made to realize his helplessness; he paused but a moment afterward, "stepped out of the circle of adoration" with which Nanak was surrounded, "took the dust of his feet" and departed, *not* having become a convert to the holy life.

Does the story mean that Nanak had not the power to convert the devil, or to overcome evil entirely? Or is it a simple tale of the perennial conflict? The Christian tradition has Jesus led by "the *Spirit*" into the wilderness to be tempted of the *devil* (cf. *Matthew* 4:1), with the *devil* taking him "into the holy city" to the very "pinnacle of the temple" and to "an exceeding high mountain," promising him the wealth and power of the world, if he would only worship him. But Jesus resisted all temptation and the devil went away, himself unconverted, and free to tempt others ever afterward. Nanak, of course, could consign the devil and all evil agents to their fate, to the operation of the eternal round of karma, the law of conduct, with its inevitable results. This was, in fact, his recourse and his refuge many times as he went about, frequently misunderstood, flagrantly misrepresented and sometimes even violently abused. Whole villages were at times quite indifferent to his presence and, of course, unresponsive to his message. Sometimes he was recognized only as the butt of pranks and jests. He was often merely deemed a queer faqir, such as India has long been tolerantly well aware of.

Sometimes the stories do indeed present their subject in the guise of a philosopher and theologian. For example, he visited Benares where the Shivite brahmans were most influential and on one occasion met a Hindu pandit, "teacher," Chatur Das. Chatur Das saluted Nanak with due respect and inquired what "way" (marga) of devotion he followed and to whom he was devoted? The Hindu pandit was unable to identify him by his outward appearance as being anything other than *some* kind of saint. Nanak at the time wore a tilak mark on his forehead, but it was not made with the white clay of the Shivite. Nor had he the spiral, perforated ammonite shalagrama commonly worn thereabouts by Vishnuites. Nor could the pandit take him for a Moslem. Nanak answered the inquiry by turning to Mardana and requesting him to play, while he himself extemporized a hymn which pleased and fascinated Chatur Das, who finally observed that Nanak must indeed be "a perfect servant of the Lord," in contrast with whom he, the pandit, must be "as drab as a white heron." Thereupon they fell to discussing doctrine. When Nanak asked what the pandit taught his pupils, the latter replied, "the words of the supreme Brahman" (Chatur Das must have been a vedanti monist, judging by this reply). Thereupon Nanak pronounced what he himself called *the* supreme Word, namely, *Onkar* (*Om*), and recited many verses, all of which so powerfully affected the Hindu that he fell at Nanak's feet, muttering humbly, "O Guru, O Guru." This teacher thus became the taught—although we are left in doubt of his actual conversion to Nanak's "way." Hindus, in fact, are not usually converted by any *doctrine*. Nor do all the details of this Benares incident make us sure of Nanak's skill as a philosopher. He remains and must remain the simple, earnest servant of Sat Nam by verbal declaration and by inner consecration. But we must follow him upon his longer journeys, as the janamsakhis have recorded them, for the sake of seeing how much altogether is contained in the Sikhs' own tradition, and out of what *total* experience of thought and life came Nanak's teachings as tradition at last framed them.

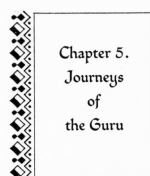

# Chapter 5. Journeys of the Guru

To follow Nanak further is to test him in a larger situation as a conscious devotee and minister of truth. On one of his longer journeys he had occasion to consider items of the Buddhist reformation, even though Buddhism was mostly a faint memory in a circumscribed locality of India in Nanak's day. Anyone brought up intelligently in the Hindu tradition, as Nanak was, somewhat loosely speaking, anyone who had any knowledge at all of the ancient Buddhist way, would think of it as nastik, or "atheistic," in contrast with various astik, or "theistic," theories among the Hindus. Perhaps the still more tangible reminder to Nanak of the older atheisms of his country were the Jains who flourished in goodly numbers, representing the Indian speculative tendency—or the tendency of Indian *speculation*—toward an atomistic, materialistic view of nature, in that older day. Every now and then attempts were made to revive and popularize one or another form of nastik theory. Nanak may have encountered in upper India one of these which emphasized man's own self-reliance. But although the greater, kindred, original Buddhist movement had long since vanished from the Indian scene, its original homeland itself endured eastward of Benares where Buddhist recollection could still be stirred. And beyond northern India in Ladakh, Tibet, and thereabouts, was the Lamaistic type which Nanak could have known about.

This journey which we have in mind, however, took him down to Gaya where he viewed the place of "enlightenment" of the Buddha, marked still by the very (?) Bo-tree under which the wandering ascetic Gotama (or Gautama, in later parlance) had experienced the vision of a more normal, middle way of life. There was something for Nanak to admire in Buddha, even while he condemned the Hindu brahman's way. The brahman ascetic (especially the sannyasi) separated himself from his fellows, whereas the Buddhist devotee had become monastic, had become one of a community of devotees. That is, such was the early Buddhist practice in protest against the brahman's ascetic role. Later brahmanism had itself taken to monasticism under the influence and leadership of certain moderns, for example, the eighth century Shankara, but ascetic individualism was still predominant and Nanak was protesting it, with no undue emphasis, however, on *self*-determination. And brahmans had long since taken charge of things in the Buddhist holy land. And the place thereof had almost forgotten the nastik faith while subjected to the brahmanical transformation. Nastik shrines had taken on the names of Hindu deities, and Hindu spirits were abroad.

Nanak found himself in controversy with ascetic brahmans within the very shadow of the Bo-tree where the Buddha had learned to reject both brahmanism and asceticism. The issue was that of spirits, of ancestral spirits, in particular. Nanak contended that the worship of them had no real value beyond respect for one's forebears and reverence for their memory, that surely they should not be *worshiped.* But Hinduism had given the ancestral cult the central place in domestic worship and the communal ritual. Nanak pleaded for a recognition of True Name alone as the center and object of devotion, and as the one sure ground of spiritual illumination. This to him was wisdom beyond anything, also, that Buddha found, for Nanak was an astik, not a nastik, with respect to God.

From Gaya Nanak went on further to the eastern coast and down to Puri in Orissa, seat of Jagannath, the "Lord of Earth." That he went partly by coastal voyage is possible, but doubtful. The land routes along the eastern side of the peninsula are normally quite open and the peoples along the way comparatively docile, allowing normally for safety in foot-passage. At Puri the deity Vishnu-Krishna, *i.e.*, Vishnu manifest in the form of Krishna, had been worshiped for many centuries under the name of Jagannath. The shrine was famous—and still is—as a goal of lengthy pilgrimage, and the scene, occasionally, of immense assemblies. A theory has prevailed that within the temple precincts all pilgrims lose or else may disregard temporarily their caste or "birth" distinctions in their worship there. This feature of Jagannath lends peculiar character to the ceremonial. However, it is not of record that the social equality conferred by Jagannath and enjoyed in his presence persists in the pilgrims' minds and conduct elsewhere outside the sacred precincts—the god had not so thoroughly transformed the Hindu order. The Sikh records themselves mention the "gorgeous and imposing worship" at this shrine and call it largely "artificial." But Jagannath is very sacred to the Hindus, and the true idol has been guarded jealously, although suffering at times vicissitudes of fortune. One account says that the Moslem emperor Firuz Tughlak of Delhi led an expedition in 1360 against Jagannath, converted many Hindus to Islam, captured the great image and sent it up to Delhi to be publicly "trodden under foot." This same expedition upset a "pillar of victory" at Puri which a Bengali Hindu Sena king had erected there in the twelfth century to commemorate his own conquest of "the earth." But the Moslems may not have secured the true image, after all. The Hindus may have hidden it, allowing their enemies to carry off a substitute. It was once, in fact, buried from enemy sight and permitted to lie hidden so long that Hindus themselves forgot about it for a season.

Nanak did not make the pilgrimage to Puri in adoration of this Lord, nor did he care what image stood within the shrine. He raised his eyes above the image to the heavens themselves. He gazed upon the heavenly lights, not on those flaring in the temple compound, on the procession of the planets and not on files of devotees moving about in idle (or idol) worship. He made his own offering of fervent utterances of Sat Nam, which sprang from the salver of his heart, and not of flowers and incense from jewel-studded platters. It is said that he composed a hymn on the occasion, one of whose lines is "What pleaseth Thee [*i.e.*, Sat Nam] is the real *arati* of the light which glows in everything" ("Arati" is the waving of lamps before the idol). And Nanak is thus contending that arati is nothing in comparison with man's recognition of the divinity in all things—or, as we might say in words of the Christian tradition, "the light that lighteth every man that cometh into the world."

Nanak and Sikh tradition make much on the whole of this Puri visit. It has rich implications in detail. He seems to have discussed with the attending priests such subjects as idols and their worship, reality and its manifestations, the many and the One, transmigration and the round of life, and matter and spirit, and so on—with what effect we are not told, save that his own gospel seems to have made no headway there. He interviewed one brahman, in particular, who kept his eyelids closed and his nostrils pinched together, the better to exercise, the brahman said, his mental vision and detect the true scent of reality. Nanak ventured playfully to test the vision and the scent. He took the brahman's lota, or water-jar (something he would not have dared to do where *caste* prevailed and the question of pollution could arise), and hid it where the brahman could not find it with his eyes and nostrils closed! At which failure Nanak chided him with deception of himself, for, said Nanak, it was false for him to assert his power of vision into the "three worlds" when he could not even see behind him in this one. And he added this caustic comment, that evidently the "Lord of Earth" did not actually bestow insight and omniscience on his worshipers.

Sikh tradition brings south India, also, into the total picture, that is, the India of Tamil culture away on beyond Puri. This region was accessible; several highways connected south and north. Moslems had already come into the south from upper India. Moslem armies themselves had penetrated below the Vindhya mountains and had instituted a line of sultans there. Wars had ensued between these sultans and the Hindu kings of regions yet further south, although the flourishing Hindu kingdom of Vijayanagar, which proved to be the last stronghold of any Indian *national* faith against Islam, had not yet been overcome. Vijayanagar was still strong in Nanak's day. Although it was a home of Hindu culture, associated especially with the worship of the sectarian god Vishnu, two of whose manifestations, Rama and Krishna, were most popular, it was tolerantly disposed toward Islam *as religion*. It had also welcomed Moslem ambassadors and had given with approval Hindu wives to Moslem soldiers—to that extent, at least, recognizing or submitting to the political power of Islam. But it was a *mad* maharaja who once made over his throne to a Moslem ally who gave him aid against a rebel. (Vijayanagar was to fall at last in 1565 by the battle of Talikota and be broken up by the Moslem conquerors.) Nanak, of course, was merely an inoffensive pilgrim, only incidentally concerned, at most, with the government of southern India. The Sikh janamsakhi does comment on his dress while he toured the south, as if he had adopted temporarily something more conventional: wooden sandals, a cloth around his waist, a sheet over his shoulder, and a turban of twisted rope on his head. This sounds Shivite, partially. But it says also that he wore on his forehead "a patch and a streak." And this looks like a combination tilak: the Vishnuite patch and the Shivite streak.

Nanak got as far some time or other as Ceylon, if we may believe the janamsakhi. In any case, the real intent may be to indicate that he wanted to take some further reckoning of the Buddhist gospel. And yet the lure of Ceylon, whose ancient capital was Lanka of the Epic story, may have been by that time purely Hindu. Tamil culture prevailed in northern Ceylon in Nanak's day, but Hinayana Buddhism was elsewhere in the island. Lanka figures prominently in the Hindu *Ramayana* story which described its vast extent and great magnificence, including seven broad moats and seven stupendous walls of stone and metal. It had been built, according to the epic, for Kuvera, a sort of Pluto, chief of the *evil* spirits living in the shades. But a Puranic story represents the island as originally the summit of the fabulous Himalayan Mt. Meru, the Indian Olympus, which was broken off by a terrific wind and carried south and hurled into the southern sea. There it became the home of the demon folk, over whom Kuvera came to rule, at last, as the epic has it. Kuvera lost his throne, however, to his demon half-brother Ravana who extended his power over into India and once seized and abducted Sita, the faithful wife of Rama. Rama, with his wife and several trusty comrades, was at the time in exile in south India, pending the conclusion of a period of wandering, after which he might return to the north as king. Rama was able, with the aid of Hanuman, especially, and his hosts of monkeys, to follow Ravana's trail to Lanka and to rescue Sita finally unharmed. Nanak may indeed have sought out the Ceylon of Hindu legend, and the janam-sakhi says he was the guest of the raja of the island!

But the Buddhist element is itself inescapable, whatever Nanak may have known of it. The Buddhist *Mahavamsa*, or *Ceylon Chronicle*, says that the raja of the time was "faithful to the religion of the Buddha." This "time," however, may have been that of the eleventh and twelfth centuries, when Ceylon's name was glorious and its rule even included southern India—prior, that is, to the rise of the Vijayanagar empire. But Buddhism, nevertheless, was in Nanak's day the national religion of the island, and many royal personages earned immortality by their protection of it, insuring the continuity of its long tradition. Raja Prakrama Bahu of the twelfth century had, perhaps, the most notable reign. He was a devoted and enlightened Buddhist who sought to renovate the doctrine and to eliminate false ritual. He built dagobas, erected statues of the Buddha, and provided residences for the priests, reading rooms for the literate and rest houses and first aid stations for travelers and the needy. Nor did he neglect the interests of his Hindu subjects. He made special provision for the brahmans of his capital, Pollanarrua, on which he lavished wealth, surrounding it with extensive ramparts and furnishing for its populace schools and libraries, halls of music and dancing, and public baths.

There had long been intercourse between Ceylon and China, also, important both for commerce and religion. Early in Nanak's own century (in 1405) a Chinese commander, Ching Ho, had visited Ceylon "as the bearer of incense and offerings to be deposited at the shrine of Buddha," and for a few years (1434-1448) Ceylon had paid China an annual tribute. Nevertheless, Hinduism itself provided the closest bonds between Ceylon and India in that century and subsequently. Tamil culture was common, as has been said, and the Tamil language was the usual channel of intercourse. And Hindu shrines were numerous, often in close proximity to Buddhist monasteries. To the casual observer the mingling seemed almost indiscriminate. And at the opening of yet another century Ceylon was destined to learn of European culture and western Christianity. The Portuguese who had come to India visited Ceylon in 1505—thirty-five years before the death of Nanak. There is an account of the arrival in Colombo harbor in 1522 of a ship of Portugal bearing "very white and beautiful people who wear boots and iron hats, eat a sort of white stone and drink blood . . . have guns with a noise louder than thunder, and a ball shot from one of them, after traversing a league, will break a marble cast."

The janamsakhi does not indicate, however, that Nanak was aware of much of this complex condition in Ceylon. It says that the raja whom he interviewed asked him his name and caste (a usual, initial question), whether he was a brahman or a trader, a Hindu or a Moslem (caste was represented among Moslems also at the time), asked him if, perhaps, he were really "Gorakhnath" from the Himalayas "above the sky"? Nanak answered, it seems, very vaguely, enigmatically, and this in itself intrigued the raja who forthwith took him to the palace and introduced him to the queen. But there is no report of any ancient Ceylonese Buddhist monuments, of any visit to the Bo-tree of Anaradhapura or to the temple of the sacred tooth at Kandy, or any comment on the Buddhist monk's own bald pate, ochre robe and rosary. The burden of the story is that Nanak expounded in Ceylon the gospel of that supreme state of man in which there is neither joy nor mourning, no castes nor any marks of caste, neither sermons nor scripture, no hopes and no desires, but only a mind at rest in God—which betrays, at least, some probable awareness on the *story-teller's* part of Buddhist doctrine. Sikhs, of course, since Nanak's day have known many Buddhists and have had occasion to consider many implications of Nanak's reputed visit to Ceylon.

Not the least interesting of Nanak's contacts on his journeys was his association with the yogis (sometimes written and pronounced in a vernacular as "jogis"). The "brahman" of the lota incident at Puri may really have been a yogi. There were yogis of many kinds. Nanak was mistaken now and then for one—for one of the mendicant type, rather than the philosophic, although he never could have been confused with the common run of nude, ash-besmeared "jogis" of the plaited locks. And, we may observe in passing, there were female yoginis, as well, in the lower orders.

Yogis generally were devotees of Shiva. They often gathered in large numbers at centers of Shiva-worship during annual festivals. Nanak came into conflict with them once on a visit to Batala, south of Amritsar, on the occasion of Shivarat, the springtime "night of Shiva." Their leader known in Sikh records as Bhanganath, or "lord of bhang" ("bhang" is a hemp-concoction), confronted Nanak and challenged the very garb he wore, declaring it to be a "mixture of sour milk and sweet," and asking how anyone could expect butter by "putting acid in his milk." To which Nanak gave this tart reply: "Your own mother, O you hemp-consumer, must have mishandled her churn when she produced a lump like you, you a yogi and a beggar and a bhang-addict in one." Bhanganath pretended to ignore this thrust. He dared Nanak to attempt a miracle, since it was noised abroad that Nanak could work such. Nanak's rejoinder then was merely this: "I have no wonder worth showing *you!* If the whole earth were moved, that would not move you. Nor could God be made to grant to such as you an undeserved reward. I have no miracle other than Sat Nam." And all the yogis cried out in derision, "True Name indeed! And who are you? One of them? a Udasi? an Audhut? maybe a Bairagi, or a Siddh—or perhaps, indeed, a *yogi?* Yes, a *yogi!*" And they forthwith bade him join their own ranks, to share with them their daily winecup (these may have been drinkers of a concoction made from molasses and a flower-extract, a common drink throughout the countryside). But Nanak held true to his own commitment. He was a devotee already of whatever might be true in *any* order, and an opponent of any error anywhere. He was already "intoxicated" with draughts of the divine nectar, the wiseman's only worthy drink.

Nanak, of course, need not have repudiated—indeed he did not repudiate—all elements of yogism. Yogis were not strict ascetics in any sense, theoretical or habitual. The higher type of yogis, those adherent to philosophic Yoga, could not, according to their theory, be ascetic. Rather, they were realists of a moderate kind, not scornful of the world, although seeking some control of it. The world was not "illusion" to them, not the realm of maya, to use an idealistic term. Nor were their own bodies maya; they, too, were real and tangible. And the final goal they sought in speculative practice was not the *sole* reality called Brahman, the idealist's Absolute. There was for them a form of matter co-eternal with their personality. And, too, they had a place within their thought for God. Nanak could agree with many elements of this higher Yoga, however widely he would be inclined to deviate from certain Yoga practices—exercises with the breath, and so on. But he, nevertheless, could not wisely countenance the ways of illiterate, shiftless wanderers—sometimes mere impostors—who ignorantly did homage from shrine to shrine and made religion their only source of livelihood.

Nanak found himself at variance also with Jains whom he met occasionally. They were the extreme ascetics of his time, although—or should we say *because?*—they held a very realistic view of earth and life. Matter and mind, body and spirit were with them, also, co-eternal, somewhat as in philosophic Yoga. On this dual basis they were *practical* ascetics, prompted by a thoroughgoing animistic theory to exercise great care with respect to "life" in everything. No notion of "illusion" (maya) minimized life's realities. In theory and in practice they emphasized ahimsa, shedding no blood and doing no injury wilfully to any living thing. Jains were not then very numerous, although their gospel had had currency for two thousand years—there may have been a million of them, only a small percentage of whom might be found on pilgrimage at any given time. Their temples stood widely distributed from Gujarat on the west of India to Bengal on the east, and in the Deccan; the most prominent were at Girnar and Shatranjaya in Kathiawar, Abu in Rajputana and Parasnath in Bihar. When Nanak passed judgment on the Jains, he charged them, fcr example, with being inconsistent: they would not inflict injury upon a living thing, but they could be stolidly indifferent to its pain and suffering! They unsympathetically strained the quality of mercy. He accused them of having more concern for life than God himself had who "both killeth and restoreth" (but Jains, of course, had no concern for God). He chided them for "plucking out their hair," lest it harbor insects and threaten them with injury, and for "carrying brooms along to sweep their way," lest they tread some life to death. And, said he, they "drink their water dirty," fearing that to strain it might injure whatever life was in it, yet oblivious of the life they actually destroyed by drinking it. He deemed them an unprogressive sect, neither "yogis, yangams, qadis nor mullas," whose food brahmans would not touch, whom Hindus generally would not recognize—for want of any tilak on their foreheads, possibly—and who were virtually denied access to "the sixty-eight" sites of Hindu pilgrimage. But now and then a Jain yielded to Nanak's argument and even sought to join his company, as he went about, including these Jain centers in his itinerary.

What, at last, of Nanak and the Moslems! Were they not the severest test of Nanak's gospel?—or by what standard shall we ultimately judge it? The janamsakhis include Islam in the picture. They say that Nanak even made the pilgrimage to Mecca and Madinah, visiting them during his "fourth or western" period of seclusion or retreat (the life-story is told in terms of five periods, altogether): He started out from north India in the company of Mardana and wearing the blue dress of a Moslem pilgrim, leather shoes (What *kind* of leather? Certainly not *pigskin*, thus defying Islam. Yet could it have been *cowhide*, thus offending Hindus?), carrying a pilgrim staff, a cup (for drinking, or ablutions, or Meccan Zam Zam water?), and a skin (doubtless a deerskin such as ascetics used, but which would serve him as a prayer-rug). But there is some hint, also, that he wore upon setting out, at least, the Hindu tilak label on his forehead and a string of bones, such as were dear to Shiva, about his neck! Yet at prayer time, they say, he would recite the Moslem "call."

A fellow pilgrim, himself a Moslem who had undertaken the hajj, or major pilgrimage to the Arabian holy cities, took occasion to question Nanak, asking if he were merely an eccentric darwish, really a Moslem, or, maybe, actually a Hindu? The hajji warned him that no Hindu could set foot in Mecca, and advised him to give up the journey, whereupon Nanak recited verses from the Koran and shouted portions of the adhan, or call to prayer, which normally includes the tashdid or "witness," namely, "I testify [ashadu] that there is no God but Allah; I testify that Allah's prophet is Muhammad." The hajji noticed that Nanak, however, omitted the tashdid, something more serious than mere irregularity of garb—pilgrims en route to Mecca might wear any dress. He therefore doubted Nanak and went on his way alone, leaving Nanak—and Mardana—to make their way in accordance with—the *Sikh* tradition! According to this tradition it had already been written in "the books" that "Nanak" would come one day and "the wells of Mecca would be filled," the well of Zam Zam, in particular, whose waters had first risen in response to miracle, and that Nanak's gospel would mean the fulfilment of Islam.

Nanak, however, was somewhat ill at ease in Mecca, as we may properly suppose! Was he unfamiliar with Moslem pilgrim practices? Or was he *defiant* of them? He lay down within the mosque to rest, but his feet were toward the qiblah, or prayer direction! When a qadi rebuked him for this disrespect, he asked the qadi in which direction after all was *not* the qiblah, since God is everywhere? Had not Mohammed himself once declared (cf. *Koran* 2:109) the same?—before his subsequent and final judgment that the Meccan Ka'bah with its black stone (*hajaru'l-aswad*) was the only rightful qiblah (*Koran* 2:129). Thereupon the qadi was convinced, recognizing in "Nanak" the coming messenger, falling at his feet and kissing them (this, of course, is Hindu, not Arab custom) and proclaiming him a "faqir of Allah." Then crowds gathered about them and Nanak preached to them the futility of rites, of whatever faith. Said he, The Hindu cries "Ram, Ram" and the Moslem, "Rahman," but both the Hindu and the Moslem are jealous of each other, and neither of them really knows Sat Nam. He recited a hymn of Kabir on the subject of "the Vedas and the Qur'an" and two Persian hymns, all of which deprecated scriptures and commended the superior virtue of humility and prayer, if one sought spiritual insight into the essence of religion and the character of God.

In Madinah, "*the* city of the prophet," Nanak met and vanquished qadis and mullas in extended argument, and astonished all the assembled pilgrims by rendering a new version of the "call to prayer." This is indeed a curious item in the Sikh tradition. Nanak substituted in the adhan in the place of the normal "Muhammad ar-rasul Allahi" (Mohammed is the messenger of Allah), "words of similar sound" in testimony that Nanak himself was the messenger of Allah and the true Guru of the age. The exact words are not given, but we might suggest these, "Om ham adar rasul Allahi," which could be made to sound like the Arabic original, although meaning "Om, we have the honor to be the messenger of Allah."

However unwilling we may be, for purposes of understanding the Sikh's own point of view, of separating arbitrarily the factual from the fanciful in the "biographies" of Nanak, we may discount the Meccan pilgrimage as fact. We may not, on the other hand, discount his Moslem contacts, especially if we understand that his complete itinerary may actually represent most of all the lands of the "five rivers" (the Panjab) and of the "two rivers," the Jamna and the Ganga, with excursions, possibly, into several farther parts of India. Moslems were numerous in the whole Indo-Gangetic region. His contacts with the Mughals, for example, include items of sheer fact, and may include actual dealing with the Mughal Babur. Nanak was, in any case, in Sayyidpur when Babur came along that way. And he had a message for these Moslems who, as the Sikh records say, came as "a bridal procession of sin, falsehood marching in the van, singing a paean of bloodshed."

Babur indeed considered his own campaign of conquest something of a crusade, at least, for he assumed the title Ghazi, which means "victor" over unbelievers. He had dreamed for twenty years of entering India. In 1519 at the age of thirty-six he made his first preliminary reconnaissance into the Panjab. In 1524 he was invited by the Lodi viceroy of Lahore to join him in deposing the Lodi king Ibrahim of Delhi (whose actual capital at the time was Agra). Early in the cool season of the following year he got under way and by January 1526 had entered India with a modest force of 12,000 men, including "servants, merchants and their servants and followers of all descriptions," as he has said in his own *Memoirs*. He estimated that Sultan Ibrahim "could bring into the field an army of five hundred thousand men," but he did not fear even such a host. He had muskets and field pieces, including a heavy cannon, and Ibrahim's numbers were more showy than efficient. Perhaps an actual hundred thousand of them faced Babur on the plain of Panipat in April 1526, and within ten days thereafter Ibrahim's head and his kingdom lay at Babur's feet.

Babur has recorded the fact that "five Musalman kings and two Pagans exercised royal authority" in India before his own conquest. The two "pagans" were Rana Sanka of Chitur in Rajputana, and the Raja of Bijnagar (*i.e.*, Vijayanagar) in the far south. Babur would end "the sway of the accursed pagan," hoping that "the Almighty would consign him to perdition at the day of judgment." He accepted from all the "heathen" (he meant non-Moslems) nothing less than "effectual repentance," that is, conversion to Islam. Nevertheless, there was little wanton slaughter. He may indeed have slain as many rival Moslems as pagan Hindus. Nanak and Mardana themselves were not molested at Sayyidpur, except to be detained under guard and pressed into Moslem service by an officer of Babur named Mir Khan, Nanak serving as a laborer and Mardana as a groom. Even so, many Hindus and Pathans (these latter, Moslems) were slain. Nanak and Mardana may have been counted "strangers," for whose safety the Koran itself makes some provision in a time of war.

Nanak recognized his "luck" and sang of it, for though a slave, he was *alive*. He bade his minstrel "drop the reins" and take up the rebeck, and the guard that stood by noticed that Mardana's horse obeyed without the reins—and that Nanak's loads seemed to carry themselves! and that later, when Nanak's task was grinding corn, the mill turned of its own free will! These and other marvels were soon reported to the emperor, and when Babur thus learned that he had punished a village that contained a holy man, he came to do Nanak homage and make amends, if possible. Whereupon Nanak humbly informed his majesty that he wanted nothing for himself, but only that all captives should be freed, those pardoned who had fled the village for safety, and the restoration to its rightful owners of all property that had been seized. Then he sang a hymn of lamentation, recounting the devastation of war, yet giving God the glory for His providence. God, said Nanak, "had parcelled time, had established the nine regions, the seven seas, the fourteen worlds, the three qualities and the four ages." And Babur, giving assent to the affirmation that all times, places and circumstances were in the hands of God, and that he would do God's will and make amends, departed. And Nanak was exalted in the eyes of all the villagers, as they set things to rights and resumed their village ways.

The legendary tale goes on to say that Nanak went afterward to visit Babur who received him and, offering him bhang (the hemp opiate), bade him sing a hymn. Nanak, of course, declined the bhang, saying that he had already taken a due amount of both stimulant and sedative whose permanent effects gave him a wholesome frame of mind, gave him a mind intent on God. He sang freely in the vein of counsel to the emperor, urging him to "deliver just judgments, revere holy men, and foreswear wine and games of chance." Babur did indeed foreswear wine, but not immediately. He admonished Nanak meanwhile to turn Moslem and thus perfect his faith, saying that Islam was *the* religion of One God. Nanak agreed to the one God of Islam, but would not grant the "association" of Mohammed. He said this qualified God's unity, and that, anyway, Sat Nam was God, and that he, Nanak, was the servant of Sat Nam, commissioned to the accomplishment of the brotherhood of Moslems, Hindus and all mankind in this comprehensive Unity.

Nanak lived five years during the reign of Babur and ten years thereafter, while Babur's son Humayun reigned (Humayun reigned really longer, but the famous Afghan Shir Shah interrupted his rule awhile). He moved about freely, there being usually comparative quiet then in upper India, but making his home, Talwandi in the Panjab, his headquarters. During all the years that he journeyed he had occasionally visited Talwandi and Batala, being welcomed by his parents in the one and by his parents-in-law in the other, while they lived. And toward the end of his life he went home to Talwandi on "an order from the Lord," to determine a successor to the headship of the movement he had instituted.

It is part of the story that a Sikh succession was established. Nanak had two sons, but one of them was dissolute. The other, Sri Chand, had given his father only a qualified devotion. But his mother was insistent that the choice should fall, nevertheless, on him. There were also many other faithful disciples by that time. And Nanak selected one of them, Angad, in preference to either of his sons. And Angad was confirmed by many signs, including an appearance of the goddess Durga [*sic!*]. Nanak himself retired to Kartarpur, a village on the Ravi river, to end his days, leaving Angad to carry the umbrella of spiritual authority over Sikhs.

The Sikh records make a good deal of Nanak's final days, for there was much at stake. Men and women who had been affected by his teachings or who had known him as a saint came from all directions to do him honor. They came to bear further witness to their loyalty, some to renew bonds of fellowship which had been weakened. And Angad himself would come to assure Nanak, especially in the days when Nanak lay dying, that there would be forever one community of Sat Nam. Nanak sat toward the very end in the open underneath an acacia tree whose leaves had withered, but which turned instantly green and full of blossoms at the Guru's presence, as if his very life was passing into it. He fell into a trance, recovered consciousness for a while, and with his last breath bade the company sing as he passed away, himself uttering "Wah Guru!" in the name of God, as they sang, meanwhile pulling over himself a sheet. As the company stood awed before the sight, a soft light glowed underneath the sheet, which spread above it and blended with a halo which had at that very moment formed about the head of Angad. Thus did the divine commission depart from one body and settle on another—or, better, link the founder of the faith with his successor.

And when, next morning, the faithful lifted up the sheet, the place was empty where Nanak's corpse had lain, while at either side of it were flowers blooming. On the previous evening some had proposed to bury Nanak, while others would cremate the body. Now they took the flowers and divided them for burial or for burning, as the case might be, both parties to be satisfied by this device, while they united in reverence for the departed Guru. Afterward one party built a shrine where the body had lain and the other built a tomb nearby. And some years later the Ravi washed them both away, lest idol-worship or else an ancestral-cult flourish where the factual Nanak died and the formless Nanak had been reborn.

With all due respect for Sikh tradition, for we understand its implications, especially in the light of the process of comparison, we may conclude the present chapter with a brief appraisal. It is plain that no one in Nanak's time could rightly gauge him, no matter with what full confidence in himself he went about his mission. Nor could he calculate his influence or even count exactly the number of those who were truly his own followers and who would continue faithful to his teachings. He made no attempt at such a calculation. He seemed to think he had a message which revealed the hidden heart of things and would propagate itself through contagion from among its early advocates. We judge him, therefore, not as we might, for example, judge Mohammed, who formulated a specific creed and organized a definite community of believers, with a view to making *all* religion Allah's. We judge him, rather, as we might judge the Buddha, the Christ, Kabir, or any other genius of a movement, who left its creedal contents largely undeveloped and its organization vague and incomplete. We are to judge this first Sikh in a fuller measure than himself, by other Sikhs and by what came after him. Meanwhile, ere we undertake a survey of his teachings in detail, we may remind ourselves that we have only scanty sources for a *history* of Nanak, although the materials are fairly adequate from which to make a reconstruction of his whole career. We may make use of Babur's *Memoirs*—save that they do not precisely mention Nanak—the *Dabistan*, the *Granth Sahib*—its "Kabir-portions" and other parts—the janamsakhis and a host of miscellaneous references to the India of Nanak's time.

That Babur's *Memoirs* do not mention Nanak is not in itself an evidence that Babur did not know him. Babur may have taken him to be merely another sufi, sadhu or faqir. Nanak and his Sikhs excited no political attention at the time. Babur indeed failed to mention many items of religion among matters in an unusually full and admirable account. He makes no reference, for example, to Kabir and the Kabir-panthis, nor to the Maratha bhakta Namdev who had greatly influenced Kabir. He does not mention the Telugu brahman Vallabhacharya (1479-1531), born in Benares, devoted to Krishna and to Krishna's spouse, Radha, and long resident at Vijayanagar (which Babur does name); nor Chaitanya (1485-1533), a Krishnaite of Puri-way who wandered and taught widely as if himself an avatara of Vishnu. These all were of no political importance, nor did they later assume any place in politics, as Sikhism, on the contrary did.

The early records which *do* mention Nanak put no stress on politics. Rather, they represent him as avoiding it. And yet, there was something in him, in his movement and in his times as he affected them which was destined to be tested by political affairs of state. Was there something worldly after all in Nanak? And are not politics in the long run an inescapable and valid test of faith? The final estimate of Nanak, therefore, is a matter of the centuries, including likewise the present fateful years of India's history.

# Chapter 6. Nanak's Message and his Book of Psalms

NANAK, both the factual and the formless, lives mostly in his message which the Sikhs have dutifully and fondly cherished, and the fundamental substance of his message has been preserved in a book of psalms, the *Japji* or *Japuji Sahib*, a "book of praise in remembrance of the Lord." Nanak himself in his later years may have made a collection of these hymns in modest compass. If not, he had at least recited them so frequently that they had lodged securely in the minds of many of his followers. There were thirty-eight of these psalms in all, a total of less than four hundred lines, which form altogether only a small proportion of the voluminous *Granth Sahib* itself. The *Granth* took on huge proportions after Nanak's day, at the direction and through the composition of several of the line of Gurus who succeeded him, but many of the most progressive Sikhs of later years have considered the *Japji* an epitome, as it was indeed the inspiration, of the larger *Granth*. It is Nanak's own peculiar contribution, and a worthy one at that, to the altogether vast and miscellaneous literature of Indian religion.

Although there is no manuscript extant of this *Japji* in Nanak's hand, he may indeed have written one. At least, he probably wrote separate psalms from time to time and bequeathed them to his followers in fragmentary form. He, of course, was literate. He could take direct account of Indian literature in his own immediate tongue, the Hindustani, whether it was written in the nagari alphabet of Hindi, in the Persian-Arabic alphabet of Urdu, or in Panjabi. He knew the blunt, unpolished Hindi of Kabir. He learned Persian and read sufi writings in that tongue. He could have read

Babur's polished Persian, even though he may never have known of Babur's own *Memoirs*. He must have had some acquaintance with the Arabic Koran, with certain portions of it, anyway, then in circulation in northwest India—there were not yet at that time anywhere any renderings of the Koran in other tongues than Arabic. There were also in circulation many "sayings" (hadith) of Mohammed, some of which Nanak doubtless heard. He was greatly interested in all these things and in Indian lore in general, and he had occasion frequently to compare his and others' teachings. Indeed he took precaution to preserve his own teachings when he designated a succession to himself. Nanak is, by the way, the most conspicuous, if not the only, Indian reformer who made definite arrangements for successors whose primary responsibility was the preservation and the spread of his own message.

The *Japji* and the later, more inclusive, *Granth* have their own peculiar language, both in alphabet and grammar. It is the Gurmukhi, Guru-mukhi, or "Guru tongue," which Nanak spoke, although he did not invent its alphabet. This peculiar alphabet, slightly disconcerting to many Sikhs and to all outsiders, was a deliberate invention of a later day. It became thus the Sikhs' own classic medium for the transmission of the founder's gospel, for their sacred scriptures and for their theology. It embraced to begin with certain old Hindui elements, many obsolescent deshi or local "country" terms, and some Arabic and Persian words, all of which were subject to Sikh reconstruction, whether by intention or from sheer circumstance—a most interesting aspect of linguistics is its religious use of terminology; a new sect, we see, creates its own vocabulary, to a marked degree. The Sikhs, therefore, have had their "classical" language in its own artificial alphabet, and a vernacular, besides, which may be called Panjabi. As a simple illustration of what Nanak and the Sikhs have done with antecedent sources, consider the word "jap" itself, an ancient Sanskrit term connoting praise. It means this to the Sikh, also, that is, "psalm or praise." In the Hindi of Nanak's day the related form japna was used with special reference to the counting of one's beads at prayer. And to the Hindu a common name for rosary was japmala, "wreath of praise," or "praiseful necklace." He called his devotion japtap, or "praise fervor," especially if it was connected with austerities. Nanak, of course, had the praise of Sat Nam in mind, not, however, by way of austerity and the counting of a string of beads, but by inward repetition of the Name.

Any such variation as this on the part of Nanak would not in itself have excluded him, however, from the ranks of Hindus, for among them the bhakta cult was fairly common, as we have seen already—bhaktas themselves emphasized the repetition of the name of deity. Nanak may actually have contributed to this practice among the Hindus. But the way of bhakti was only one of several ways among the Hindus, and Hindus sang the praise of many gods, repeated the names of many gods. Hindu bhakta, for example, is well illustrated in the miscellaneous verse of Tulsi Das, author of the modern, popular version of the *Ramayana*, who flourished in India only a few years after Nanak. He made use of forms of *japna* in the common bhakti manner:

> Tulsi jape to Prabhu jape aur nam mat le,
> Prabhu nam shamsher hai jam ke sir men de,

or,

> Tulsi, when you praise, praise none other than the Lord,
> The Lord's name is a sword to decapitate death's angel.

Although this is in the mood and manner of Nanak and Kabir, "the Lord" had for Tulsi Das several, more specific, connotations than Sat Nam, within the compass of which (or whom) Nanak did include *all* lesser names. Nanak explicitly disapproved, as he himself said, singing "the manifestations of the remote" (gavai ko japai disai duri), by which he meant the Rama and Krishna avataras of Vishnu, while Tulsi himself sang with special reference to Rama as the highest Lord (prabhu).

Nanak repudiated also the japtap which consisted of "countless repetitions, countless obeisances, countless acts of ritual, and innumerable austerities" (asankh jap asankh bhau asankh puja asankh tap tau). And the Name (nam) he praised represented a supreme and radiant Lord (prabhu) even more inclusive than Krishna, Rama, Vishnu, Shiva, Shakti, Brahma, Indra and—Allah. His Name was higher than the high (*cf. Japji* 24, 35), its truth the ultimate beyond any wisdom of the Vedas or the Koran (*cf. Japji* 22). He sang in full obedience and prompt attention to the "divine command" (hukm) of this Ultimate, recognizing that

> By His will are all things formed [hukm hovani akar . . .],
> No one blessed save by His will,
> And by His will alone doth nature run her course
> [ik na hukm bakhsis iki hukmi sada bhavai ahi].
> All are under His command, and none may act without it
> [hukmai andari sabhu ko bahari hukm na koi].

The *Japji* in its traditional form has a prelude to its thirty-eight verses, and also a postlude, the former professing to set the "basic theme" (mul mantra) and the latter providing six lines of reiteration in conclusion (in Nanak's name, if not by his own hand). By the usual arrangement the whole work amounts to three hundred and seventy-five lines, something far less bulky, for example, than the seven thousand lines of the one hundred and fifty Hebrew *Psalms*, and only a few of them bulk severally as large even as Psalm 23.

The prevailing type of versification of the *Japji* is what is known as the doha, or rhymed "couplet," each line consisting of twelve plus ten mantras, or "syllables." The longer verses are composed mostly of slokas of six lines each—or multiples of six—although some slokas contain only five or multiples of five each. The rhythm is not that of polished regularity, but that, rather, of extemporaneous recital—to Mardana's accompaniment, of course. There is, consequently, great freedom of movement, and a free, often baffling, use of words, with an exhibition of a grammar all their own. Repetition is frequently indulged in, for certain words, phrases and lines are favorites with Nanak. The following doha, for example, represents a recurring theme of slokas, or hymns, Nos. 9, 10 and 11:

> Nanak bhagta sada vigasu
> Suniai dukh pap ka nasu,

which means,

> O Nanak [or possibly merely Nanak saith], the faithful are ever happy,
> Sorrow and sin are destroyed by their devotion [by their hearkening, that is].

And there is a buoyant movement to the lines, a vigorous incentive in their very repetition. Nor did the average villager find objectionable monotony in frequent, continuous repetition, for the method was a common practice of recital by strolling poets and musicians whose presence for entertainment was always welcome in the villages.

The *Japji's* mul mantra, or prelude, was very commonly repeated and may have acquired thus its "basic" quality, may have taken on a speculative form, although it lacks consistency and is not at all profound. It is, nevertheless, typically Hindu Indian. Villagers themselves were, of course, not *thoughtful*, nor did they look for any depth of thought in their minstrels and in wandering teachers of religion. Rhythmic verse with reverent intonation and with stringed accompaniment was the standard, effectual medium of religious education. "Devotional" instruction, at least, could not be carried on through labored prose, itself precise, profound and logical. Nanak may have toyed with vague ideas, putting them experimentally into modulated phrases until something of a synthesis took shape in his sensitive and often puzzled mind. Higher thoughts may have run at inconsistent random through his brain, until an essence was distilled to which he could give expression in his own words as something basic. His utterance, in this instance, was a succession of single words, each with its own intonation which in itself would excite in many hearers some startling conviction and incline them to accept his message. Each word would register according to the listener's intelligence, and the listener's own reaction would provide the necessary commentary. And Mardana, perhaps, was playing on the rebeck all the while.

Ik . . . Onkar . . . satinamu . . . karta purakhu nirbhau
  nirvairu . . .
Akalmurti . . . ajuni . . . saibhang . . . gur prasadi . . .
Japu . . . japu . . . japu . . .
Adi sachu . . . jugadi sachu . . .
Hebhi sachu . . . hosi bhi sachu . . .

One! . . . Om! . . . True Name! . . . He that works within
  and without, devoid of fear and lacking enmity . . .
Image of the Timeless! . . . Ageless! . . . Self-existent! . . .
  Matchless Guru! . . .
Praise . . . praise . . . praise . . .
Truth as it ever was . . . Truth that shall ever be . . .
Truth indeed! . . . that was and is and will be! . . .

The bare recitation is impressive, and if not conclusive gives opportunity and incentive for discussion that is more congenial than dogmatic prose would prompt. Mere words? But not devoid of sound. Composed of transient syllables, each with its separate letters? Yet all are signs of the eternal, of primal sound that bursts into temporal eloquence (as some Indian mystic might affirm). Reality lies behind them, whose humble agents they may be, according to their reception. The interpretation of these simple words might vary, but never be at full variance from truth. There was extreme flexibility, therefore, in their recital, they were seeds scattered about the village fields in preparation for any crop the hearer might accommodate. The occasional thinker might even make a system from the simple symbols, or at least express them in more highly speculative fashion—for example:

> Unity, uncaused original existence, the truth itself, for which the True Name stands. It is all-pervasive truth, here, there and everywhere, with full accord between its essence and its form. It is essentially devoid of attributes, even while its inner essence has been manifested. And what is manifest is not illusion, but reality. Its forms may be detected by the senses, and though the forms may vary, they are channels of committal to the real which is itself potential.
>
> Self-activity makes for this potential, and creates the actuality, and this is represented by the Name which is at once the inner and the outer, real in time and space, yet timeless and without dimension. The devotee sings the True Name's praise, and his praise is highest, most effective when he realizes first the Name within him and then becomes aware of the Name in everything about him, for all is One, as the Guru's grace reveals it. Let all men everywhere, therefore, praise the One, the only Om, the True Name that is eternal.

Such speculation is no more conclusive, probably, than Nanak's bare recital. Nanak himself never resorted to such abstraction, but there was much of the sort in circulation all about him, which he or any Sikh could largely make his own by referring it to the Sikh's Sat Nam, and by expressing it in his own Gurmukhi.

And the concluding sloka of the *Japji* is in something of a similar quasi-speculative mood. If Nanak did not write it, the next Guru, Angad, did. Tradition tends to make Angad the author, and if he is, the sloka not only links the first two Gurus intimately, but establishes a peculiar continuity to reach beyond them. It puts Angad's seal of approval on Nanak's gospel, even while it retains Nanak's name in the last line as signature. The content and the form are both all its own. If an imitation of the rhythm be attempted, with no great violence to the meaning, the English of it might be this:

> Breath of life the Guru, water's father-mother the extensive earth,
> Daily and nightly both act as nurses, while the world rolls playfully on,
> The goodly deeds and evil deeds are filed in the presence of Duty,
> By the deeds which they have done, some are near and some are distant,
> Those who on the Name have pondered are free at last from labor,
> How their faces glow, saith Nanak, who join the hosts of his salvation.

The meaning seems to be this:

> Man is born of the great earth-mother impregnated by the rains and finds himself in possession of the breath of life. Maturing in nature's nursery, attended by day and by night in his play, he learns to give himself to conduct which in the end decides his destiny—unless, indeed, he calls upon the Name and finds release in the company of those whose faces glow in the very light of God's own presence.

The doctrinal content is simple, by whatever analysis and exegesis. Sikhs themselves still take it at its mere face value, regardless of philology or historical examination. Indeed Sikhs have really had no heritage of historical method, either from the Hindus who themselves had none, or from the Moslems who had one that was at once out of reach of Sikhs. That is, Sikhs had in the early days of their movement little chance to learn this sort of mental or religious discipline from any Moslems.

The *Japji* itself is of a texture similar to that of its own prologue and its postlude—it embodies spontaneous, loosely woven bits of doctrine which, despite some incoherence in their presentation, have peculiar force, a forcefulness which increases with the telling. And although there may be scant novelty of thought throughout the work, no hymn is less effective for want of Nanak's own originality. The psalms expound a socially and spiritually extensive and inclusive religion in the name of Him who is introduced in the prelude, in the mul mantra, who is the one, universal, all-powerful, loving God, the creator and supreme spirit who makes no unfavorable distinctions among men, even though they themselves are born "high and low by his will" (Hymn 2), the God who looks upon men's hearts rather than upon their deeds, and who takes account of the potential goodness in all mankind—a slightly optimistic note unusual in Hindu India. They present the view that God may be called by any name, Brahma, Hari, Rama or Allah, for example, *provided* that those who call upon him by any one of these affirm that God is not only any one of them—but indeed also more than all of them in one. Nanak, however, was not himself a pantheist or a polytheist nor yet a monotheist. His psalms repudiate, at least, most of the popular ideas and practices of loose, contemporary Hinduism and soften the rigors of Islamic deism. They do not treat the gods as a fiction worthy only of men's imperfect minds, nor the world as the sphere of maya or "illusion"; nevertheless, they are not altogether free of evidences of traditional and environmental influence. There are implications of pantheism in the indescribable Unity sung in many hymns. Other hymns sing of world-renunciation in very realistic terms. The world is maya-bhumi, the "abode of wickedness or deception" that is real enough, but is as well a place for the exercise of "pity" toward one's fellowmen.

The type of world-renunciation which Nanak recommended was not to be professed or realized by "works"—through pilgrimages, by ritual exercises or by ascetic solitude, for instance. Rather, the profession and the comprehension of the Name was itself all-rewarding. He could sing that the Name is equal to any pilgrimage to Kashi (*i.e.*, Benares), Mecca, Hardwar, anywhere. If the devotee will but attend upon the Name he will come to know all places and all worlds and in the end may become as any god who himself must realize the Name. If one would free himself of sin with which the world defiles him, let him speak the Name and comprehend its love, for within the Name sin and sorrow are no more. Even the blind, if they listen for and hear the Name, may find the way and keep it through the gates of destiny, for there is sure salvation through the Name.

But an escape from the world and the grasping of salvation is not quite simple, after all, as Nanak must have realized. There are traces throughout his *Japji* of the prevalent, traditional, indigenous theories of karma and transmigration—two aspects of one theory, in fact. No strictly Indian thinker or reformer during the last two thousand years has been able to ignore them, or has ignored them, and Nanak was to that extent an Indian. Transmigration as an Indian theory meant rebirth amidst all living creatures in an indefinite series of existences, unless or until the creature in transition found release and an end of the process through some conclusive marga or "way." And karma was inherent in the process, amounting to a directive and controlling force equivalent to what the Moslem, for example, would call "fate" (qadr, referring usually to the "power" of God, however). Nanak himself does not mention "the power of the Name" or any such association of karma with Sat Nam. It is Sat Nam that *frees* the devotee from the control of karma and from the round of transmigration. But there is a touch of fatalism every now and then in Nanak's gospel: "Whatever he wills comes to pass" (kita jaka hovai—Psalm 21); "Whatsoever pleases him, that will he do subject to no command at all" (jo tisu bhavai soi karsi hukmu na karna jai). Notice the hukm, "command." Hukm and a companion word hadd served among Moslems, in particular, to represent the necessity under which Allah's own "people" (ummah) labored—by Allah's order or in bonds to him. As among Moslems Allah himself was behadd, "bondless" and under no constraint outside himself, so also with Nanak, Sat Nam acted independently. With Nanak, however, there is some qualification of Sat Nam's arbitrary will. The devotee of Sat Nam might be in bondage to Sat Nam and subject to Sat Nam's command, but in such bondage lay his freedom! Nanak was preaching a gospel of "devotion" (bhakti), not one of karmik determination. Special vision and immediate experience had taught him this. He had learned and experienced the loving-kindness of Sat Nam and believed it infinite (bhakhia bhau aparu—Psalm 4); had come to realize that men have some power of their own in life, not only to sow but also to reap (ape biji apehi khahu, "one's own self sows and the same self reaps"—Psalm 20), and had learned that God gives liberally to those who ask him (akhahi mangahi dehi dehi dati kare dataru, "to those who crave and ask he gives and gives with generous liberality"—Psalm 20). This was the Sat Nam of virtually the bhakti-marga, whose sovereignty was qualified by grace.

The *Japji* is worth reading as a whole, if it be read with sympathy and understanding. Its general tenor is readily discernible, even when the flow of Nanak's thought is ragged, splashy. His relative clauses are sometimes not in sequence. The hymns abound in quaint, colloquial expressions, epithets, nicknames and allusions. There is little in them which might be deemed essentially descriptive. Description in such connection might quickly become dogmatic—whether on the part of Nanak or offered by a commentator. A usual theme with Nanak himself is that Sat Nam the Ultimate is *in*describable—or yet to be described on occasion by any devotee himself in response to his own immediate experience of the Absolute. But there is, after all, a substance and an essence in Nanak's quaint Gurmukhi, which translations might possibly depict even while avoiding free indulgence in Nanak's sometimes ragged method of expression. Translation into English may itself be deemed authentic, if the reader has a mind to make it so. The gist of things can be expressed in English even while rhythm is attempted, with some regard for English style, which does not match too closely the form of the original. A rendering of the *Japji* is offered here with sincere consideration for both the content and the style of Nanak's own original. The author has had the benefit of other renderings, Trumpp's and Macauliffe's, for example, but was peculiarly indebted to a then unpublished version by Bhai Jodh Singh, principal of the Sikhs' Khalsa College in Amritsar. The translation offered here seeks to be as literal as possible while taking due account of both the sound and the sense of the original Gurmukhi. Essential meanings are retained whenever verbal equivalents could be found through which to give them. The intention as a whole and generally is a faithful rendering for the sympathetic English reader's benefit of Nanak's gospel of the Sach Khand, the Truth Portion—such portion of the Truth, at least, as Nanak himself professed to comprehend.[1]

[1] Cf. Psalm 37 of the *Japji*.

ੴ

# THE JAPUJI

## A BOOK OF PSALMS
## OF GURU NANAK NIRANKARI

Unity, Active Om, True Name!
Actor, Pervader, Fearless, devoid of Enmity,
Whom Time and the Ages do not cumber,
Self-existent, perceptible Gurū—
Praise!
Pre-eminent Truth, primordial Truth,
Truth that is, saith Nanak, and will abide forever.

1. Thinking comprehendeth him not, although there be thoughts by the thousands,
Silence discovers him not, though it be continuous silence;
Man is persistently hungry, though he eats of tasty abundance;
Not one of a hundred thousand artful devices avails him!
How may the truth be attained, the bonds of falsehood be broken?
By obeying the will of God as surely recorded, saith Nanak.

2. Forms have come of his order, but his order goes still undetected;
Life has come by his will, through which comes life's exaltation.
High and low are his will, and joy and sorrow his pleasure;
In his will alone is he blessed who runs the round of his nature.
All are subject to him, not one beyond his jurisdiction.
If any perceives his will, he humbles himself, saith Nanak.

3. Some sing his power who themselves are feeble,
Some sing his gifts—such as they may know;
Some sing his attributes, his glory and his precepts,
Some sing the substance of his vital wisdom;

Some sing his altering of bodies into ashes,
Some sing his gift of vitality to matter,

Some proclaim him manifest, albeit at a distance,
Some sing him present and immediately beholding;

There is no end of the multitude of sayings—
Sayings, sayings by the million millions;
He bestows and men grow weary getting,
And go on eating, eating through the ages;

He goes on ever willing his good pleasure,
Making progress undismayed, saith Nanak.

4. The Lord is true, plainly known, his loving kindness infinite;
To those who crave and seek he gives, gives with full abandon.
What indeed must he be offered to throw his court wide open?
What words must lips be uttering to make his love responsive?

At deathless dawn give Sat Nam thought and glory,
Put on the garb of deeds—and salvation's way is open!
Be sure that he himself is fully true, saith Nanak.

5. He is not fabrication, nor subject to man's making,
Intrinsically devoid is he of passion;
Who does him homage meets in turn with honor.

Whoever sings, saith Nanak, of the home of virtue,
Who sings and listens, heart-felt praise retaining,
His sorrows fade and he will dwell in blessing.

The Guru[2] has a voice, speaks wisdom, teaches patience,
Whether he be Shiva, Vishnu, Brahmā, Parbati—
If indeed I knew him, would I not describe him?

Words are vain, but teach me the mystery, O Guru,
Of him who giveth life—such wisdom may I cherish!

6. At the place of pilgrimage no bath avails without his favor,
The whole creation that I see, it came of his exertion,
Counsel glows like priceless gems, if one harkens to the Guru.

[2] The meaning of Guru varies from the Supreme to an avatara.

Teach me the mystery, O Guru,
Of the life thou givest—such wisdom may I cherish!

7. To live four ages or even ten times longer,
Winning ninefold fame with every man's devotion,
Winning a good name through the whole earth published—
Lacking God's good grace, none will care about him.

A worm is but a worm, and sin rests on the sinner,
But he forgives, saith Nanak, adds virtue unto virtue—
No man exists who needs not added virtue.

8. Responding to the Name come lords, gods, saints and masters,[3]
The white bull earth[4] and sky are made by harkening,
Worlds, nether regions, islands came by harkening,
Death itself is overcome by harkening.

Devotion leads to happiness, saith Nanak,
Sins and sorrow are destroyed by harkening.

9. Brahmā, Shiva and Indra came by harkening,
Which prompts their lips the Gayatri[5] to utter,
Yoga skill and mystery come by harkening,
By harkening come Vedic praise and wisdom.

Devotion leads to happiness, saith Nanak,
Sins and sorrow are destroyed by harkening.

10. Truth, knowledge and contentment come by harkening
By harkening comes the bathing places' merit,
Honor and the art of reading come by harkening,
And by it the last stage of meditation.

[3] Sidh pir suri nath, in the original, meaning those straight and perfect, saints and spiritual guides, heroes, and lords—designations variously applied.

[4] i.e., the earth on the white bull's shoulders; cf. v. 16, also. The word here is dhaval; in Psalm 16 it is dhaulu; both are equivalent to dhaula, the "white" bull.

[5] The Hindu Gayatri or Savitri, the daily prayer of brahmans, "Of Savitar the heavenly, may we win the longed-for glory, and may he himself inspire our prayers!" —*Rig Veda*, 3:62, 10, whatever its interpretation.

Devotion leads to happiness, saith Nanak,
Sins and sorrow are destroyed by harkening.

11. By harkening one knows the *avataras*,[6]
The role of prelates, saints and rulers comes by harkening,
The blind find their own paths by harkening,
By harkening streams impassable are forded.

Devotion leads to happiness, saith Nanak,
Sins and sorrow are destroyed by harkening.

12. His state is indescribable who keeps the Name in mind,
He repents it afterwards who undertakes description,
No use of pen or paper is availing,—
Let them think it in the pose of meditation.

The Name is such to him devoid of passion,
He knows him in his heart on due reflection.

13. Wisdom comes and understanding by reflection,
By reflection comes the knowledge of creation,
Slights and slaps are nothing by reflection,
Death's ties are cut asunder by reflection.

The Name is such to him devoid of passion,
Who knows him in his heart by due reflection.

14. One's path is rid of hindrance through reflection,
Through reflection one appears at last with honor,
By reflection one may journey quite unshaken
And find companionship at last with Dharma.[7]

The Name is such to him devoid of passion,
Who knows him in his heart by due reflection.

15. Salvation's doors are opened by obedience,
And one may save his family by obedience,

---

[6] Various "descents," that is, of Vishnu.

[7] The word does duty variously in India; it may mean here simply "religion" and its ideal state. *Cf.* verse 26, line 5; 27, lines 5, 6; 35, line 1, etc.

Obedience to the Guru gets salvation,
Who obeys, saith Nanak, is ne'er a lifelong beggar.

The Name is such to him devoid of passion,
Who knows him in his heart by due reflection.

16. Some saints are genuine and some impostors,
Some receive their honor at the threshold,
Some saints shine at the gateway of the ruler,
And some think sincerely of the Guru.

Though thought and speech be far extended,
This measures not the works of the creator,
Not by the bull[8] but by the law of mercy
Joy becomes man's guardian and guidance.

Who comprehendeth this hath truth discovered,
Nor rests his burden faithless on the bull,
There are so many earths, another and another,
A burden far beyond his power to uphold it.

Creatures, castes, of many shades of color,
Have ever been described in varied phrase,
Many who have known the art of writing
Have written many essays on such themes.

Impressive are the varied forms of beauty,
Who knows the generous bounty of the whole?
How many issues out of one source flowing—
A hundred thousand rivers from one spring.

What mighty power for man to fix his thought on!
No self-denial comprehends it all,
To please thee is a man's best aspiration,
O thou who art eternal, ever dwelling in repose.

[8] Not by "the bull" but by dharmu, "religion" which may be the true bull; cf. v. 8. Indra was sometimes conceived of as a bull. Soma, too, was sometimes a sharp-horned bull and the waters were his cows. In the ancient ritual a bull was sometimes sacrificed to Soma, Agni or Indra. But, doubtless, Nanak refers to the bull of Shiva, to the milky white Nandi, chief of Shiva's personal attendants.

17. Countless repetitions,[9] countless salutations,
Countless genuflections and numberless tabus,
Countless recitations[10] of the Vedic writings,
Yogis beyond number all indifferent to the world;

Countless devotees[11] with minds intent on virtue,
Countless the generous and those who are sincere,
Countless warriors[12] with their steel unflinching,—
Incomparable the minds in their silent, fixed attention.

What mighty power for one to fix his mind on!
No self-denial comprehends it all,
To please thee is man's best aspiration,
O thou who art eternal,[13] dwelling ever in repose.

18. Countless the fools who are devoid of vision,
Countless the thieves with their illicit gain,
Countless the rulers who dispense their judgments,
Countless the assassins inflicting wanton pain;

Countless the sinners living in their sin,
Countless the liars tangled in their lies,
Countless the outcastes[14] grovelling in dirt,
Countless the slanderers whom all good men despise.

Nanak very humbly undertakes expression,
Saying self-denial is of slight avail;
To please thee is man's best aspiration,
O thou who art eternal, dwelling ever in repose.

19. Countless names and countless places,
Regions too numerous to name,
Countless praises humbly uttered,
Names and praises couched in written signs.
Knowledge, songs and recitation,
Writing, speaking—all the while by signs.
In symbol also is the tale of final union.

[9] Jap is itself the word here.
[10] Garanth (granth).
[11] Bhagats.
[12] Sur, heroes. *Cf.* v. 8, note 3, above.
[13] Nirankar, "formless," etc. The word is used in the last line of each of verses 16, 17, 18, 19, and in 37.
[14] Mlechhas.

Destiny is not disclosed in writing,
As he alone commands, so it befalls;
Everything created has its designation,
Not a thing exists that is devoid of name.

What mighty power for man to fix his mind on!
No self-denial comprehends it all;
To please thee is man's best aspiration,
O thou who art eternal, dwelling ever in repose.

20. When body, foot, hand or trunk is fouled,
One uses water for the cleansing,
And soap is used to cleanse again
The garment that was soiled by urine.

When sense has been befouled by sin,[15]
The Name alone will cleanse it,
Vice and virtue are not words alone,
Yet conduct writes them most indelibly;

A man's self sows and likewise reaps
While under his command, saith Nanak.

21. Pilgrimage and penance and free-will giving
Gain for one no single grain of merit,
Unless one harken and his heart be loving,
Cleansed within by a meditative bath.
All good is thine, no single virtue have I,
And without it what avails devotion?[16]
By word of mouth the brahmans utter blessing,
While the True One blesses with sincere desire.

What indeed of sun-course, moon-phase, week-day,
What of months and seasons and their varied forms?
Pandits fail to gauge them, though Purans inform them,
And qadis[17] do not know the times of the Koran,
Neither does the yogi know the times and seasons,
He alone doth know them by whom they have been made.

---

[15] Papa (pap), "sin"; in line 7, papi.
[16] Bhagati.
[17] Moslem "judges."

Who then am I to know, relate and praise,
If not to use the clever words of others?
Saith Nanak of the Lord,[18] his name and will are great
And pride of self meets in the end dishonor.

22. Myriad skies above and myriad hells below—
One tires of counting all. The Veds give their own figure,
Eighteen thousand, thick as horsehairs, say the Moslems,
But could the sum be written, it would fade away,
He only counts them truly who only knows, saith Nanak.

23. With all my hymns[19] I win but scant attention—
Yet streams and floods do not disturb the ocean;
And the lords of sea-borne trade of wealth abundant
Are less than any ant that keeps not God in mind.

24. There is no end to his praises' recitation,
No end to his works and none to all his giving,
His seeing, too, is endless and his hearing, also,
The wisdom of his mind exceeds all knowledge,
There is no final knowledge of the forms he takes,
Nor any limit within which to know him.[20]

It is not possible to find his boundary,
There is no one this sort of end to know,
The more that's said leaves more yet for the saying,
Upon a lofty plane the great Lord[21] dwells,
His name is higher than the very high,
If we could only be as high as he,
He only even then his height would know.

He only knows of his own greatness,
And gives to us, saith Nanak, of his mercy.

25. Mercy in abundance far beyond description
Is that which he the giver gives us without stint,
However limitless may be some warriors' requests

[18] The expression here used is Bara Sahib, "Great Sir."

[19] Salahi salahi, "all sorts of praises."

[20] The translation of these three lines may represent more the sense than the literal words.

[21] Sahibu.

Who neither reckon nor give his mercy thought.
Many men are broken and consumed by passion
And some repudiate the very gifts they gain.
How many fools there are who go on eating, eating
And yet are hungry when days of sorrow come—
Verily, O Giver, all the gifts are thine.

Bonds and release are both by thy decree,
Nor may any other with either interfere;
He will learn whose abuse succeeds his eating
What knocks also his mouth must then consume;[22]
He truly comprehends who himself has given—
And there are some indeed who thus can understand,
To whom he delegates his goodness and his praises—
He is none other than the King of Kings,[23] saith Nanak.

26. Priceless values, trade beyond compare,
Priceless traders and their stock of stores,
Precious customers, precious bearers, also,
Precious those, the humble and the high,
Precious dharma and its precious dispensation,
Precious the scales and the precious weights,
Priceless bounty and its tokens priceless,
Incalculable karma and its sure demands—
Priceless pricelessness defying calculation,
However devotedly one catalogue them all.

Vedas and Purans attest these values
Which learned men discover and confirm,
Which have to do with Brahma and Indra,
Likewise with the gopis and their lord;[24]
By Shiva and many saints proclaimed,
As also by many kinds of sages,
Proclaimed by demons and also by gods
Whom many kinds of men and sages serve.
Much has been proclaimed and is yet to be expounded,

[22] If one who has eaten is abusive, he will learn how many blows, in consequence, his mouth will eat.

[23] Patisahi patisahu.

[24] The gopis' Lord is Gopal Krishna (Govind).

Some have given utterance, others ceased proclaiming—
His creatures have been many and more will be created,
Yet none can tell the fullness of his plan.

This fullness is a matter of his pleasure,
The True One only, saith Nanak, truly knows;
Whoever giveth utterance to harmful speech,
Let him be written down the fool of fools.

27. Where the door and even where the house,
Wherein he sits who doth uphold it all?
Many are the players, the sounds and instruments,
And the singers sing their many, varied tunes;
Water, wind and fire sing—and dharmraj singeth at the door,
Angels sing what hath been written of the thoughts of dharma,
The goddess, Shiv and Brahmā find honor in remembrance,
Indra and his hosts sit and sing thy praises,
Devotees and saints sing from deep reflection,
The truthful, the contented and hardy heroes sing,
Pandits and the abstinent read and sing the Vedas,
Enchanting women sing and scatter spells about them,
The jewelled sing to pilgrims at the eight-and-sixty centers,
Doughty warriors[25] sing and every quarter answers,
The lands and regions sing of the world Thou dost sustain.

So many please with song in this realm of Thine abode,
A vastly greater multitude than Nanak can remember;
He is Lord forever whose truth can never perish,
Whatever the vicissitude of things that he hath made;
Maya[26] indeed arises of many forms and colors,
Whose varieties he watches from his plane on high;
In the end he willeth what to him is pleasing—
He is ever Lord of Lords, saith Nanak of his rule.

28. Bowl and wallet, smug contentment, are no more than cow-dung ashes,
The body's patched-up cloak is death if faith be not the staff;
He first subdues his heart who the world aipanthi-like[27] subdues—

[25] Jodh, with which compare the Sanskrit yudh, a warrior; cf. 37, line 3.

[26] Maia; cf. mai of verse 30.

[27] In the manner of certain yogis who have banished enmity.

Hail to him, all hail!
Ever spotless, unbeginning and immortal,
Whose vestments are the same in all the ages.

29. The food is knowledge, the cook is mercy—to such repast the summons comes,
With the Lord of Lords[28] is increase, enjoyment, and every satisfaction,
Unity and separation alternate in the process fate records.
Hail to him, all hail!
Ever spotless, unbeginning and immortal,
Whose vestments are the same in all the ages.

30. One pregnant maya with great power bore three disciples,
A creator, a nourishment-conserver, a dispenser-of-the-law.
But he according to his pleasure impels their varied action,
He sees, but, how marvellous, he does not to them appear.
Hail to him, all hail!
Ever spotless, unbeginning and immortal,
Whose vestments are the same in all the ages.

31. Everywhere his seat and everywhere his stores,
His deposits are completed once for all,
He looks upon the creatures he has made,
The product of the True One, saith Nanak, must be true.
Hail to him, all hail!
Ever spotless, unbeginning and immortal,
Whose vestments are the same in all the ages.

32. If a tongue or two become a hundred thousand, and they two million in their turn,
However great their number, the Lord's name is the one of praise among them all.
Are the steps not one-and-twenty which lead a person upward!
Even worms that hear the Name become enamoured of the sky.
His glance reveals himself, saith Nanak,
E'en amidst assertions that are false.

33. In neither speech nor silence is there virtue,
And none in begging nor in giving alms,

[28] This time nathu nathi.

No power in living, nor any won by dying,
No power in rule, in the goods of world or mind,
No power in sheer reflection, contemplation, knowledge,
Nor can cunning break the one eternal round—
He bestows the virtue in whose hand the power lies,
And men are nothing, Nanak saith, be they low or high.

34. Nights and days and months and seasons,
Air and water and the fires of hell—
'Midst all such forms and hues the court of justice stands,
'Midst variegated forms and hues,
Their names alone as limitless as varied.
Deeds of all sorts come to its attention,
The judge himself is true and true his court,
Where the pious and the worthy meet with honor.
And the crude may by the law attain perfection,
Doing deeds which prompt their own reward.
Whoever runs may know this court, saith Nanak.

35. Religion[29] may indeed be so much custom,
A fund of knowledge or a round of deeds.
How many winds, waters, fires, Shivs and Krishnas,
Many Brahmās creating hue and form,
Many Merus,[30] whence works and sage instruction,
Indras, suns and moons, many lands and dwellings,
Siddhs and buddhs and yogis, many kinds of godlings,
Devas, danavs, munis, and many gems and oceans,
Many mines and builders, many lords and rulers—
Custom, saith Nanak, provides a host to worship.

36. Religion, too, may be a fund of knowledge,[31]
Whence blisses and delights portrayed in words,
Symbols which at most have partial value,
Falling short of power for describing

[29] Nanak here speaks of religion as dharm khand, and refers in the line following to the "knowledge portion" (giana khand), or the saving fund of the classical jnana-marga, the "way of knowledge."

[30] Meru, the Olympus of the Hindus at the center of the earth.

[31] Nanak continues to discuss "religion"—his expression here is gian khand, the "knowledge portion."

That which of itself assumes incalculable forms;
Who leans on words repents of their employment.
The exercise of mind may lead to knowledge,
But discernment in the end must come by insight.

37. The way of works[32] has its peculiar value,
Might seem to be religion's total way;
Great heroes of military fame have used it,
Amongst whom pre-eminent stands lordly Ram,
With whom majestic Sita keeps her calm,
A twain whose glory may not be described—
In whose hearts the holy Ram abides,
Life cannot cheat them and they do not die.
Bhagats in goodly number tread the way,
But with a special joy from truth within the mind.

*Nirankar* the formless commends the way of *truth*,[33]
He who made creation and rules it with delight.
Such is the portion of kingdoms, worlds and regions,
All numberless to any who would count them—
Realms and realms with never any ending,
All coming into life at his command.
Who sets his thought on this expands his vision,
Finds excellence, saith Nanak, quite beyond destruction.

38. Continence the work-shop, fortitude the goldsmith,
Reason is the anvil and the hammer wisdom,
Fear is the bellows, the fire is self-denial,
Love is the crucible in which the nectar melts—
Such is the judgment of the true assembly.
He keeps this in mind who desires to conquer,
Who observes it closely finds delight, saith Nanak.

### POSTLUDE

Breath is the Guru, water is the father, the mother is the potent earth,
Childhood's life is nurtured both by day and night,
Goodness and evil are distinguished by religion,

[32] This is the karam khand as evidence and means of religion.

[33] The sach khand, or "truth portion," as something higher than both works and knowledge.

Men's deeds indicate if God is near or far—
  Salvation comes at last to those whose thought rests on the Name,
  Their faces glow, saith Nanak, and they have become immortal.

The footnotes which accompany this English version of the *Japji* have sought to make some of the most obscure details a little clearer to the western reader. Particular attention may still be called to a climax of theory which the psalms portray. Nanak proposes the superiority of "the way of truth," which Nirankar commends, over the "knowledge portion" and the "action portion," over the way of "knowledge" and the way of "works." He even commends this way of truth as superior to the bhakti-way of salvation—truth is more valid than devotion! And yet, as has been observed already in these pages, Nanak was virtually preaching the bhakti or "devotion" way whose inspiration, support and destination would be realized, as he thought and said, in Sat Nam, True Name. The bhakti-marga is to Nanak, we might say, the true way if pursued in the true Name. He proposed, even though not deliberately, a *fourth* way of salvation, more instrumental and effective than any one or all of the other three.

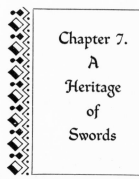

# Chapter 7. A Heritage of Swords

By his death Guru Nanak became Nanak Nirankari, a spirit rather than merely man, passing into legend out of history and virtually bequeathing to his followers the problem of succession, that of the Guruship.[1] Whether by his own intention or otherwise, his legacy of the *Japji* became eventually the fundamental item in the solution of this problem, but meanwhile the Guruship continued to be very personal. His life career was carried forward by personal custodians and heirs. He himself, in fact, effected this personal succession, and Sikhism as it has survived was not the fruit of accident and circumstance—no great movement in the history of religions is, in fact, ever merely accidental. Sikhism was itself expressive of something in the very life of India, although several decades were required for it to take the form which made of it a unique expression of Indian history, which enabled it to take a form measurably in harmony with Nanak's legacy and his own intention. Nanak himself knew that whatever he had achieved for himself, he had not fulfilled for *others* his own essential promise.

Nanak may have effected a personal succession, but otherwise had worked out no details of an organized society. He did establish a precedent through which could be established a community beyond the ties of family. He barred, that is, his own sons from succession to him, and clothed the Guruship by his own liberal ordination with more than family prestige, with due dignity and supreme importance. Toward the end of his life specific leadership became his chief con-

[1] The reference here, of course, is primarily to the human leadership, although God also has been designated Guru. The guru is, in any case, someone "most highly respected."

cern, however flexible the doctrine he was ready to bequeath. He had come, for example, to take the State for granted—perhaps he *always* took the State for granted. He recognized certain legal aspects of a Sikh's life in the world, although he undertook no formal legal code, either criminal or civil. He did not even offer, for example, a modification *as such* of either the Hindu "code of Manu" or any Moslem code of fiqh, or canon law, although he must have been acquainted with at least portions of both of them. Nor did he suggest any specific alterations in the immemorial legal usages of Indian tribes and clans.

He laid great stress on excellence of conduct beyond the requirements of any formal code of law, and bade his followers always to be *sikhs* or "learners"—he gave them for their own use no other title, with some intimation, in the title he bestowed, that there was much to learn. He would have them, it seems, take increasing advantage of opportunities to improve their condition as men free of convention and with inherent power to realize their own high ends. There is some indication that he thought time and circumstance to be on the side of progress and that India, his homeland, would some day be the scene of a new order affecting all her racial and religious elements. Nanak may have somewhat missed his timing of "the timeless," but that he could hold out such an eventuality may constitute in itself an occasion, a motive and a reason for the survival of his faith. The times of *truth* recurred and might still serve the ends of understanding and cooperation among all Indian peoples.

The period of adjustment after Nanak extended to A.D. 1606, during which four gurus in succession, Angad, Amar Das, Ram Das and Arjun, were the leaders. They gave their attention and activity to an analysis of their heritage and to its use as leaven and control for their community. And they were intimately concerned with the relation of the Sikh gospel with Hindu, Moslem and other Indian elements.

Angad himself "obtained the gift from Nanak," as a later hymn records, and found himself confronting tendencies which, on the one hand, would make Sikhism a distinctive sect, and, on the other hand, would dissipate it, neither of which eventualities was in the mind of Nanak. Angad was possibly more aware of the risk of dissipation—eradication by Indian Islam or absorption into Hinduism. He would indeed avoid the formation of a sect, but he would preserve Sikhism as a party of *reform*—and a *medium* of reconciliation. How indeed can "reconciliation" be accomplished unless there be a medium? But, Angad, how personal need the medium be? And how indispensable are you to the good work of leaven? How impersonal, after all, is leaven? How effectual can it be apart from personality? How, then, may Hinduism and Islam be reconciled? Had they in common that which might ultimately unite them? If so, who would point it out, expound it, and persuade the faithful to agree upon it? Nanak would have been happy to decrease while reconciliation prospered. If only reformers might make themselves dispensable! The history of religions might then include far fewer sects. However, good seed must be sown, if progress be the rule, and although the earth which receives it should bear fruit *of itself*, there is need of men for gathering in the harvest—and, most certainly, a need for separating wheat from tares. And this is all so largely a *personal* performance. Well, Angad felt the responsibility of a definite commission and charged himself with fulfilling its details.

Angad, whose name at first was Lahna, we may remember, was by birth and occupation a Hindu, but before the death of Nanak he had amply proved his virtue as a Sikh. He was born a tradesman in a trader's family in a Rajputana village where he spent his early years. When the Moslems sacked the village, the family removed to the Panjab, to the village of Khadur, beside the Beas river near Tarn Taran. While still a pious Hindu, however, he was once in charge of a pilgrimage to jwala mukhi, or "fire mouth," a volcanic vent in the lower, neighboring Himalayas, from which flame came consecrated to the goddess Durga. He was to have led the Durga-dance around the mount of fire, clad in a robe of office and in a harness of jingling bells. But, it seems, Nanak —then living—had gone to Fire-mouth to preach his gospel to the Durga-devotees on this festival occasion, and Angad listened to the sermon. He had known something of the Sikhs before this. He had met in his own village, and had been favorably impressed by, a certain Jodh, a conscientious devotee very zealous at his "morning prayer" and at quotations from the *Japji*. He met Nanak himself at Fire-mouth and there and then became a convert. He resigned at once from the leadership of the Hindu pilgrimage, made over the bells and the symbols of his office, returned home and adjusted his own personal affairs with a view to some itinerant advocacy of Sikh doctrine. He would at least attach himself to Nanak's staff at Kartarpur, the Sikh headquarters. Thither he proceeded with a bag of salt (salt has been especially valuable in India) as a gift to Nanak's public kitchen, and there he devoted himself so zealously to the common cause that Bhagirath, Buddha, Sudhara and others of Nanak's small community looked upon him as a good example. Nanak soon came to think of him, in fact, as his favorite disciple, a role which most of the community in its turn subscribed to.

When Angad became actually the Guru he undertook at once two things: an enlargement of the kitchen and an extension of its operation, and the formulation of a language —alphabet and all—which might be a sacred medium of expression for the hymns and prayers. Nanak himself had made the public kitchen a distinctive feature of the Sikhs, had invited guests and friends to eat with him and his disciples as one family, regardless of race, wealth, sex, caste, occupation or religion. Angad enlarged this ministry, of which many took advantage, including many Jats of indistinguishable Hindu-Moslem heritage and some of the poorer and less fortunate folk who were practically "without the pale." And Angad is somehow intimately connected with Gurmukhi, the "guru-tongue" which the Sikhs have used as their sacred language. He himself did not invent the tongue. It rests upon and utilizes the vernacular of Nanak's day, but it borrowed and invented an alphabet for its written expression. Did this mean in itself that thus early Sikhism would be a separate community? An arbitrarily distinct and independent alphabet, nevertheless, was formed through which to put on record, among other things, words with peculiar meaning in Sikh usage.

There were many dialects among Panjabis at the time. Many Sanskrit, Arabic and Persian terms were current, and many words were undergoing change of form, of pronunciation and, sometimes, of their very meaning. Among the learned folk the Panjabi was still written in the Devanagari (nagari, for short), or Sanskrit-Hindi characters. The Urdu, or "camp" language of the Moslems, written in Arabic-Persian characters had not become by that time common—was then strange, in fact, to Angad. And not only was the villager's colloquial often greatly different from the language of the learned, but words among the learned sometimes looked or sounded strange through transliteration. The Panjabi used, for example, a *j* to express either a Sanskrit y or a Persian z. Any preacher, prophet or religious leader faced, therefore, the problem of expression in the language of the people—how can a hearer be converted if he does not understand! But there was a further problem for the Sikhs. Their leaders were soon disinclined to use for their own peculiarly religious purposes either a Moslem tongue or one predominantly Hindu. The Hindui vernacular of Ramananda and

Kabir might have served the Sikhs in worship, had it not become by Angad's time entirely and exclusively a Hindu medium. The Urdu which was gaining currency represented in itself the Moslems who had invaded India, was a medium of alien culture and control and was used by Moslem mullas in religious propaganda. Nanak's *Japji* hymns, as he had recited them, were expressed in the language of the village folk, however numerous its content of words carried over from Moslem and Hindu tradition. Angad, then, would provide for these hymns their own, distinctive alphabet, and through his effort arose Gurmukhi as a new language of religion—which, incidentally, has provided Sikh and other theologians, subsequently, many acute problems of etymology, syntax and interpretation!

Angad died in 1552 after a dozen years in office, and Amar Das succeeded him at Angad's own designation, thus making further sure the exclusion of Nanak's own son, Sri Chand, from the direct guruship, and giving further opportunity for distinction between the Sikhs and the order of Udasis which meanwhile Sri Chand had instituted. Nor was Amar Das Angad's *son*, but only a god-son who had learned of Sikhism and had become a convert to it through one of Angad's relatives. Amar Das's chief qualification was, perhaps, that he possessed the barkat, "blessing"—he was, that is, in spiritual succession. And his career in office gave further emphasis to the development of Sikhism as something more than a mere sect of Hinduism, as it doubtless would have become shortly under Nanak's son Sri Chand. Amar Das was, of course, of Hindu ancestry, but proved to be a very active and efficient agent of the new community, giving close attention to certain practical reforms. He was in true succession not only as guru but also as poet, and, as in the case of Nanak, verse became the channel of his message of reform. He faced the question, for example, of sati, or "widow-burning," a Hindu custom which had continued also among

Sikhs; and he denounced the practice. Instead, he gave sati a figuratively spiritual interpretation—thus opening the way, we may ask, to widow-remarriage among Sikhs? He registered his view in the following verse:

> They are called satis who burn themselves with the burning corpse;
> We Nanakis deem them satis who perish of the very shock of separation,[2]
> Or those who in separation live content and virtuous,
> Who every morn on rising commemorate their Lord.

The themes were numerous and characteristic to which Angad addressed his many verses, among which, for example, were such topics as the grave defects of Hindu scriptures, the evils of idolatry and polytheism, the cupidity of brah mans, the sad state of the world, the risks of worldly love, man's obstinate perversion, the virtue of humility and penitence, God's indwelling in men's hearts, the supremacy of God, the sure happiness of the holy, and the high quality of the office of the guru. One of his most notable compositions is the forty-stanza *Anand*, or Song of Joy, commonly used at wedding festivals.

The Sikhs, we may suppose, were left mostly to their own affairs during these early years. If the Mughal government took any notice of them, it was no more than mere routine attention—they were only another local enterprise, a transitory movement! But among the Sikhs themselves the guruship itself remained somewhat in question. Angad's own son Datu had pressed a *family* claim to office and had engendered some dissension, but had made peace with Amar Das through the good counsel of Bhai Buddha. Sri Chand, however, pressed both a family and an *ideal* claim. If he could

[2] "Satiam ehin akhiani jo madia lagi jalani
Nanak satiam janiani ji birhe chot marani,"—to which he added the comment that true satihood was recollection of the Lord.

not have the guruship, he nevertheless insisted on a strictly otherworldly interpretation of his father Nanak's gospel. When it had become clear that no such view would be officially promoted, Sri Chand and his partisans began to "mourn" about it. At least, they set themselves apart as udasis, "mourners" over the sad state of man in an evil world, if not for sorrow over being barred from office. Perhaps the other Sikhs themselves applied this title to them and for themselves determined that, if possible, there would be more of anand (joy) than of udas (sorrow), in their movement, that Sikhism should *not* become mere negative asceticism.

But the Udasis, nonetheless, may have exerted some slight, effectual pressure on the family principle. Although Amar Das did not designate one of his own sons to follow him in office, he named a daughter's husband, Jetha, who took office as Ram Das, with the provision that the guruship should remain in *his* family. But the office was not even destined to become matriarchal. Amar Das had been guru a dozen years; his son-in-law was in office six. Ram Das was a pious, peaceful man who filled the office acceptably, but without distinction—unless indeed his kinship with the influential Sodhi khatri family of Lahore was such. And, perhaps, it was he whose name is rightly associated with the Amristar site on which the Darbar Sahib stands. He lived there, maintained there a public kitchen, and many devotees flocked about his residence; and the settlement acquired the name of Ramdaspur, that is, "village of Ram Das." It was one of many villages on land which the Mughal emperor Akbar, Babur's grandson, had made over to the Sikhs. Within the grant lay also the village Govindwal where Amar Das had lived, who while he was guru had inclosed a great well of water reached by many steps, in which devotees might bathe. Ram Das likewise made provision for a well by renovating an ancient Hindu property which included a temple and a pool. The temple was itself a Hari-mandir, or seat of Vishnu, and Ram Das may then have had no other name to give it! But the pool, tank, or talau, held for the Sikhs amritsar, "water of immortality."

Hindu atmosphere, however, lingered on these premises. Ram Das's marriage to guru Amar Das's daughter had been approved because he was a khatri according to the Hindu social scale. And Hindus insisted on their own privilege of worship at the Hari-mandir. A bairagi[3] even disputed Sikh occupation of it, affirming that the spot was sacred to Ram Chandra, seventh avatara of Vishnu, the tutelary divinity of the bairagi devotee's own brotherhood. But the bairagi was at last persuaded that Ram Chandra himself favored Sikh possession. Moreover, the Government itself had made the Sikhs a grant of this very site! Despite the general atmosphere the momentum of the Sikh administration was perceptibly enhanced, and when Ram Das died in 1581, his own son Arjun, who succeeded him by his father's own appointment, faced opportunity for notable advance.

Arjun (1581-1606), the fifth Guru, came into a large inheritance, and Sikhism during his term of office began to assume more definite proportions as an actually new community. Its numbers had been growing, although the total was not yet large. There were members of the order in many villages—"eighty-four" in one of them—and there had been various "capitals" or centers of the gurus—for example, Kartarpur, Khadur, Gondwal, Govindwal (or are these latter two one and the same?) and Ramdaspur, all villages within one larger neighborhood. Arjun himself became the greatest of the early leaders and the fashioner of a second sword. Amritsar became his capital after seven years of his guruship elsewhere, and its permanence was established as the central

[3] Or, perhaps, more exactly a vairagi, traditionally a recluse, or one "detached" from passion and its worldly objects. Actually many vairagis were of coarser fabric.

home of Sikhism. Tarn Taran[4] was his seat during the first seven years.

Arjun's term of office coincided with the latter half of the Mughal Akbar's reign (Akbar was emperor from 1556 to 1605), with that portion of it in which Abkar's restless intellect sought absolute truth *somewhere* in religion. The sectarianism of Islam, his own religion, had disturbed him. His inquiries for truth were made in many quarters. He had welcomed Jesuits to his court in 1578 and again in February 1580. He had issued the decree of Iman-i-Adl, or a "religion of justice," in 1579, and had frankly admitted that he himself had ceased to be a Moslem. And a year after Arjun the Sikh took office, Akbar had proclaimed the Din-i-Ilahi, or "Divine Faith." It was a season in which Sikhism might have hoped to make impressive progress, but we are not sure how much account Arjun and the Sikhs took either of Islam or of Akbar's own innovations. Circumstances, at any rate, compelled the Sikhs to take serious account of political Islam, but there are no references in Arjun's memoirs to Islam as religion, to the Arabic Koran, or to any strictly Moslem doctrine. There are many references, on the other hand, to Hindu "vedas, puranas and smritis."[5] And yet it may be that Moslems were, after all, the greatest factors in determining Sikh destiny. Guru Arjun's era was a momentous time of turning in Sikh fortune, a time of utter transformation in the mission of the Sikhs. The time had come for a reappraisal of the mission, to determine further its relations with Islam, Hinduism and any other faiths. Arjun could still offer Sikhism as the essential, and an all-inclusive, gospel, if a reinterpretation could be achieved of common elements within the total Indian setting, but Sikhism was

[4] See illustration No. 7 for what this seat became more recently.

[5] These are all somewhat indefinite titles, but altogether inclusive of the Hindu sacred writings.

tending to become a *church* within that setting, a movement within non-ecclesiastical Hinduism, an order by the side of ecclesiastical Islam and a *state* within the empire of the Mughals. For the Sikhs, matters creedal, ritual, financial, political and social became public issues in a special sense—and the problem of the guruship itself persisted!

The guru's place of residence, thus the headquarters of the Sikhs, was itself a matter of concern. In Arjun's day Tarn Taran was a humble village and Amritsar was not at all pretentious. Their prominence developed, rather, in the nineteenth century under Maharaja Ranjit Singh after the Sikhs had organized a ruling state. Arjun merely lived in Tarn Taran seven years, but on removing to Amritsar he began to construct there a more distinctive capital. He built—or rebuilt?—in the center of the lake, at a low level symbolic of humility, a modest structure of burnt brick as a sanctuary, giving it the name of Har Mandir, "everybody's temple"—a deliberate modification, perhaps, of the name Harimandir,[6] "temple of Vishnu," of the former Hindu temple on that site. The building was doubtless soon completed and it stood, subject to occasional repair, until demolished in 1761 by the Persian invader Ahmad Shah. Whereas a Hindu temple is usually closed on three sides, with its one doorway open toward the east, toward the rising sun, and available to Hindus only, Arjun's temple was provided with doorways on all four sides as a general invitation to all worshipers. Only the very center of the shrine was denied to any worshiper—even to the Guru—and that was occupied by the *Adi Granth*, the basic scripture, as soon as

[6] "Har" in the colloquial was probably a word of mixed ancestry, although probably Indo-European, at least. In the manner of the Persian it might mean any, each or every (e.g., har ek, each or every one). In the manner of its Sanskrit lineage it was a name for Mahadeva (Shiva), although usually applied to Vishnu. The form "hari" itself was applied specifically to the "green" god Vishnu, leaving "hara" to apply to the "destroyer" Shiva.

Arjun could arrange its compilation. In substance this temple was merely a gurdwara, but it soon acquired for Sikhs a value beyond that of any such local village shrine. Arjun himself intended, as he said in a commemorative ode, that the Har Mandir in its holy lake should have the value of *all* the Hindu "sixty-eight goals of pilgrimage" (a phrase he quoted from *Japji* 10).

The assembling of the *Adi* or "original" *Granth Sahib* into compact, coherent form, and its elevation as authoritative scripture was a significant achievement—Arjun's noblest, probably. It incorporated Nanak's *Japji,* the religious poetry which gurus Amar Das and Ram Das had composed, many verses of Kabir and other bhagats (theistic-minded devotees), and many of Arjun's own compositions, notably his lengthy *Sukhmani,* or "Peace-jewel," or psalm of "peace" of mind, and the long acrostic *Bawan Akhari,* "the fifty-two." All of these writings proclaimed in simple, sometimes childlike, manner the typical Sikh gospel. Arjun's own verse sang the praise of the One God, the divine Guru, who dwells everywhere, especially in men's hearts, and is accessible to all; and his hymns might be as effective for worship and meditation as, for example, the psalms of David, of Asaph or of Solomon, except that they are not so well known or as widely read. They are likewise scarcely as *thoughtful* as, for example, many psalms of the Buddhist "brothers" (thera) and "sisters" (theri) who early addressed themselves more to abstraction than to God—in imitation of Buddha's own mindfulness and concentration.[7]

But of more than passing interest for us at the moment—of interest for substance of doctrine, for example—are the writings which were deliberately excluded from the *Adi*

[7] These early brothers and sisters belonged to the more original, Hinayana type of Buddhism long before any bhakti type of religion had appeared in India. The Hebrew, Buddhist and Sikh scriptures differ much in content, after all.

*Granth*. The bare fact of canon-making has a meaning in itself. The Sikhs were intent upon a *book*. The Hindus had their shastras[8] and the Moslems their kitab.[9] The Sikhs, of course, had nothing as extensive as the former and were sceptical of Hindu scriptures, anyway. They were doubtful, likewise, of Moslem writings. They had their own *Japji* and a good deal more besides, and a word had become current among them which needed their own definition of it—the word was *granth*. This, it soon appeared, would serve them as a proper designation. "Grantha" was an ancient term descended from the Sanskrit and meaning, among other things, treatise, book and composition. For Sikhs it would henceforth be *the* Book of selected, authoritative sayings. And there would be an adi, original or primary edition exclusive of much miscellaneous "wisdom" then in circulation in the form of verse—much of which, to be sure, was read by Sikhs themselves.

The *Gyan Ratnavali*, "nuggets of sound wisdom" by Arjun's own scribe, Gur Das (Bhai Gurdas Bhalla), and popular with Sikhs, was excluded—on grounds not readily to be determined. Were some of the "nuggets" indiscreet in their vehement condemnation of Hindu "holy" men and of Moslem bigotry? Were some Sikhs offended by Gur Das's reference to Arjun's lack—as *he*, the poet, said—of formal investiture and consecration as the guru, and were some likewise displeased by his reference to Nanak as an avatara (a manifestation of Vishnu, that is)? Was there some uneasiness over the Hindu and Moslem association Gur Das imposed on Nanak? That is, he portrays Nanak in the company of Vyasa,

[8] "Shastra" has for the Hindu such meanings as command, code, law, treatise, book and scripture—so many, in fact, that particular shastras must be further specified.

[9] To Moslems their Qur'an, or "reading," is pre-eminently al-Kitab, the Book, such being the first of fifty-five special titles given it, including al-Kalam, the Word, an-Nur, the Light, and al-Haqq, the Truth.

the "compiler" of the Hindu *Mahabharata* epic, and in Mohammed's company, the "hearer" of the Koran. And yet, Gur Das's mood, in general, was consistently Sikh, if religious reconciliation was the theme, and he portrays Nanak as the prophet of the age who would reconcile Hindu, Islamic and other sects and purify the world of social ills! Here is a fair specimen of the *Ratnavali* "wisdom" in a free translation:

> Four races and four creeds were in the world 'mongst Musulmans and Hindus,
> And all were uniformly selfish, jealous, proud—
> Hindus by the Ganga at Banaras, and by the distant Ka'bah Musulmans.
> Muslims mark by circumcision, and Hindus by the tilak and the thread;
> Muslims Rahim, and Hindus Ram implore, and miss the way that leads to either god;
> Forgetful of the Veds and the Qur'an, the present age's snares entangle them.
> Truth stood idly by, the while unwanted, as brahman priests and Muslim mullas clashed—
> And there was no salvation for the world.
>
> God heard the plaint of virtue and despatched the guru Nanak to the rescue of the world:
> As Nanak set example, chelas wash their guru's feet, and drink the water freely afterward. . . .
> Nanak showed that all the many gods are One, that one are all the several castes of men;
> He ordained the salutation of the feet, whereby disciples high and low are equal,
> Reversing the very order of man's nature by making heads submissive to the feet.
> He offered to this darkest age salvation by means of worship of the one True Name—
> Nanak came indeed to give this age salvation.[10]

[10] Notes on this specimen: Musulman is Muslim or Moslem, Ganga the Ganges, Banaras Benares; the tilak is a forehead mark of Hindus, the mulla is a learned man (mulla is the Persian form of the Arabic maulawi), and a chela is a student, pupil.

Many less pretentious items, also, were excluded, including some nuggets which, they say, the authors themselves offered directly to Guru Arjun. It seems that Arjun had been accustomed to watch the building of the temple from a nearby "office" which he continued to use during the compilation of the *Granth*, and that "four religious men of Lahore," Kahna, Chhajju, Shah Lal Husayn and Pilo,[11] by name, came there one day with their offerings of verse—it was a pleasant spot to which they came, the records say, green herbage providing it a carpet, and jand, wild caper, fig and pipal trees providing shade.

Kahna offered this verse:

> I am He, I am He
> Sung by Vedas and Puranas,
> Where none have found me yet by searching.

This is very brief, to be sure, but may contain much by implication, or by interpretation. It may seem at first like typical sufi or bhagat sentiment, but may have meant something else to Arjun, may have seemed to tend unduly toward the impersonal and pantheistic. It might have been expressive of an extraordinary sufi notion that a man may himself be God. A certain Moslem poet once was slain by order of the khalifah (caliph) for supposedly calling himself al-haqq, "the truth," which in the khalifah's view was sacrilege or worse, since according to the Koran Allah himself is al-Haqq. And there was in Hinduism a remotely similar analogy in the philosophic dogma "tat tvam asi" (that thou art), meaning that individuals are essentially one with the Absolute and not what they merely seem to be. Such idealism was too extreme for realistic Arjun.

Chhajju offered this verse:

> Look thou not upon a woman,
> Not even on her figure cut from paper;

[11] *Cf.* Macauliffe, *The Sikh Religion*, III, pp. 62ff., for reference to the verses of these four.

Women are like sly Baluchi raiders
Who carry off their men to slay them.

Here was bhagat sentiment—of such was Chhajju who even against "pin-up girls" would lodge objection. He had passed through life's earlier "stages" and had come to that of the strict ascetic. But Sikhism had already questioned the ascetic ideal which figured so conspicuously in the Hindu round of life. Nanak himself had not depreciated or repudiated women, had not condemned the state of the householder. He, of course, had had a wife and family and his separation from them had not been absolute. Arjun himself had had more than one wife—no doubt had more than one at that very time. In any case, Sikhs were working out their own peculiar ideas of womanhood, which differed more or less from either the Hindu or the Moslem view of woman, as we shall see. The *Granth* had no place for such a verse as this one of Chhajju's, therefore.

Shah Lal Husayn submitted this:

Be silent, oh, be silent!
  What need, my friend, for speaking?
  There is no need for speaking.
Without, within us is the Lord,
To whom in silence we address us.
In every heart the One Beloved,
Nor is there anywhere a second.
  Saith faqir Husayn quite humbly,
  I'm an offering to the Guru.

The objection to this verse could not have come from its reference to a "second," although this may have been suggestive of a Moslem dogma that Allah is God "alone." To Sikhs also God is "one." The reference to "the One Beloved," however, is in the sufi manner, somewhat different from the Sikh. But the gospel of "silence" was incompatible with Sikhism. Hindu sadhus, for example, might take vows of silence, but Sikhs were vocal, missionary and advocates of conversion through "harkening to the Name."

Nor had Sikhism a place for the pessimistic despair of Pilo's verse:

> Those who have died at birth
> Are better off by far than we;
> We live amidst the filth of earth
> Which they're not doomed to see.

Sikhs themselves were not disposed to quit the scene at the very outset! Even had Arjun and others known then of the seasons of distress ahead of them, of the bitter struggles and disasters not far distant, they would not have yielded to a counsel of despair. Struggle, also, was God's gift to them —or, at least, their heritage in God.

The compilation of the *Granth* was a process at once indicative in itself of what Sikhism was to be. Arjun, the compiler, was an observant, keen and sound critic of all about him, and the trend of practicality and realism in his movement was proving stronger than tendencies toward the mystical and negative. He commented freely on the virtues and the defects of the various religions. His rejection of Chhajju's verse and of Pilo's confirmed a judgment of his predecessors—Chhajju died a solitary recluse. Nor would he travel with Husayn who after practicing Islamic rites for many years, lost faith in them as effectual in "this world of sport," or *chance*, that is, and became a dancing darwish. He had his own notion of sainthood, as may be seen in his comment upon a monk who had taken a vow to "touch nothing." He doubted if there could be a "true touch-nothing saint," for the tongue of such would never "touch" a lie, his gaze would never touch the womenfolk of other households, nor would he ever let slander touch his ears!

Arjun held the view that men saw "according to their lights," but since the seed of the True Name was sown in every heart, anyone of the four castes (!)[12] who practiced the Name might obtain salvation. The true saint, said he, not only cherishes the Name within himself, but sees the Name in others and takes pains to make them realize the Name in all its fullness. For example, he considered him to be a *true* Vishnuite whose body and mind were so pervaded by the Name that he had no desire of self nor thought of personal reward, that he was a *true pandit* who disciplined his mind and cultivated his soul in the service of Sat Nam, while knowing "the essence of the Vedas, the Upanishads and the Puranas." He held that these scriptures had been "created out of a single letter of the Name," that is, contained truth, but were only partial revelations of True Name. A very telling comment of his was that the Vedas "knew nothing of bhakta or 'faith'." He considered him to be a *true* bhakta who had mercy toward all God's creatures and emphasized "love of the True Name." In all this we recognize the process by which former values can be utilized by inclusion within the scope of a later reformation. It is a slightly different process from that of reformation within an older order. It makes itself the fulfillment of the past, the completion of the partial. Arjun's Sikhism thus provided men a fuller light and opportunity for them to realize its fullness in Sat Nam. And yet, as has so often happened in the history of religion, theory is one thing and accomplishment another. For the Sikhs there was a defect of their Hindu origin which lingered in them. Arjun seemed, at least, to have toward the panchamas, or "fifth" caste of "untouchables," the sweepers, scavengers and such, the consciousness that they were outcastes—an attitude destined to revision when many of these panchamas themselves turned Sikh, thus altering a social question by a change of faith.

[12] Whether such an allusion is a general reference to the human species or is yet more specific and technical, the "caste" atmosphere is dominant in India.

Was there, then, a major principle which governed Arjun's compilation of the *Granth?* No literary tests, it seems, were used, although grantha sometimes meant traditionally a 32-syllable affair. There were no strict theological tests. Verses were included of the Moslem shaykh Farid—verses, by the way, which gave a rather pessimistic picture of the world! Arjun himself could be almost as pantheistic as a sufi when writing of "the Lord without form, feature or hue, beyond the world of senses." This, no doubt, reflected something of the theological "attribute controversy" in which Hindus, Moslems and other theistic peoples have engaged. And there were no puristic linguistic tests to apply to the compilation, for many types of words were indiscriminately included—foreign words, vague words, words fitting into accidental phrases with inconsistency and sometimes contradiction. The governing principle was rather the Sikh communal consciousness, instead of anything more definite. Nor did it dictate a closing of the canon, although it had rejected certain elements.

There were matters of importance other than ritual and scripture which Arjun had to deal with, and we must understand them, also. We must see the Sikhs in the total situation during Arjun's guruship. Finance was one of his concerns. The public kitchen called for maintenance. Gyanis and granthis had to be employed for the temple ritual. Gurdwaras had to be provided and supplied with oversight as the Sikh membership increased. Voluntary alms could no longer be depended on to meet increased, legitimate expenses. A church and even a state were virtually in process of formation. Arjun called, therefore, for tithing, called upon every adult Sikh to pay a tenth of his gross income to support the kitchens, the sanctuaries and the office of the Guruship. A map was made with subdivisions of all Sikh landed properties, with some estimate of their annual production. For each manja, or subdivision, tithe-gatherers were appointed under a masand or supervisor, and every year at the time of the Vaisakhi festival (in spite of Nanak or any other, the Sikh calendar could not escape its special days!) a public reckoning was made. This was not merely provision for finance—Sikhs were getting acquainted with and practicing self-government!

And there was trade, also, to be attended to. Although the Sikh community was mainly agricultural, there was a natural increment of trade, and Arjun encouraged it as a means of wealth and power. He himself engaged in it, for example, sending his agents abroad as far as Turkestan to trade in horses. His aim in this may not have been, however, entirely commercial—it was at least missionary, also. Arjun was, in fact, the first Sikh missionary, in the sense of a propagation of the faith by an organized community. Foreign trade thus brought both its financial profit and its converts, and tended, even though unconsciously, to preclude from among the Sikhs the common Hindu notion that foreign travel was taboo, since harmful to religion. High-caste Hindus at the time would have felt themselves defiled by foreign travel, and if, for any proper or necessary reason, they had been abroad, they conscientiously submitted to ceremonial cleansing on their return. Sikhs themselves have traveled freely anywhere, uninhibited by any such tradition.

There were political considerations, also, with their own social and religious implications. The outer, larger world of the Mughals took increasing notice of the Sikhs. Although there was during Arjun's term of office no open conflict between Sikhs and Mughals, his "martyrdom" in 1606 may have been indirectly connected with Mughal rule. But there was, at any rate, no conflict between Akbar and Arjun, only complications with two of Akbar's ministers, Chandu Shah and Birbal, and with his grandson Khusraw. Birbal, Akbar's Hindu prime minister, made an effort to impose tribute on the Sikhs. It was a political, not financial, move and nothing came of it. But Akbar's finance minister, Chandu Shah, proposed an intermarriage. Chandu Shah was himself a high-caste Panjabi Hindu. He had a daughter, Sada Kawr, beautiful, the heiress of a wealthy dowry, but feeble-minded. He offered her in marriage to Arjun's son, Har Govind, after a period of prospecting and divination by the family priest and the local barber. The village barber, we may remark, had long had many functions, was also marriage-broker, surgeon, chiropodist and quack.

Sada Kawr's mother had initiated the marriage quest, reminding Chandu Shah of the risks young virgins ran in those days—the daughter was only seven at the time—from roving "Turks" who often kidnaped children. Mughals and Hindus both had had trouble with the various "Turks," as she called them—Turanian tribesmen, that is, of the northwest. And Chandu commissioned the barber and the priest to find a bridegroom. These two finally came to Amritsar, having heard that a young man was there who answered their requirements, an unwed son of the Sikh guru who might welcome an important new connection and the wealth it might entail. A tentative "arrangement" (bandobast) was entered into—tentative because Chandu's wife had considered the Sikhs socially inferior and Chandu himself had thought their religious habits most irregular. And some Sikhs also questioned the wisdom of an alliance. Meanwhile a new contingency arose during a darbar which Arjun had summoned in Amritsar: One day as the guru sat in state, a prominent Sikh, Narayan Das, approached and offered his own daughter in marriage to the guru's son. He announced that he was proposing this on the very day which his astrologer had discovered to be appropriate for the girl's betrothal! And he offered a substantial dowry. The proposal caught the fancy of the Sikhs, and Arjun himself accepted it at once. He called for his son, Har Govind, presented him in public and had marked on his brow the saffron token of betrothal. Whereupon another loyal Sikh, Hari Chand, arose and offered his own daughter also in marriage to the guru's son, saying that he, at her birth, had vowed her to the guru, and adding, How could anyone repudiate a sacred vow? Moreover, Hari Chand proceeded immediately to give Har Govind gifts and to daub a *second* saffron mark upon his brow. Here, then, was polygamy in principle, at least, and we may assume that Arjun accepted the proposal, making ultimately for polygamy in practice. But Chandu's daughter was herself not added as a third; the alliance with the Mughal minister was rejected—which amounted to official insult, leaving Chandu thirsty for some adequate revenge.

Of greater consequence was the episode of Akbar's grandson Khusraw—it brought on a greater crisis, Arjun suffering for his connection with it, at the suggestion, presumably, of Akbar's minister, this same Chandu Shah. Khusraw plotted to secure the Mughal throne; he sought to supersede his own father, Salim Jahangir, as heir in succession to his own grandfather Akbar. And in some way he involved the Sikhs in his conspiracy. The Sikhs, unfortunately, misjudged the circumstances and met disaster, because Jahangir himself won the throne and exacted reparation for any aid which they had given Khusraw—including hospitality, at least, and a subvention to him while he was a fugitive. That is, Khusraw became openly a rebel after his own father had ascended the throne and enlisted many Sikhs in his rebellion. Khusraw may indeed have seemed to the Sikhs a better man than Jahangir. They may have known the latter in his youth when he was dissolute (he never overcame his early love of drink), notorious for vice and cruelty, and himself a rebel against his father Akbar. Or they may have wanted Khusraw to be the governor of the Panjab and northwest India. But Jahangir, nevertheless, was an abler man than Khusraw and was in quite immediate succession. He changed many of his ways on becoming emperor and made in time a good name for himself as an exponent of Akbar's wisdom, statesmanship and love of justice.

Khusraw, on the other hand, although a very amiable young man of commendable moral character, was a misguided youth of weak disposition and susceptible to flattery. On April 6, 1606, after his father had ascended the throne in Agra, Khusraw fled from the Fort in the capital and proceeded by way of Tarn Taran to Lahore where he thought he might become the governor. Arjun, they say, who had just then become the Guru in Tarn Taran, was cordial to him, made him a gift (or a loan?) of five thousand rupees cash, and encouraged many Sikhs to join his forces. Khusraw reached Lahore with about 12,000 men, but met repulse by the loyal Mughal governor, Dilvar Khan. He retreated to Sultanpur, near the confluence of the Beas and the Sutlej, where he encountered an army of the emperor himself, was defeated, taken prisoner and brought before his imperial father who had meanwhile journeyed to Lahore. There the rebel[13] was publicly humiliated, "seven hundred"—so Jahangir himself says—of his followers were impaled on stakes about the city and a host of sympathizers suffered fines.

Guru Arjun was among those fined! But shortly afterward he was imprisoned—at Chandu Shah's suggestion? And soon after that he was put to death with torture in the Fort (Lahore), thus becoming "the first martyr of the Sikhs." The Sikh records themselves modify the story by reporting that Arjun was not really put to death, but while he was bathing in the Ravi under prison guard, he vanished in the waters of the river. And they add that "thus did Arjun for his sanctity, for his conversion of the Hindus and Muhammadans . . .

[13] The story of the flight, rebellion and fate of the Prince may be found in Jahangir's *Waki'at* in H. Elliot, *History of India*, VI, pp. 291-301.

fall victim to the bigotry and inhumanity of a Muslim emperor." It was martyrdom in any case, and his career may be reviewed in the light of the total office that he came to fill, including martyrdom.

Arjun became deva to his people—deified by the peculiar Indian process. In their memory and for purposes of a special annual occasion he is "Guru Arjun Deva" in the martyr's role, and his fate in itself has doubtless contributed to Sikh survival. He was otherwise, also, worthy of remembrance. His guruship fell within a most unusual period of Indian history, when Sikhism as an agency of reconciliation among religions might have hoped for great accomplishment, either in its own name or indirectly. But however conscious Sikhs and Mughals were of one another,[14] the Mughal leader Akbar was himself at work on a reconciliation of religions! And, of course, Akbar enjoyed extraordinary prestige and advantage. What could the humble Sikhs accomplish in such a circumstance? Did it occur to them at any time to throw their modest strength into the general enterprise? Did it occur to Akbar to utilize them? Akbar may not even have been aware of the Sikh experiment in its original proportions and intention. Was Sikhism as *religion* not yet something to be reckoned with in comparison with the religions Akbar knew and made some use of, namely, Hinduism, Christianity, Judaism, Jainism, Buddhism, Zoroastrianism and his own Islam? How strong *must* a movement be to bring about the effective reconciliation of religions? What, after all, *is* the means to such an end? And by what signs can such an end be known, if it should ever be accomplished?

Akbar's own experiment is of lasting interest, and we

[14] The Sikhs' own records say much more about the Mughals than the Mughal records say about the Sikhs!

should examine its details.[15] He had been born a Sunni Moslem—Sunnah was the "way" of orthodoxy—and had been so reared, but when he had become the emperor engaged in affairs of state, with occasion to reflect upon religion's place in politics, he had had a change of view, in which personal inclination and political expediency may have mingled. He had been emperor six years when in 1562 (Amar Das was guru of the Sikhs and Nanak had been dead a dozen years) he paid a visit to the tomb of the Moslem saint, Mu'inu'd-din Chishti in Ajmir, Rajputana, giving some special thought to Moslem-Hindu rapprochement. Soon afterward he abandoned the jizyah, a capitation tax which Moslem rulers had customarily imposed on subjects of other faiths, ceased collecting pilgrim fees and took other measures for the promotion of good will and of religious exercise.

A liberal atmosphere developed in the court. Free-thinking Moslems saw their opportunity, and may have induced in Akbar further doubt of the perfection of Islam. He began to question Islamic ritual and dogma, and soon found himself in the position of one "whose sole object is to ascertain the truth"—an intriguing but probably deceptive formula. He began to search for truth in *all* directions! A new headquarters of the state had been established, the city of Fathpur Sikri had been built, and there in 1575 (while Ram Das was guru of the Sikhs—no connection between Sikh and Sikri; the latter is the name of the place where shaykh *Salim* Chishti, a follower of Mu'inu'd-din of Ajmir, had lived as a hermit, near the very field on which Babur in 1527 had defeated the Rajput army), there in 1575 Akbar had built the Ibadat-khana, or "hall of religions," in which public discussions were carried on among devotees of various faiths. A

[15] See V. A. Smith's *Akbar* and Nizamu'd-Din Ahmad's *Tabakat-i-Akbari* in Elliot's *History*, vol. v, pp. 177-476, especially pp. 390, 409. However, a better source on religion is pp. 526f. (Budauni's *Tarikh*).

court historian has recorded that "this house of wisdom shone resplendent on Friday nights with the light of holy minds . . . sufis, doctors, preachers, lawyers, Sunnis, Shiites, brahmans, Jains, Buddhists, Charvakas, Christians, Jews, Zoroastrians and learned men of every belief"—not mentioning the Sikhs. Learned Hindus discoursed on the ten avataras (of Vishnu, that is) as the complete channel of salvation, "as the medium of raising men's minds to the comprehension of the supreme God." The Moslem historian Budauni (Budayuni)—himself an orthodox Sunni—says that certain Shiite missionaries from near the Caspian Sea came and "attached themselves to the emperor, flattered him, adapted themselves to his changes in religious ideas, spoke derogatorily of the Companions of the Prophet, and tried hard to make a Shiite of him." Others also had their day at court, but, says Budayuni, "the various sects at length took to calling each other infidels and perverts" and "His Majesty who sought after the truth, but was surrounded by low, irreligious persons to whom he gave his confidence, was plunged into scepticism. Doubt accumulated upon doubt and the object of his search was lost . . . and not one trace of Islam was left in him. . . . He cast aside the Islamic revelations regarding resurrection, the day of judgment, and all the ordinances." This may have been on Budayuni's part unduly severe condemnation. Akbar may have been somewhat justified in thinking that if some truth was everywhere to be found, he was scarcely to believe that Islam, a comparatively new religion in an ancient world, could hold it all. He at least did not believe in Islam as the *consummation* of the truth! He was aware that it had sometimes forced conversion to itself. He confessed that he himself had one time compelled Hindus to accept the creed. And he had observed that repetition of the creed, performance of circumcision, and prostration were in themselves nothing in God's sight, apart from sincere obedience.

In May 1578 came a further influential episode. While Akbar was on tour along the Jhelum river, he experienced a fit of ecstasy, entertained a special vision, and as a consequence took suddenly to the doctrine of ahimsa, "non-injury," of which the Jains were the strictest devotees. Perhaps the Jains had emphasized this doctrine in their Ibadat-khana colloquies and had rehearsed the story of the ancient Asoka's conversion to it. Akbar, however, did not resort, as Asoka did, to a proclamation that ahimsa was henceforth a policy of state. He was still at heart a Moslem. As late as 1581, he had a mind to make the pilgrimage to Mecca, but desisted for fear of leaving India. But by 1582 (Arjun had taken up his office by that time in Tarn Taran), he undertook the exploitation of a *new religion*—it had come at last to that! He gave it the name of Din-i-Ilahi, merely "the religion of God"—not Dinu Allah, or any such combination with the Islamic God. "Din" itself was used by Moslems for "religion," but it was not their exclusive property. It may indeed have come to them at first from Zoroastrians. It was commonly in use as a designation of religion. And Akbar had in mind a *universal* faith to which all faithful might subscribe. Meanwhile he had designated himself the Chakravartin, or "universal emperor," expressed in terms familiar in Hindu history—the Vishnu Purana calls him a chakravarti who is born with the print of Vishnu's discus in his hand; he is one, at any rate, whose chakra or dominion is extensive. Bharata, the great epic hero of the *Mahabharata*, was the first chakravartin—unless the conception was brought to India by the early "Aryans." Monarchs at times contended with each other for the title. Akbar would combine in himself universal pre-eminence in both political dominion and religious faith. But in religion he was doomed to disappointment. At least, his Din evaporated, and all the faiths severally persisted which it sought to merge. Sikhism itself with which Akbar had not actually reckoned was itself much more potent at the very time the Din was advertised. It may have found already more truth than Akbar knew, although Akbar, doubtless, had found more of it than Pilate, for example, had discovered, who *asked* for truth but did not tarry for reply.

How indeed may one set out "to ascertain the truth"? What conditions must first be met if ever one sets out? Was there an auspicious background at the time in India? Which might have served the inquirer better, Hinduism as in Nanak's case, or Islam as in Akbar's? And what was there still in both which the Sikhs themselves might use? By what *method*, furthermore, might truth be realized? Nanak and the Sikhs had relied upon the "formal" and upon the "formless," also. Akbar had acted somewhat similarly. He had been a formal Moslem (although not so literal and fundamentalist as Mahmud of Ghazni, for example), and had found that Islamic orthodoxy was inadequate to meet the needs even of all its own adherents, not to mention the needs of all humanity. He knew that Islam had largely won its way as an *organized* religion, regardless of how influential its many Sunni mystics may have been, and that it would hold its place, if at all, in India by being organized—even if the civil government itself were to pass into non-Islamic hands. He also knew how loosely bound was Hinduism—practically unorganized—and how ineffectual its spiritual character was in many ways. And in the end he learned how futile it may be to attempt to *organize the truth!* He was caught in a very practical dilemma in the way of speculation. It is unlikely that he found more truth than Islam contained already, and what he found apart from Islam was evanescent, ephemeral and negligible as compared with Hindu spirit. Perhaps, instead of searching for truth as if it lay *beyond* anything immediate, he should have had recourse to the method of recognizing and utilizing truth-at-hand, truth that had already been discovered. But in this way he might not have been able to organize a *new* religion!

Were the Sikhs also tampering with fate and circumstance? Had they misunderstood the very process of reconciliation? Was Sikhism actually surviving by becoming organized? And was it by becoming organized becoming less efficient as a reconciling agent? Could organic Sikhism escape politics, was there not inevitable some conflict with the Mughal state?

All of this, together with whatever answers the many questions call for, is not merely ancient history. This era of Arjun and Akbar is suggestive for these days wherever sects and religions are concerned with comity and a permanent alignment of the truth with life. The interactions of great world religions, the relations of sects and denominations within a single faith—for example, the problem of a "united Church" in India, the questions which Moslems have raised, as well as Christians, with reference to unity among themselves—all these are matters of increasing moment in these times today. And we might ask at last in the light of them, what *is* religion (din, dharma, daath, religio, threskeia, panth, or whatever be the name applied to it) and to what degree in bulk and quality do the many faiths exhibit it? How does religion operate? If not through the many faiths, how then? Is there anything abstract which we may rightly call *religion?* Perhaps it is, after all, both abstract and concrete, also! This duality may not have been obvious to Akbar, or to Nanak, or to Arjun. And who can know religion? How may *he* discover it, tune himself to it, utilize it?

To what extent are the various faiths religious—any one of them, or all of them together? Could any one of them be justified in calling itself final? *Was* it final, *is* it final, or will it *eventually* be final? Is there a "universal faith," a Din-i-Ilahi, "God's religion"? If any one of many faiths lays claim to, or holds the consciousness of, finality, what practical adjustment can it make with other faiths? May such consciousness be made organic for the sake of visible finality, actual unity, throughout the whole range of religion? If, on the other hand, any one religion has a consciousness of incompleteness, or of imperfection, what profitable course might best be followed by it with respect to other bodies? If one religion would convert another, can it do so by absorption in any formal way? Do not even organisms operate by principles? Can an organism ever fully typify a principle? Can anything organic ever reach perfection? And still another query quite as practical, Can the *formless*—Nirankari Sikhism, for example—be satisfactory and efficient?

We have not meant to ask these many questions hurriedly, but rather in the mood and tempo of the mul mantra of the *Japji*, pausing after each one and giving thought while perhaps the minstrel Mardana with his rebeck strummed an accompaniment. Or we might look further into the Indian scene during the many intervals and learn of religious individuals and agencies which may have offered answers to many of the questions.

We have observed already that organization was either ignored or minimized by Hindus. Moslem sufis, too, at first disdained it, but in the end established brotherhoods and monasteries. Among the sufi orders in the time of Akbar were the Chishti (the reader will recall Salim and Mu'inu'd-din), the Suhrawardi, the Qadiri, the Naqshbandi, and several less important, all together having shrines throughout the empire. Even Hindu bhagats who commonly in theory rejected creed and ritual, just as commonly had use for both. There were very few exclusive solitaries, anchorites. Most "saints" were themselves members of some band or order. The Kabirpanthis, it will be remembered (cf. p. 56), and many others had established definite societies and had provided shrines for local worship. Although all the orders laid stress on the conduct of the individual devotee and on the character which the individual should attain. They were loosely bound communities in an evil, transitory world from which each member of them must escape. They had so modified—or restricted—their theory of transmigration, for example, that, in general, they, the sufis and the bhagats, did not anticipate a transformation on the earth itself whereby an ideal order would be established. The meager extent of their organization was not a means to such an end. In this there was a difference between them and the Sikhs. For Sikhs an organization became incidental, even essential, to survival, and for the accomplishment of even an earthly transformation. Their own order was a communal instrument.

The Sunni Moslems not only held prescribed doctrines and observed the daily, weekly and seasonal calendar of ritual, not only held a theory of unity in terms of the Daru'l-Islam, or "household of Islam," in contrast with the non-Moslem Daru'l-Harb, or "house" against whose "unbelievers" the Moslems should make harb or "war," but they construed Islam to include ultimately the converted adherents of *all* non-Moslem religions. Although not all Moslems have ever held the view that Islam would be the final faith by force, Islam in general has been consistently institutional and has considered its religion *instrumental.*

Hinduism would have furnished in the negative many answers to our many questions. Some Hindus, for example, counted nothing perfect short of the Ultimate, the Absolute. They saw only defects in the present, the immediate, and for them no *part* had virtue in itself—all were parts of a stupendous whole which alone was real. As for scriptures, they were, like Nanak's "words," made up of signs. Hindus looked on other faiths with tolerance, knowing that they also were imperfect. They were unconcerned about conversion, save in a transmigratory sense in which all beings were involved, but not in the sense of transfer from one household to another. This was very different from the Moslem view, we understand. Hindus and Moslems could very promptly have called each other "infidels and perverts," in Budayuni's phrase which he applied to all non-Moslems. They held very different concepts of religion, these two peoples.

There were Christians, also, on the scene. The *Akbar-namah* records that "Padre Rodolph" proposed in the *Ibadat-khana* a very concrete test of revelation, a fiery-furnace test of the comparative merits of the Koran and the Bible as "the true word of God"—there was no way then and there to make a test of Christianity and of Islam as organisms; at least, Christianity had not yet reached that part of India as an order with ecclesiastical prestige. The Moslem 'ulama, says the *Akbar-namah*, "shrank from the proposal" made by Father Rodolph at which reluctance the emperor was "much annoyed." The burning of the books would not have been in itself convincing, because the books were only symbols. Had Akbar known it, there was indeed an ecclesia behind the Bible more compact than any order in Islam. Padre Rodolph and other Christians at the court carried on more immediately a *doctrinal* controversy, not an institutional one. Budayuni speaks bitterly of Christians and their "chief Pontiff known as Papa" and says that they "advanced proofs of the Trinity and affirmed the [sole] truth of the religion of Jesus." And he adds that "the attributes of the abhorred anti-Christ were ascribed to our holy Prophet by these lying impostors." They had come out to India as representatives of organized religion and were offering Moslems and other Indians an actual transfer of membership into another order. Akbar might welcome Christians, but he was scarcely more than an observer on (or *at*) the *Ibadat-khana* stage.

He welcomed Parsis, also. Budayuni tells us that these proclaimed "the religion of Zardusht as the true one, declaring reverence to fire to be superior to every other kind of worship." Akbar admitted and recognized their influence to the extent of keeping sacred fire burning in his Hindu women's quarters and himself performing homage to the sun.[16] He did not realize, nor did Hindus, how close was the connection between Hindus and Parsis in the theory and ritual of fire, although the Hindu cult of Agni, god of fire, was common in the homes and elsewhere.

And, according to the Sikh tradition itself, Akbar once received a hymn in praise of the Sikh's True Name, which pleased him very much. It was written in a mixture of Arabic and Hindi, says the legend—its presentation can be no more than legend, yet indicating even so the Sikh concern. It is, at least, an expression of the possibility and hope of a community of worship between the two religions, Sikhism and Islam:

> One man calls on Rama, on Khuda another,
> One implores Gosayan, to Allah others pray;
> Some bathe at tirths and others visit Mecca,
> Some engage in puja and some perform salat,
> Some read the Veds, the Qur'an some others,
> Some affirm them Hindus, some say Musulmans,
> Some look to swarga and others to the Garden,
> But he fulfils the will of God, saith Nanak,
> Who knows God in the secret of True Name.

Two camps are thus represented until the True Name is proposed, the items on the left hand being Hindu and those on the right Mohammedan. Rama is a manifestation of Hindu Vishnu and practically god in his own right, and Khuda is itself a Moslem name for God. Gosayan is Krishna in shepherd form who is yet another manifestation of Vishnu. Allah, of course, is the standard name for God among the Moslems, the "essential name" which Mohammed himself learned comparatively early in his mission. Tirths are places where the Hindu pilgrim bathes, while

[16] Parsis are not sun-worshipers, however.

Mecca is the chief goal of Moslem pilgrimage. Puja is Hindu worship and salat is Moslem, public worship, in particular. The Veds or Vedas are Hindu scriptures, generally, but might refer to the earliest of them. In comparison even with the very earliest, the *Rig Veda*, the Moslem Koran is a very recent and very little work, but one with vastly greater influence. Swarga is one of several Hindu heavens, and the Garden (jannat) is the Moslem paradise. The hymn as a whole is in the spirit of the *Japji*, unless its intention was to recognize with approval the various elements in the two households of faith, and to intimate that Sikhism offered the consummation of them all. In which latter case, the hymn is still in the mood of Arjun. If Akbar is justly represented as pleased with it, he could have seen in "True Name" something akin to, or even identical with, his "Ilah."

Akbar's own experiment was ultimately clearly syncretistic, *by abstraction*, at least, rather than by combination. But it may have come to grief not so much on that account as on account of politics. His religious quest, in spite of having made him doubtful of or hostile toward Islam, might have been indifferently considered as an expression of the spirit of the times, *if* he had not taken steps to make himself the head of all Islam—or it seemed to many that Akbar would thus exalt himself. Akbar issued his famous gold coin bearing the inscription, "The Great Sultan, the Exalted Khalifah." Was this indeed an assumption of the headship of Islam, or only a declaration of independence on the part of Indian Islam? He did indeed call his capital Daru'l-Khilafat, "the residence of the khalifah." The central Moslem Khilafat rested at the time among the Osmanli in Istanbul (Constantinople) who mostly used the title Sultan, and their rule was comparatively weak. Akbar had never really thought of acknowledging the Turkish overlordship. Indeed, the prevalent theory of the central office did not itself suggest the submission or obeisance of all Moslems to any one authority. Akbar's action, therefore, was by no means defiant. No, the real political difficulty was represented in his assumption, according to general Moslem accusation, of the nature and prerogatives of God! He was accused of making the "Allahu akbar" (God is great) of the public call to prayer, mean "Akbar is God." In the public mind he had himself become in his own estimation the divinity of his Din-i-Ilahi!

Or was it all politics of his own peculiar brand, by which he would offset the effects of certain millennial demonstrations which were in themselves some evidence of the spirit of those times? There was among Moslems an extensive expectation of the millennium. A mahdi[17] of theirs was due to appear in "the last days" who would "fill the world with justice." One such, Raushani Jalala, son of a "prophet" named Bayazid, appeared in 1588 by way of the Khaibar Pass, only to be met and slain by Mughal forces. No civil state could ignore these mahdist demonstrations, for they usually had political implications, also. Akbar himself may have wished to fill the role of mahdi? And there was a somewhat similar mind among the Hindus—there was expectation, for example, of the Kalki-avatara, Vishnu, that is, coming on "the white horse" at the end of this Iron Age, to destroy the wicked and to restore the world to purity. This advent, too, had its political implications. But Akbar's declaration of his *own* "divinity" would not in itself have disturbed the Hindus, at least, among whom many of the better educated sought themselves to realize divinity, who were quite familiar with the classic phrase aham brahman, "I am God," as indicative of the just end of any sincere man's quest.

[17] The mahdi is to the Moslem a "directed" guide, of either blood or spiritual descent from Mohammed, who will appear in the last days upon the earth. He is Allah's chosen messenger then to men. There have been, mistakenly, many Moslem mahdis, and a true one is still expected by his partisans.

Now let us return directly to the Sikhs and to Guru Arjun as factors in this total situation, a total which must be kept in view if Sikhism is to be accurately interpreted. Sikhism was actually during the guruship of Arjun in the way of becoming a militant religion, with something of political significance in consequence. It was not the martyrdom alone of Arjun which made Sikhs warlike—nor was it, we may add, the death of Jesus on the Cross which made among Christians the Church militant. In both instances the martyr's garments were parted among bystanders, garments which thereafter, with little stretch of the imagination, could be woven into a martial fabric. No, not the martyrdom itself; Sikhs were slowly getting organized and as an organism they came to be confronted by some circumstantial need of war. "Formless" religion, of course, cannot wage war! But formlessness was giving way, perhaps, to a communal consciousness. A new gospel may win its way with individuals who in time find it expedient to band together for their common safety and for the preservation of their gospel. The gospel thus becomes embodied, and when offices arise and officials fill them, the "church" is organized and visible, and becomes custodian of the cherished services and sacrifice and of the ideals which at first inspired them. The Church becomes as visible as any civil state and may often find itself in competition with it—or, it may seek to be itself the State.

This, then, is the turn that Sikh affairs were taking as an inheritance from Guru Arjun. If there was any strain in Arjun's time between his own people and the Mughals, it came by way of one or two of Akbar's own ministers, Chandu Shah and Birbal, either one of them or both, perhaps. Birbal, it seems, was more or less ill-disposed toward Arjun and the Sikhs until his death in 1586. It was Birbal the politician, however, not Birbal the brahman Hindu who was inimical. Of course, as a brahman he would take offense at some religious practices which did not conform to his own brahman code, but Sikhs as such held no doctrines abhorrent to him. He had actually subscribed to Akbar's Din, was the only Hindu, in fact, whose name appears in its official membership, and he was devoted also to the Parsi Sun-cult. But he seems to have been politically somewhat jealous of the Sikhs, and he served notice on them that their temple would be sacked and their capital destroyed (does this mean Tarn Taran, or Amritsar? the larger temple in Amritsar had not yet been built). Guru Arjun had himself offended Birbal by declining to pay a levy in support of a campaign of the Mughals against some frontier rebel Yusufzais in the valley of the Swat, in the far northwest of India. But Birbal lost his life later in this very campaign, and thus ended the threat against the Sikhs.

Although neither in Nanak's *Japji* nor in Arjun's *Sukhmani* is there a hint that war is a just expression of Sikh power and a righteous means of accomplishing Sikhism's mission, the martial mood was nevertheless in the making —to be seen as the guruship itself continued. Not one of the first five gurus ever themselves handled arms—in general, there was no occasion for it. Arjun himself had declared that "the divine Guru is Peace." He built a shrine in Lahore which bore an inscription of his own composition in which he urged his "brothers" to perform their ablutions, remember God, and read, hear and sing the hymns of God. Guru Nanak previously had said, as the legend has it, "Take up arms that will harm no one; let your coat of mail be understanding; convert your enemies into friends; fight with valor, but with no weapon but the word of God." Nevertheless, Sikh tradition includes also a legend traced from Bhai Buddha which foretells that Har Govind, Arjun's successor, would wear "two swords, one temporal, one spiritual"; and "words of Arjun" have been read back into the record, words of Arjun's "parting message" to his people, which serve as warrant—or, at least, apologetic—for a change of character in the Sikh religion:

> I have succeeded in effecting the object of my life. Go to my son, the holy Har Govind, and give him from me an ample consolation. Bid him not mourn me, nor indulge in unmanly lamentation, but sing God's praises.
>
> Let him sit fully armed upon the gaddi[18] and maintain an army to the best of his ability.
>
> Let him fix the mark of Guruship upon his forehead, as now the custom is, and ever treat his Sikhs with utmost courtesy.
>
> Let him hold Bhai Buddha in due honor, and observe the precedents to which now is added bearing arms!
>
> Do not cremate my body; let it float away on the bosom of the Ravi.
>
> I bear all my torture to set a good example to the teachers of True Name, that they may not lose patience, nor rail at God in their affliction. The true test of faith comes in the very hour of misery.[19]

It was not long before rumor, whether couched in terms of the last "words of Arjun" or in others, began to pass through the Indian bazaars and along the pilgrim routes that a change of mood prevailed among the Sikhs. In the Greater Garden some ploughshares were being beaten into swords and there were pruning hooks becoming spears. A fellowship of reconciliation was assuming martial form.[20]

18 Throne.

19 *Cf.* Macauliffe, *Religion*, III, p. 99.

20 See illustrations Nos. 9 and 10 which indicate the later role which Arjun has assumed.

# Chapter 8. The Khalsa of Gobind Singh

ARJUN'S successor, his "holy" son Har Gobind (a nephew who had become a "son"?) served in the guruship forty years (1606-1645). We shall drop into the way of spelling Gobind with a *b* and not a *v*, chiefly for the sake of indicating that the *b* fits better into later Sikh tradition. The *v* is more particularly Hindu—Govind, the "cow-herd," is, for example, a Hindu name for Krishna. The distinction between the letters in the name is never, however, consistently observed in Sikh tradition. And there were four other gurus besides Har Gobind in the line before that visible personal form of guruship came to an end—ten gurus altogether, of whom Gobind Singh was last, although the episode of Banda Singh, an "eleventh" guru, seems to have been necessary as a final test of the transformation in the institution and theory of the guruship.

Har Gobind was about ten years of age when inducted into office. The fact that one so very young could be made guru may be altogether circumstantial, but more likely means that Sikhism had achieved sufficient solidarity to treat the guruship more symbolically. There was, however, great virtue in the lad himself, and he soon displayed some military competence, a mastery of the two swords—with arrows and leaden bullets, also, to give assistance to the second sword. He commonly went about with a personal guard of sixty matchlock men and a mounted troop of three hundred horsemen in attendance. The warrant for such precaution was the Sikh consciousness of "enmity with the Musalmans," Har Gobind himself being conscious of sonship to a martyr whose very last words assured him that God was on the side of those adequately armed. The Sikh attitude, to be sure, was not aggressive, but the principle of mutual antagonism between Sikhs and Moslems was by this time well established. One of the guru's earliest official orders, for example, to his alms collectors was that they should bring in arms and horses as well as money. The nation in-the-making must defend itself, he thought, and be ready likewise for offense, if necessary.

Sikh communal consciousness was not only aware of Moslems, it also took account of many Hindus, with whom on occasion there was enmity. There were certain Hindu rajas in the neighborhood whose counselors apparently misjudged the Sikhs as potential trouble-makers. At least, Sikhs actively resented whatever they deemed imposition and were now and then in conflict with the rajas, the Moslem overlordship paying, meanwhile, no particular attention to this strife. Indeed, before any overt hostilities between communal Sikhism and Moslems had begun, Har Gobind and other Sikhs sometimes took service in the Moslem state administration. Har Gobind once served Emperor Jahangir (d. 1627) on a royal hunting expedition—and was not averse at the time, it is worth remembering, to eating flesh. The Mughals did not recognize the Sikhs as a community. The Sikh community was still crude, its members mostly villagers, tradesmen, hillmen and nondescripts. Many outlaws even joined the guru's ranks. Some irresponsible Sikh guerrillas committed outrages, but the government dealt with these offenders individually. They captured horses and kidnapped women, for example. There is some evidence that the guru himself was once captured by a band of irregulars, whether they were Sikhs or Rajputs, and was detained by them in Gwaliyar fortress until a fine was paid for his release! A Sikh once made off with two prime horses from the stables of the emperor, Shah Jahan, in Lahore. On two occasions imperial squads pursued outlaws into Amritsar and met then each time with forceful opposition from the Sikhs, although once the guru saw fit to withdraw a while for safety beyond the Sutlej river. Times were so uncertain at the very end of his guruship that he died a practical fugitive at Kiratpur on the Sutlej. All this reflects, as we mean to show, something of the gathering storm.

Meanwhile Har Gobind maintained a sure but not distinguished guruship. He was a loyal, faithful Sikh, assiduous in public worship and the maintenance of Sikh institutions, contending for the faith of Sat Nam against yogis, sadhus, bhagats and faqirs, and surviving contentions in his own household—he himself slew two rivals to his office. He completed a shrine which Arjun had begun, the Akal Takht,[1] or "throne of the Timeless," which stood beside the principal Har Mandir in Amritsar, and dedicated it both to peace and war. He "churned the nectar [amrit] and took his stand upon eternal truth" and under God's instruction "filled what could not otherwise have been fulfilled, and dispelled both doubt and fear," said the poet Gur Das[2]—presumably with reference to Har Gobind—, who died half way through Har Gobind's term of office. Sikh devotion to their guru was so great that several of his followers would have cast themselves in 1645 into the very flames of his funeral pyre.

Although Gur Das himself died in 1627, his estimate of Arjun and various things is valuable. He undertook a survey of the guruship in general and an appraisal of the whole experiment which the Sikhs had carried on up to the year of his death. He had known Arjun and was well acquainted with much of the history of Hinduism and Islam, and he cites many eras, sects and persons of importance in Asiatic history. He is very critical of the old religions. He observes that India had long been on the verge of ruin and its peoples long depraved because of the errors into which the Hindus

[1] *Cf.* illustration No. 6.

[2] *Cf.* above, pp. 146f.

fell, when along came "Muhammad Yar" spreading further ruin and corruption. The reference must be to Mahmud Ghazni or to some other invader who had taken the title Yar-i-Khuda, an equivalent to the Arabic Khalilu'llah, "friend of God." Gur Das was certain that Islam had more sects than the traditional "seventy-two,"[3] and had added confusion to already degenerate times by its rites, distinctions, seasons, offices and institutions. He classes Moslems and Hindus into one community of the greedy, violent and bigoted, and warns Sikhs against all of them, their wiles and ways. If, says he, Sikhs themselves are ever perverse, it comes not of their religion, but of their own weak devotion. It is the Hindu religion and the Moslem religion which have corrupted their adherents, says Gur Das. Let the Hindus keep Banaras, however, and the Moslems Mecca, says he, for whatever good may come of these religious centers, but let the Sikhs understand that their own holy land is *everywhere*. He suggests that Sikhs sever their connections with the past and as a distinct group within the Hindu-Moslem setting be true "Sikhs of the Guru," with utmost loyalty and no backsliding or division. All Sikhs, he claims, are really one under God who is One without a second, but if they are to bear distinction, let it be something of their own. Let them, for example, adopt a distinctive salutation, such as "Pairi pawana" (I fall at your feet), avoiding both Hindu and Islamic formulae. He deems Sikhism actually "superior to other faiths" and something tangible, and Sikhs themselves superior to, for example, "Armenians, Arabs, Christians, Turks and Jews."

Har Rai (1645-1661), a grandson of Har Gobind, succeeded to the guruship—the office had become by this time hereditary, but by another principle than that of primogeniture. In the entire line of gurus only three sons, each in his

[3] According to an hadith, or "saying" of Mohammed, and as catalogued in al-Shahrastani's *Sects.*

own turn, succeeded their fathers—Arjun, Har Kishan and Gobind Singh, the fifth, eighth and tenth gurus, respectively. Har Kishan (Har Krishna?) was Har Rai's son, and Gobind Singh was Teg Bahadur's son. Har Rai's sixteen years in office promoted Sikh solidarity, as if Gur Das's advice were then being followed, together with the circumstance that Sikhs became remotely involved in a civil war among the Mughals. This civil strife came about in this way: the emperor Shah Jahan's four sons, Dara, Shuja, Aurangzib and Murad, fell into dispute over the succession. Dara, the eldest, was the father's choice, but Aurangzib, the third, eventually succeeded. In the struggle, the Sikh guru, Har Rai, took sides with the unsuccessful Dara who, as it happened, was a very liberal Moslem, although not in the manner of his great-grandfather Akbar's liberalism. But when Aurangzib, a Sunni bigot with more pious, religious pretense than real inner character, secured the throne, he called on the Sikhs to make amends for their guru's partisanship. Har Rai sent his own son Ram Rai, accordingly, as a hostage to the Mughal court as a guarantee of future good relations. But, whatever their status, Aurangzib had had occasion to reckon with the Sikhs!

If their apology could itself prevent his using force against them, he could, nevertheless, assail them otherwise, and so he chose to criticize their *Adi Granth.* He charged that it contained sentiments disrespectful toward Islam—toward Moslems, at least, if not also toward the Prophet and the Book. A real or an imagined insult to either the Prophet or the Book would have indeed entailed dire consequences, for no "unbeliever" could insult Mohammed or the Koran and be allowed to live. Sometimes the sacred writings of non-Moslems had themselves suffered at the hands of Moslem bigots by comparison with the Koran as the only sacred scripture—although by no means as frequently as a common western story would make out! The western tale reports, for instance, that the Moslems who captured Alexandria (Alexandria capitulated once in 641 and had to be recaptured five years later) destroyed the "library" there on the ground that if the books agreed with the Koran, they were useless and if they disagreed they were pernicious! The destruction, as commonly erroneously reported, was at the khalifah 'Umar's command by his general 'Amr. The tale is as fabulous, however, as that of "Omar's letter" which he wrote and had cast into the Nile to induce the river's "fertilizing tide to begin to rise abundantly." The early Moslems had actually more respect for books, including especially Christian and Jewish works, and, furthermore, there was then no Koran as such (*i.e.*, codified, etc.) in 'Umar's day; nor had many books been left of the library of Alexandria. But the story has done duty on various occasions in explanation of certain Moslem acts of bigotry. Indian scriptures were, of course, not themselves within the range of the Koran's own compass of toleration, but they could come ultimately, in the Moslem mind, into inclusion and association with the tolerated *Injil* (New Testament) of the Christian and the Jewish *Torah*, if only by analogy, except that all Moslems did not recognize the principle of analogy (qiyas) in the operation of their canon law. The scriptures of the Sikhs were scarcely known as such, were certainly further removed from recognition than were the Hindu writings, where such a Moslem as Aurangzib was concerned.

If Aurangzib had knowledge of Sikh scriptures, it was doubtless fragmentary, at the most. He once cited as Sikh scripture certain doubtful lines which, he contended, slighted "Musulmans," namely:

> Mitti musulman ki pere pai kumiar
> Ghar bhande itan kian jaldi kare pukar.[4]

[4] These lines, whatever their true form, may be found in Rag Asa of the *Adi Granth*. *Cf.* Trumpp, p. 639.

Which might be put into these English lines:

> Ashes of Moslems are mixed with potter's clay;
> Bricks and vessels of the mixture cry out as they burn.

Although these lines are doubtful, their use by Aurangzib, as the story goes, serves to raise some question of the currency of Sikh scriptures and some problem of textual criticism. The Sikhs' own tradition of these lines is quite uncritical—and probably untrustworthy. It says that Nanak and a certain shaykh (!) Brahm (the name is Hindu, although the title may be Moslem. He must have been a Hindu, nonetheless, regardless of his very common title) were one time discussing the relative merits of burial and of cremation for the disposal of the dead. The shaykh contended that one could not rise again on the Last Day whose body had been burned, according to Hindu (and Sikh custom). The resurrection of the body (*cf.* the "reassembling of the bones" on "the day of standing up"—*Koran* 75:1-3) was orthodox Moslem dogma, despite any practical scepticism on the issue, such as that of the disputer (hasim) in *Koran* 36:77-78, who asked, "Who shall give life to bones after they have rotted?" But we may not fully know to what extent Nanak was concerned with or took account of a "last day" by whatever name (the Koran uses six or seven for it) and a "resurrection" at the time. In ordinary Hinduism, at any rate, there was no such doctrine. We do know that Nanak once remarked that it was far better for a body to be burned to ashes than to be desecrated at the hands of the grave-digger (grave-diggers were outcastes of the potter class). However, the tradition, as carried in Aurangzib's quotation, tends to indicate some ignorance on Nanak's (?) part of Moslem custom—unless, indeed, as Aurangzib may have contended, some misuse had been made of Moslems' remains, whence the "insult" to Islam in these words of

CUPOLA OF THE TEMPLE AT TARN TARAN, AND THE SACRED POOL

WORSHIPERS AT THE TEMPLE OF TARN TARAN

Nanak. But what were, what could have been, Nanak's or a Sikh's own words?

When Aurangzib confronted his hostage, Ram Rai, with these lines, he did not say whence he had found them; he did not claim that they were part of the *Japji*, for example; he merely ascribed them to the Sikhs. And Ram Rai, it seems, had himself some knowledge of them. At least, he suggested cautiously that the lines first be verified, since his majesty, possibly, was in general misinformed, may have misread the text, or may have got it by some misquotation. Ram Rai intimated that Nanak's actual words may have been

> Mitti be-iman ki pere pai kumiar
> Ghar bhande itan kian jaldi kare pukar,

which might be translated as "Ashes of the faithless," etc.—*be*, "without" and iman, "faith," the latter being a standard term with Moslems. The emperor could be well content to have the ashes of infidels mixed with potters' clay and made into vessels that sizzled at the fireside, and he, therefore, as the story goes, was pleased with Ram Rai's explanation!

But there is still more to the Sikhs' own tradition. It reports that the Sikhs themselves were displeased with Ram Rai's version, contending that he had no right to question Guru Nanak's words—as if Aurangzib had correctly quoted them, or as if the Sikhs would welcome controversy. And this accounts for the Sikhs' repudiation of Ram Rai, the guru's son, and his loss of the succession!

Assuming that Nanak was somehow represented, we may suppose that he had used neither "musalman" nor "be-iman." The former had no real relevancy in the line, if indicative of a Moslem practice of cremation, and the use of "be-iman" was equally irrelevant, if attributed to Nanak—at least, neither "be-iman" nor "iman" may be found in Nanak's *Japji*. The gyanis and the granthis themselves have been unable to explain the matter—they have not, at least, explained it with any satisfaction. A certain western scholar[5] has offered a solution by a somewhat promiscuous use of words and meanings from several sources, making the first line read "Mitti musul man ki pere, . . ."—in which "man" means "clay," as in the *Marathi*, although Hindustani had given up this use of it, and musul means "pestle," although there are commoner Panjabi words for this, and "kumiar" means "potter" (good enough!), and "per" a "lump" (also good!), etc., and making the couplet as a whole to mean:

> Clay from the earth is worked by the pestle into a potter's lump,
> Made into vessels and bricks which sizzle in the burning,

which may truly represent, after all, what Nanak may have said in description of a common, humble occupation.

There were still other than scriptural items blown about by the winds of the gathering storm, some of which were not to be as amicably settled as was that of the doubtful couplet. Some had to do with festivals on which both Hindus and Moslems had various opinions. The Indian year's religious calendar affects the total population one way or another. Nor could the new sect of Sikhs ignore it. They might despise one event and look with favor on another, but something of their own to celebrate was necessary. Possibly there was some natural disposition toward the Hindu calendar, in spite of any communal trend on their part toward isolation? They might at least adapt some features from the Hindu heritage. Take the annual Holi, for example; they might make it their own and call it Hola, whatever Hindus or Moslems might thereafter think of it. Guru Arjun had once given this advice, according to the Sikh tradition:

> Let us worship God, make obeisance to him,
> Today is our day of rejoicing [while Hindu Holi was going on],

[5] Trumpp. *Cf.* Macauliffe, I, p. 226; IV, p. 309.

Today we celebrate our own Phagan [*i.e.*, Phalgune, the month of Holi];
Service to God's companions shall be *our* Holi,
And the red color of Sat Nam will cling to us.

That is, Sikhs would, by the guru's own pronouncement, adapt the festival, even to a figurative use on the occasion of the red powder scattered actually by thè Hindus when they celebrated.

Holi was a Hindu springtime (February-March) festival,[6] a veritable saturnalia centering about bonfires of sacred cow-dung, and offering to children of the "twice-born" (dvijas), especially, opportunity to make merry, and providing for all a special time of omens, auguries and divination—and of ribaldry with indecent songs, the throwing of dust and red powder, and of giving gali, or "abuse." It was traditionally an annual celebration of the burning of a witch named Holika who had once tormented and terrorized the whole of India. The innumerable fires in the homes and in the village compounds were reminiscent of the burning. It is not of record, however, that the Sikhs entirely purified the occasion for themselves. In fact, many of them have kept the holiday questionably, somewhat in the manner of some "Christians" on All-Hallows Eve, and have indulged in frivolity, wine-drinking, throwing dust and mud and color, and blackening their faces.

Nanak had once remarked, "In the beginning there were no sacred feasts," but new needs arose among the Sikhs by Arjun's time, and subsequently the Sikh calendar of celebration included also days of martyrdom. These latter in themselves enhanced the tension with the Moslems who were the first occasion of Sikh martyrdom.

[6] See J. C. Oman, *Brahmans, Theists and Muslims of India*, pp. 241ff.

Har Kishan[7] (1661-1664), a son of Har Rai, came after him into the guruship—an appointment which, it appears, Aurangzib also approved, having once summoned him to audience in Delhi, one of the emperor's ministers, himself a Sikh, extending the royal invitation. His term of office was short and comparatively uneventful. He, like his predecessor, left no words of wisdom for his people's canon, he may indeed have had no fixed place of residence, and he died of small-pox.

The career of Teg Bahadur, the ninth guru (1664-1675), however, takes on more importance. Sikh affairs had not been till then in the best of order, except for the strength of a common mind which held together the local groups in many scattered villages and found expression in a certain uniformity of worship chiefly at Tarn Taran and Amritsar, but also in gurdwaras in many of the villages. The question of the guruship itself continued to be troublesome. Ram Rai, the erstwhile hostage at the court of Aurangzib and a brother of Har Kishan, had claimed succession and had established himself in Dehra Dun as a pretender. "Twenty-two Sodhi" clansmen of Bakala, themselves, contested the office on behalf of someone. After Teg Bahadur had been prevailed upon to take the office and had been generally acknowledged, a rival employed an assassin whose bullet struck the guru but not fatally. Aurangzib continued to be uneasy and suspicious of many Sikh activities and would have taken measures to repress them, save that a leading Rajput chieftain, probably Jai Singh of Jaipur, interceded for them. Their numbers did indeed include many undesirables—an unsympathetic writer of the day, in fact, called all Sikhs "scavengers."[8]

[7] "Kishan" is preferable to "Krishna," an alternative, for the former is at least *less* Hindu. Preferable, also, to "Krishan" as in Khazan Singh's *History*, pp. 145f.

[8] D. Ibbetson, *Punjab Castes*, p. 285. *Cf.* p. 6, above.

Teg Bahadur himself had good qualities bequeathed to him by the sixth guru, Har Gobind, whose son he was. "Sword hero" was his very name—he had a blade his father himself had bequeathed him. "Teg" was an old Panjabi word for "sword"—used, for example, in a proverb which matches our own "might makes right": "Jeh di teg use di degh" (He who holds the sword is owner of the cooking-pot). And "bahadur" is an honorific title which at least could be made to indicate that he who wore it had some claim to social elevation.

Teg Bahadur came into office at forty years of age, held it a dozen years and died a martyr. They were eventful years, 1664-1675. He was not by nature a bold, aggressive person, but he rallied about him many thousand warlike men and filled the office boldly. He had had experience, of course, had traveled widely and had often "roughed it." He and his family had spent some time as far away as Patna, on the lower reaches of the Ganges, where, incidentally, he had become fluent in a high-grade Hindi. He may actually have been in the Mughal service at this distance, or in service under the Mughal retainer, Raja Jai Singh (cited above) of Jaipur, whom Aurangzib sent into Bengal and Assam to quell disturbances. It appears that Teg Bahadur took part in the expedition against the Hindu raja of Kamrup (Assam), whom he converted then and there to the Sikh religion. Jai Singh approved this interest in religion.

As guru, Teg Bahadur chose to live in Anandpur, a village on the Sutlej a hundred miles eastward from Amritsar and in the shadow of the Himalayas. This was off-center and remote, but expediency warranted the choice, as circumstances soon confirmed its wisdom—trouble was fast brewing. Aurangzib's uneasiness has been mentioned. There were many disturbing factors in his empire. Many Sikhs engaged in outrage and sometimes leagued themselves with other restless elements—for example, with the Moslem zealot,

Adam Hafiz, who moved about among the peasants with immunity, while taking toll of Moslems and Hindus who were wealthy. Sikhs had a formal opportunity to aid Kashmiri brahmans against their Moslem overlords who were forcibly converting Hindus to Islam, but Teg Bahadur doubted that Sikhs could then muster force enough for an overt *military* expedition, and an excuse was offered instead of aid. The Sikhs declined the brahmans' invitation.

The Sikhs' initiative was soon taken from them and Teg Bahadur at last came face to face with Aurangzib, who was himself finally aroused to action. There is some conflict of opinion over the emperor's basic motive, the Sikhs making out a case of persecution in connection with attempts at forcible conversion.[9] That Aurangzib might have been of this mind is readily conceivable, but it is more likely that his object was more security in those parts where Sikhs were operating. One record plainly says that Aurangzib was suppressing outlaws[10] and deemed Teg Bahadur a rebel against the government. The manner of the guru's appearance in Delhi in response to the royal "summons" is likewise variously described. A tale has been preserved that the guru roamed from place to place with groups of his disciples, somewhat in the manner of Udasis. He did wander, but not in the guise of an ascetic. And the tale relates a visit to the neighborhood of Agra, where he tried to pawn a signet-ring in exchange for some provisions, at which the shop-keeper's suspicions were aroused and the matter was reported to the kotwal, or superintendent of the market, himself a constable. The kotwal interviewed the guru and then sent word to Delhi, whence orders were received to

[9] Khazan Singh quotes in his *History*, pp. 152f., Muhammad Latif's *History of the Panjab*. Cf. also Musta'id Khan's *Ma'asir-i-'Alamgiri* in Elliot's *History*, VII, pp. 183f.

[10] *Ma'asir-i-'Alamgiri*, in Elliot, VII, pp. 185f.: ". . . bloody, miserable rebels . . . braggarts . . . unbelievers . . . desperate men."

bring him thither. In another version, the emperor sends a summons to Anandpur, calling on the guru to report in Delhi—a journey of about two hundred miles. The guru at first hesitated to obey, but eventually set out, only to be met en route by troops which had been dispatched to apprehend him.[11]

The substance of the different versions is simply that Teg Bahadur went to Delhi under guard, arrested as a public enemy. He may have been tried also as an "unbeliever"—there were many prisoners of the sort in Delhi and elsewhere. The outcome was a sentence of death and he was soon publicly executed, in a space which later became the Chandni Chauk, by a method variously reported. He was, in fact, beheaded, his headless body remaining long exposed in public, or else, as one Moslem account has it, which many Sikhs accept, his body was quartered and a portion of it hung at each of the city's four gates. Faithful followers of the guru took his head to Anandpur where it was cremated with appropriate ceremonial—Sikh tradition makes the pyre of sandalwood with attar of roses sprinkled over it. The mul mantra of the *Japji* was recited at the lighting of the pyre and the assembled Sikhs sang hymns as the "sacred" head was burned to ashes. The Sohila, an evening prayer, followed by a benediction, was recited at the end of the cremation. Or did the head actually remain in Delhi in the first instance, being burnt there by faithful Sikhs and entombed in a sis-ganj, or "head stack"? In which case, the body or a portion of it was taken to Anandpur and burned, carried thither by Sikhs who in the guise of sweepers were able to secure it. It all amounts to "martyrdom" in any case, according to the Sikh tradition.

Teg Bahadur's life and death passed into legend, whatever may have been the bare facts of his career, and both life and

[11] *Cf.* Cunningham's *History* (ed. Garratt), pp. 63-66.

death had political and religious value. His son, Gobind Singh, composed these lines in his father's memory:

> He protected the frontal marks and sacrificial threads,
> Displayed great bravery in this Kaliyug,
> Gave up his life in aid of worthy men,
> Gave up his head and uttered not a groan,
> Suffered martyrdom for the sake of his religion,
> Could have saved himself, had he not scorned to do so.[12]

And lines are cherished which are attributed to the martyr himself, for example:

> Give thine own head and not forsake
> Whom thou hast undertaken to protect;
> Give up thy life, but give not up the faith.[13]

Other writings attributed to him have been included in later editions of the *Granth.* He must have had in some way the "gift" which was essential to the office, and he gave expression to it while he served. Perhaps some of his utterances were orally transmitted until they could be written. Accounts of him often fail to distinguish details of his career from those in the life of his son Gobind who was his companion for many years and who succeeded to the guruship. It is clear, however, that Sikhism as expressed in the guru's leadership had taken on a martial character and he was more than a harmless guide in spiritual concerns. It can be seen that Sikhism and Islam—that is, the orthodoxy of Aurangzib and the party of Teg Bahadur—were incompatible. And by that token it may be understood that

[12] Khazan Singh, II, p. 652, gives two lines of Gurmukhi:

> Dharam het saka jin kiya
> Sir diya par sirar na diya,

which he translates in I, p. 161. We prefer to render them: "He gave his life for his religion, Gave up his head but not his consecration."

[13] If these are not actually Teg Bahadur's lines, they and the lines ascribed above to Gobind Singh are two versions of the one theme. Perhaps the original words were "Sir dadam magar sar-i-Khuda na dadam." "He gave his head, but yielded not God's trust" (although Khuda is a *Moslem* term for God).

Sikhism continued somewhat compatible with Hinduism, virtually serving itself heir to that phase of Hinduism, the warrior-cult, which was itself militant. Notice that Gobind's verse refers to Teg Bahadur as protector of "the frontal marks," that is, the tilak in the manner of the Hindus, a sign of ritual observance and sect loyalty, and of the "sacrificial threads," undoubtedly a reference to the dusuti, or "double" thread, worn about the neck by the "twice-born" Hindus.

And Teg Bahadur's own writings refer to Hindu scriptures as having foreshadowed the advent of the religion of Sat Nam, making Sikhism the fulfilment of Hindu India's own search for God. He appropriates and uses the Hindu Hari as practically equivalent to, if not identical with, the Sikh Sat Nam, indicating to that extent, at least, an affinity with Vishnuism. Yet he also identified Hari as "Brahm, Narayan, and Ram," and as the One Lord who, in this Kaliyuga in which men are blinded by intoxicating Maya and tangled in the noose of Yama, god of hell, has come "by the favor of the True Guru" to destroy fear, to remove folly, and to be the friend of the friendless and the savior of all men. All this was in keeping with sentiment commonly expressed in religious circles in which the guru moved, and his son makes it more explicit for his own followers in his own time of office.

Gobind Singh (1675-1708), the tenth guru, became a champion of the lowly peoples of north India and an irreconcilable foe of Moslem rule, affording Sikhism opportunity for further integration and ultimate expansion. Up to and including his time Sikhs had dwelt mostly within the triangular region inclosed by the Beas and the Sutlej rivers and the Himalaya Mountains, nor had they for all purposes a headquarters. Moslems in this area were chiefly there as overlords, and Sikhs became increasingly aware of them as taskmasters. Islam as religion was still extraneous to this region, and prevalent Hinduism was of a mediocre quality, and static.

Gobind Singh was only fifteen years of age when his father died, leaving him the guruship, but he had shared his father's company and had become imbued with the consciousness of mission. He was an intelligent and loyal Sikh, and his wife Jita, whom he married in 1677, gave him capable support in attention to community affairs and herself set a prominent example for all Sikh women. Gobindji and Jita shared a heritage of hate, for her family as well as his had suffered at the Mughals' hands. He awaited the day of revenge when he might inflict upon them something to compensate for his father's martyrdom. He had long to wait, but he continued steadfast. His life was quite uncertain for over twenty years and throughout his entire guruship he occupied a shifting gaddi, "throne." It was a time of general restlessness in India.

Even while Gobind was assuming leadership in Anandpur under the shadow of the Himalayas, rumor reached him that rebel bands were moving among the western ghats on the Bombay side. The Marathas down that way had risen against Aurangzib's officials, and a leader in the person of Shivaji[14] had appeared and had made sufficient progress to be crowned on June 6, 1674, at his hill-capital Raigarh as Maharaja, with the special title of Chhatrapati, "Lord of the Umbrella"—of sovereignty, that is. He won his way eventually to recognition by the neighboring kings of Golkonda and Bijapur and won the assignment to himself and his Maratha state of a blackmail levy of a chauth, or "fourth," of the annual revenue of the Mughal provinces of all south India. His was a very effectual example of defiance and of Hindu independence. Other peoples still nearer Delhi

[14] Khafi Khan gives in his excellent *Muntakhabu'l-Lubab* (also called *Tarikh-i-Khafi Khan*) a detailed account of Shivaji. See Elliot's *History*, VII, pp. 269-306, in particular.

(Dehli) had resisted Aurangzib, the Jats, in particular. Although these Jats had been badly beaten by the Mughals in 1670, they continued their resistance. And tribesmen in the northwest had given the Mughal government serious concern, without having been at last altogether pacified. There were disorderly elements in Bengal, and pirates along the Bengal coast, which had kept the Mughal governor, Shayista Khan, busily engaged. And a hundred miles southwest of Delhi a curiously named sect of Satnamis (!),[15] "true name" devotees, had taken up arms in 1672, had seized several villages and had held them until defeated by the government in March. This movement with its curious name was not then a part of Sikhism, despite its devotion to Sat Nam. It was, rather, a local demonstration of general restlessness. Rumors and information of all these disturbances came to Gobind's ears. And he had learned indefinitely of the arrival of Europeans in parts closer to north India—they had actually been settled twenty-five years in Bengal and ten in Bombay when Gobind Singh took office. He inherited no judgment with reference to the Europeans, although Sikh records tell of Teg Bahadur's standing on the roof of his prison in Delhi and saying as he gazed off toward Bombay that India would one day be conquered by the British! But Gobind *had* received this counsel from his father, "Keep your seat fearlessly at Anandpur and destroy the Turks"—*i.e.*, the Mughals.[16]

Not until near the end of the century, however, was Gobind able to establish a permanent, effective order, the Khalsa, expressive of Sikh solidarity and political ambition. Meanwhile he and his people lived precariously at times and always waiting for their opportunity, not at the guru's "seat

[15] See Khafi Khan's *History* in Elliot, VII, pp. 294f.

[16] Among the sources for the story of Gobind Singh are W. L. McGregor, *History of the Sikhs*, I, pp. 69-104; Khazan Singh's *History*, pp. 162-204; Cunningham-Garrett, *History*, pp. 66-85.

at Anandpur," but among the hills. Gobind hunted the wild boar and the tiger, welcomed recruits to his gradually increasing forces, and drilled them in martial exercises, mastered his inheritance of legend and religion, attended faithfully to his devotions as a Sikh, studied a little Persian, read a good deal of Hindi,[17] and received "ambassadors" occasionally from nearby chieftains with whom he could discuss possible alliances. Raja Ram Singh of Bengal sent gifts to him: five horses in full trappings, a sagacious elephant, a miniature throne with attendant puppets, a peculiar composite weapon useful as a pistol, sword, lance, dagger and club, a drinking-cup and some personal adornments, jewels and a garment. Sikhs in various quarters sent in gifts and revenues. A semblance of a state was undertaken, assemblies were held in "the castle of the hills" at the call of a big drum constructed as a symbol of authority.

It had become apparent by 1695 to many keen and interested observers that the once mighty empire of the Mughals was in the process of decay. Shivaji and the Marathas alone had exhausted much of its waning strength, although Aurangzib had collected for the struggle with them the largest army that India had ever known till then, and he had waged for a decade, 1683 and following, so unremitting a campaign in several directions that there was brought under his nominal control the most extensive empire that the Mughals knew. The campaign, however, was expensive and exhausting, and incited much ill-will. Guerrilla bands continued operation, some of the Mughal army officers proved to be untrustworthy, two of the emperor's own sons, Mu'azzam and 'Azam Shah, rebelled against him, and nature itself sometimes played havoc with his forces—once twelve thousand men with their arms and stores were de-

[17] Khazan Singh's observation that "Guru Gobind Singh was a great scholar in Gurmukhi, Sanskrit and Persian" (I, p. 166) is somewhat extravagant.

stroyed by sudden flood. And Aurangzib became aware at last that the English controlled the seas around his empire, cutting the sea route, for example, from India to the Hijaz in Arabia and blocking pilgrimage. And by 1695 Guru Gobind Singh was finally prepared for action outside the confines of his hill-retreat. The great drum sounded out its summons to assembly, the troops were marshalled which had been drilled for the offensive, and the base of operations was moved out of the hills back to Anandpur.

The guru and the Sikhs were not declaring war—not openly, at least. There was still great caution in the movement, but the Khalsa was nonetheless in process of formation, the shadowy state was ready to take form. Gobind was a man then (1699) of forty years, mature, seasoned and resourceful, with an enhanced sense of divine assistance in his discharge of sacred duty, and enjoying the confidence of a large following and the general public. He chose to act under cover of a mela, a religious gathering, which would not in itself arouse the government's suspicions. It was the occasion of the Baisakhi festival of spring (April), and Gobind summoned all Sikhs to attend it, announcing that the goddess Durga herself had already bestowed her blessing upon his enterprise. He had for some time made Durga the special object of his worship, a matter which occasioned no surprise or anxiety among the Sikhs—nor would this have troubled any of them, even had they been disposed to theological discussion. Durga was a deity familiar to all Indians in those parts, Hindu, Sikh and animist. She was known by many names, according to locality (in Bengal, for example, she was known as Kali), or merely as Mahadevi, the "great goddess" or the Mother. She was probably Teg Bahadur's own deity on occasion. She was indeed Hari's shakti, the female aspect or "power" of Mahadeva, to whom both men and women were devoted. Gobind knew the value of appeal to her or of any plea made in her name, nor saw anything in her worship necessarily incongruous with Sikhism. Once while at Naina-devi in the hills he had enlisted Hindu pandits to assist him in her worship, making then a burnt offering of hundreds of pounds of ghi, raw sugar and molasses. This in itself did not make Gobind Singh a Hindu, even as also his choice of a title, Khalsa (see below), for the state did not make a Moslem of him! He was proceeding with some independence and sound judgment of his own.

During this Baisakhi mela, then, he organized the Khalsa. Although khalsa was an Arabic term in use among the Moslems, Gobind found in it something singular, something distinctive for his purpose. Its root is "khalis," meaning "pure" or "free" and emphasizing sincerity in religion. The Koranic sura of Unity bears it in its title, that is Sura 112, one which Moslems say has, with its fifteen Arabic words, one-third the value of the whole Koran,[18] declaring as it does the creed of the pure and undefiled: "Say: He alone is God, God the eternal, He begetteth not nor is he begotten, and there is (has been) none like unto him." And an Arabic derivative of "khalis," *i.e.*, "mukhallis," could be, sometimes was, used for "savior." Indian Christians of the north came in a later time to call Jesus Christ, among other names, al-Mukhallis, The Savior. Gobind's use of the term indicates, however, no compromise with Islam—he certainly did not seek Moslem favor thus, although he was not forgetful of the Sikhs' great duty *somehow* to affect Islam. He intended that the Khalsa should nevertheless become the instrument of Sikh development.

The actual initiation of the order was dramatic, an occasion of exacting trial for his followers whom he assembled about his tent amidst the mela. In the presence of the company he called for attention, drew from its scabbard his martyred father's blade, and asked as he poised the blade aloft

[18] Whose total vocabulary is 77,639 words, in the Moslem count.

if there was a Sikh who would yield himself to death then and there in the guru's stead to insure success to the cause for which the guru stood? There was no immediate response but silence on the part of all, as if no one fully understood. The guru added that Durga required sacrifice, actual blood-sacrifice, if the Sikh cause were to be successful, and this time there was at least thoughtful silence. Gobind spoke a third time in sincere, appealing vehemence, and five men, one by one, responded, offering themselves. It was a solemn moment and Gobind expressed deep satisfaction. Then he led them at intervals, one by one, into his tent, the place of sacrifice. Each time there could be heard by those without the fateful cry, "Ya Durga," and the sound of the falling blade—no other sound or utterance. Thereafter, on each occasion, Gobind emerged with the sword-blade dripping blood. The bystanders were at first awe-struck, soon many trembled in great anxiety and at the last some fled in mortal terror. But the solemn rite was slowly executed, and five loyal Sikhs, apparently, had gone to death as willing victims to Durga's pleasure. Then it was that Gobind spoke again with reassurance to the company, and turning toward the tent called the five men out again—who came at once to meet a still wondering but transformed audience. *They* had not been slain, those five. The blood was goat's blood, an animal dear to Durga as an offering, and the five willing, would-be victims were yet alive, to live as influential heroes wherever the Sikh cause led. They had become the immortal nucleus of the Khalsa! They were, by name, Daya Ram, a khatri of Lahore; Dharm Das, a Jat shudra of Delhi; Muhakam Chand, a shudra cloth-printer of Dwarka; Sahib Chand, a brahman of Bidar, and Himmat, a shudra kahar, or bearer, of Jagannath—three shudras, a khatri and a brahman, now in a new casteless fellowship.

What these five men had endured as a test of loyalty had a very great effect on all who were assembled at the mela, and was destined to become a cherished, influential memory among all Sikhs. But there was need of something more continually effective if the Sikh cause was to prosper permanently. The Khalsa must depend on something more than newly kindled enthusiasm—such might wane—and the cherished memory of heroic acts and a sacrificial episode. Not that the sacrifice, even with the blood of goats, should be repeated and become habitual. This was hardly in keeping with the true Sikh religion. Gobind would provide, however, something quite as definite and likewise appropriate. What he actually did at this time was manifold—there would be *several* unifying factors which would make the Khalsa Sikhs unique, without any necessarily violent departure from their whole tradition. He instituted a baptismal rite, the pahul, the assumption of a new name, singh, the wearing of tangible symbols of membership, the kakkas, a communion, with the sipping of nectar, amrit, and a managing committee, the panchayat.

The five heroes of Anandpur were the first to be baptized and immediately afterward the pahul or baptismal "cleansing" was administered to all, and all assumed the new name singh, or "lion." The communion likewise was administered to all, beginning with the five. The original ceremony went somewhat in this fashion: Gobind took pure water in an iron vessel, stirred it with a two-edged dagger as he recited some verses of the *Japji* and some other verses of his own composition, while his wife Jita threw in some sweets (patase). The result was amrit, nectar, the "water of immortality." The "baptism," then, consisted in sipping the liquid and submitting to a sprinkling with it—a rite altogether different from anything in Moslem or in Hindu ritual, although possibly reminiscent of a Christian sacrament. The drinking of the liquid was in itself "communion" —all drank from the one vessel, thereby breaking caste! The five drank first as the guru held the vessel, then the guru sprinkled some of the sweet water on their hair and dashed some in their faces, causing them to repeat after him Wah Guruji ka Khalsa, Wah Guruji ki Fatah (Hail the Khalsa of the Guru, Hail the triumph of the Guru). These five in their turn administered the rite to Gobind and to "mother" Jita and the rest—to the number of 20,000 altogether. This pahul has been a custom ever since with Singhs, although in recent times they have partaken of a sweetened paste at the formal ceremony, instead of sipping amrit or having amrit sprinkled on them. Thus no vestige remains among the Singhs of the ancient Hindu custom of chelas, "pupils" of the guru, "teacher," drinking, as evidence of devotion, the charan-pahul, or "foot-wash," the water with which the guru had bathed his feet at the time of prayer. However, the Hindu custom, rather than the Christian sacrament, may have prompted the first exercise.

Sikh tradition not only links the first five "brothers," the panch piyare, "five beloved," with the initial rite, but has added five others, the panch mukte, "five saved," namely Ram Singh, Deva Singh, Tahil Singh, Ishar Singh and Fatah Singh, thus establishing a more extensive apostolic base. And it includes yet another "five," the panchayat, but one not altogether distinct, because two of this group belong also among the panch piyare. This panchayat five included Daya Singh (the former Daya Ram), Dharm Singh (formerly Dharm Das), Man Singh, Sangat Singh and Sant Singh. This committee directed community affairs in Anandpur in an emergency, and were empowered to conduct gurdwara services. This set a precedent for Sikhs in imitation of an ancient Hindu administrative custom. Each local community of Sikhs since then has had its own panchayat in control of the gurdwara. It came to be a saying among Sikhs that where five of them were met together there the guru was also. (*Cf.* the Christian "Where two or three are met together in my name, there am I in the midst of them.")

The kakkas, too, are linked with the initial Anandpura ceremony, although we may suppose that they are the result actually of some development out of that occasion. These five are items or tokens whose names begin with the letter *k*, namely:

> *kesh*, the hair of the head, that of the man, especially, left uncut and usually wound into a top-knot [jura],
> *kangha*, a comb worn in the hair behind the knot,
> *kara*, a steel bracelet worn on the left arm,
> *kachch*, a pair of shorts worn about the body's middle,
> *kirpan*, or *khanda*, a two-edged dagger worn at the belt.

These have since been for every Singh the marks of his membership in the Khalsa.

From the first guru Gobind Singh committed all the Sikhs to the exercise of arms, pledged them never to turn their backs upon the enemy in time of battle and never to surrender. Nor did he forget the former elements of their religion. He not only set a personal example in devotional observance, but urged his people specifically to worship God, to practice ablution and prayer, to read the sacred scriptures, to avoid any semblance of idolatry, not only not to worship in the presence of idols, but to avoid also cemeteries and cremation-grounds, and to abstain from eating the flesh of animals killed in the Semitic, Moslem manner. The cremation-grounds were Hindu, the cemeteries were mainly Moslem, therefore to be avoided. Although Hindus, generally, neither killed animals nor ate their flesh, Moslems ate the flesh of animals (not pork, of course), slaughtered by a sort of Semitic ritual, during their annual festival of Baqr 'Id, for instance. Sikhs themselves have eaten many kinds of flesh. Gobind also warned them to keep pure their family ties by having no dealings, matrimonial or other, with men who smoke or who kill their daughters, as some of the ruder tribes of north India have done (cf. the *Koran* 17:33; also, a reminder by Mohammed to his own people of the crime of female infanticide). They were to protect the weak and give assistance to the poor. And they were to have no dealings with false Sikhs and their descendants.

Obviously, all this could not have been details of an *inaugural* address at Anandpur! Gobind had said some of these things previously, and he said some others later on. They may be taken in connection with Sikh tradition as ingredients of Gobind's constitution. One thing is certain—there was instituted an *imposing order*, adequately free, on the whole, of contaminations from Hinduism and Islam. There is no reference to strong drink, Sikhs have never been abstainers. Nor are any specific injunctions given with respect to mortuary rites. Sikhs may dispose of their dead as they choose, and they have not held it to be a mortal sin sometimes to let corpses remain unburied—as the fortunes of war might at times decree. This early order, with or without certain elements, is most significant, and not the least important aspect of it is a suggestion that *the content* of the guruship was undergoing change, to which the Anandpur initiatory invocation lends some evidence: Hail the Khalsa of the Guru, Hail the triumph of the Guru!

There are indications borne out by subsequent developments that although the Khalsa and its triumph were invoked, it was not Gobind explicitly who was invoked as "Guru." Nor was the reference itself explicit—the content and the connotation of the title were in process of revision, even though no Sikh at the moment could foresee the outcome. Gobind had had twenty-five years of experience in the office and had known about it through his father. He had learned of its vicissitudes which seemed at times a demonstration of impermanence. Perhaps something more permanent and substantial than a line of *persons* might be found. The lives of persons are uncertain, personalities vary, are at times unfortunate, even unexemplary, and no one principle or process of succession had been generally, agreeably, accepted. Of course, from the very first, in an exalted sense, God or Sat Nam wás Guru in the Sikh tradition, even while the earthly office was filled by someone under *him*. But there was need of human guidance more immediate and tangible—and such consciousness of need was a current mood of India at the time. The Vishnuite Hindus had their avataras in reasonable proximity, but Sikhs had not accepted such a theory for their own. Moreover, they were opposed to idols! The Shivite Hindus felt the prevalence of Shiva's power through Durga, Kali and other female deities, but polytheism was as much to be avoided as distasteful idols. The Moslems had a book—and the Sikhs also had one. It was indeed the *Granth* which came to fill the earthly guruship, a revision and enlargement of the *Adi Granth*, nevertheless a concrete, immediate and enduring guide. This may be taken for the moment to indicate the thought in Gobind's own mind and the trend of circumstance.

The Khalsa itself meanwhile was to prove for Gobind and his people a most exacting venture. Its first years, which were likewise Gobind's last, were years of fiery trial. Although the newly organized society may have seemed to many a mere incident among the multitudes, a tolerable religious demonstration, its activities the first year or two brought it into public notice as something more significant. The word first passed on to the Mughals was simply that a revival was going on among the "unbelievers," and possibly a "third religion" being organized, but it was soon apparent that the "revival" was anti-Moslem, was especially a menace to the Moslem Sunnis. In 1701 Aurangzib took serious notice of it. It had enlisted a motley crowd, not only a respectable nucleus, but hosts of sweepers, scavengers and others who were socially despised, and many outlaws. But they had attained a new dignity through membership in this virile, hopeful order. Perhaps Jat stock predominated—and Jats were then inspired by the notion of a kingdom of their own which would displace the too familiar and oppressive "Turks." Jats were men of sturdy frame and stolid mien who could be very active in the fervor of religious consecration. There were also in the crowd Pathans (pronounced pa-*tan*), soldiers of fortune from the northwest frontier, rugged adventurers for the sheer love of war and pillage. Some of the hill rajas had at least pledged their aid, but may have made their aid contingent on success, although Gobind had been actively allied with the rebel raja of Kuhlur. Gobind had actually launched his offensive against some other rajas in the hills, who were lesser allies of Aurangzib—for example, the chiefs of Nahan and of Nalagarh.

Aurangzib launched his attack by dispatching flanking forces, one under command of the governor of Lahore, the other under the command of the governor of Sirhind, whose seat was only thirty miles south of Anandpur. Gobind had expected such a move, but was not prepared to encounter as large a force as that which actually arrived. On learning of the Mughal strength, he dared not risk a battle. The Mughals previously had temporized, he knew, enabling his father Teg Bahadur to win some skirmishes in the vicinity of Amritsar, but now he knew that something more than a mere skirmish loomed for him. Some of the weaker Sikhs deserted him, and some others he dismissed with curses for their cowardice. For a faithful few he counseled flight as being most expedient. His immediate family, for example, with the exception of his eldest sons, fled southward, but suffered loss en route—two younger sons were captured and taken to Sirhind for execution. The Sikhs have marked the spot where they were slain, and to this day as they pass it, they cast stones derisively in token of revenge, and offer prayers for the youthful victims. The guru himself, his elder sons, and many hundreds of the most faithful and the hardiest retreated from the neighborhood of Anandpur and took refuge at Chamkaur, one of their hill forts.

The Mughal forces pursued the fugitives to Chamkaur and besieged the fortress, in due time taking it, the Sikhs losing many men, including Gobind's sons. Gobind himself escaped under cover of the night to the nearby town of Bahlul and thence in the disguise of a Moslem darwish fled farther to the wastes of Bhatinda, a hundred miles below Amritsar. Many of the besieged escaped and in good season rejoined the guru in Bhatinda. It was a comparatively safe retreat, this desert region south of the bend of the Sutlej river. Many of its Jat inhabitants were friendly. It was usually dangerous and futile for a hostile expedition to venture into this recess of sand and distance. A Mughal force essayed it but lost a brief action at Muktsar. Gobind and the members of his Khalsa were then left undisturbed for several years—from 1705 to 1707, until the death of Aurangzib. When Aurangzib sent the fugitive a "summons" to appear in Delhi, Gobind penned his famous *Zafar Namah*, or "victorious epistle," in defiance. This letter reproached the emperor for his false dealings, bad faith, high crimes and misdemeanors and rehearsed the merits of the Sikh religion and the Khalsa, assuring him that the Khalsa would one day take vengeance on him for his injuries to it and for his abuse of India. Gobind meanwhile took pains to keep the Khalsa organized and active.

These months of retirement gave Gobind opportunity for literary composition. He wrote a *Japji* of his own, but wrote a long a in the title (*Jāpji*). It, too, was a book of "psalms." He composed also additional materials for the *Granth*, namely, his *Akal Ustat*, or "praise of the Timeless," and his autobiographical *Vichitra Natak*, or "wonder tale." He also collaborated with several of his more learned associates in an abridgment of Hindu Puranic writings, which he entitled *The Twenty-Four Avataras*, a fanciful adaptation of his own of the fantastic, mythological stories of the Hindu gods, especially the ten "descents," with additions of his own to those descents, including the spiritual appearance of *himself*.

Gobind had accepted with approval the earlier *Adi Granth*, thus establishing to such degree a scriptural succession, and his own *Jāpji* itself subscribes to the gist of Nanak's *Jāpji*. Nor do his additions to the *Adi Granth* alter the general temper of the Sikh tradition, except that they are predominantly martial. Among the items added were other slokas of Teg Bahadur, his father, and a dohra (doha) of his own which he had written in Anandpur to his father in the Delhi prison awaiting execution:

> Strength is available, fetters can be broken, and expedients abound,
> All is at thine own disposal and thou art thine own assistant.

The Bhatinda period was making inevitably a most significant contribution to Sikh history, for in it, a period of armed truce or, at least, of suspension of hostilities, a literary reconstruction of the guruship was taking place, in spite of Gobind's own conception of himself as the divine instrumentality of progress in his time. Gobind may indeed have offered himself as the final avatara, since he was the tenth in the Sikhs' own line—and ten represented the ultimate in all Hindu reckoning. But he did not attribute to himself divinity. Rather, he emphasized the power and sovereignty of God. He adopted as his own Nanak's "root assertion," the mul mantra, and grafted branches to it, for example:

> Ek onkar satigurprasadi
> Chakr chihan aru baran jati sru pati nahin jih
> Rup rang ar rekh bhekh kou kahi na sakti kih
> Achal murti anabhau prakas amitoj kahi jai
> Koti Indra Indrani sah sahani gani jai
> Tribhavan mahip sur nar asur net net ban trin kahat
> Tva sarab nam kathai kavan karam nam sumati,

which might be appropriately translated as follows:

> The one, true, wise and pure Guru
> Hath no contour, countenance, color, caste or lineage,
> No form, complexion, nor any lines by which one may describe him,
> A being limitless in might, fearless, luminous and steady,
> Enduring Lord of multitudes of Indras and Indranis,
> Sovereign of nature's types, heroes, men and demons,
> Indistinct to dwellers of the vale and woodland,
> Who indeed can name thee whose names are legion by thine actions.

This is in the vein of long tradition, but Gobind did make some attempt to "name" the Lord, resorting to warlike vocabulary often, to such terms, for example, as:

> *A-kal*, the timeless, deathless,
> *Sarb-kal*, all-death, or the end of all who die,
> *Mahan-kal*, great death, or the death that overtakes the faithless,
> *Sarb-loh*, all-steel,
> *Mahan-loh*, great steel,
> *Asi-pani*, sword-in-hand, and
> *Asi-dhuj*, sword-on-the-banner,

some of which were used in one of the invocations of Gobind's *Jāpji*, namely:

> May *Akal* protect us,
> May *Sarbloh* protect us,
> May *Sarbkal* protect us,
> Yea, *Sarbloh* protect us!
>
> O thou who art deathless,
> Who hast amply armed us,
> To whom we go in dying,
> Do thou in arms protect us!

This may have been a favorite invocation, because Gobind attributed to loh, sword-metal, a mysterious virtue on which his life had depended on more than one occasion. He was a man of the sword, reliant upon it and upon all weapons. In the *Zafar Namah* which he wrote to Aurangzib were these lines (in Persian):[19]

> Chaukar az huma hilat dar guzasht
> Halal asat bar din bih shamsher dast,
>
> When all other means have proven ineffective,
> It is right then to take up the sword.

And in his *Vichitra Natak* these lines occur as comment on his theory—or theology?—of war:

> I bow to the scimitar and the two-edged sword, to the falchion and also to the dagger,
> I bow to the arrow, to the musket and the mace, to lance, shaft, cannon, rapier and sword,
> I bow to all the weapons known as *shastar* [*i.e.*, held in hand],
> And I bow to all the weapons known as *astar* [*i.e.*, which hurl projectiles]

But with all his military ardor he exalted above warfare the devoted worship of True Name. He composed quatrains to be recited at the time of pahul, which not only contained injunction to fight nobly, but declared also that armed kings with their ponderous elephants and fleet horses, and with their many trained soldiers clad in mail, were inevitably as nothing compared with devotion to the Name—or did he actually mean to say that such kings with their equipment could not stand up before pious Sikhs! before valiant Sikhs baptized to conflict with the enemies of Sat Nam. In any case, Gobind had a theology distinct from war, and his favorite name for Sat Nam was Akal, the Timeless—Gobind was himself pre-eminently a disciple of "*timeless* truth." His exposition of Akal is chiefly contained in his *Akal Ustat* ("akal stuti, in the Hindi, "praise of the Timeless"), which might be adequately represented by this digest:

[19] *Cf.* Ganda Singh, *Banda Singh Bahadur,* preceding the Foreword.

Akal is primordial being, primal divinity and the creator of all; unborn and free of death, immortal, invisible, distinct from all creation, of changeless purpose;

He has made millions of Indras and Brahmas, made and unmade Shivas and Vishnus and the fourteen worlds, all blended with himself; deities, demons, celestial singers, serpents, yakshases he has made innumerable;

He is at once far from all and near to all, dwelling in the sea and on the land, in the upper air and in the lower regions; Brahma and Vishnu have not found his limits, but his light is seen in all the fourteen worlds and is contained also within all souls—in the ant as in the elephant;

He knows of every heart its secrets, deems the rich and poor as equals, doth not exercise a partial love, but recognizes every place and all the peoples;

He removes all sickness, sorrow, sin, gives milk and sons—tho he has no son himself—is life's preserver, the seal of purity, the attractiveness of youth, the torment of our enemies, the life of friends, the giver of great gifts, the king of kings;

He is the one true, wise and pure Guru, hath no contour, countenance, color, caste or lineage, . . . etc. [cf. the *mul mantra* above in Gobind's version].[20]

All this is a rehearsal of familiar terminology but is referred here to *Akal*, is a more or less random description of divinity in the manner of any bhagat, for example—but in this instance, as may be known from our other sources, the bhagat Gobind was a man of war. And Gobind is more monotheist than mystic, save as he assumes a unity in which other than Sikh elements are merged. He reminds the Hindus often that their Veds and their gods all get their meaning from Sat Nam, that they all, in fact, testify to Sat Nam, in so far as they have a meaning. He tells Hindus and Moslems that "mosque and mundir ['temple'] are the same," that Allah and Abhekh ("a-bhekh" was an expression of the Hindus, meaning "without qualities" or "unmanifested") are one, that the "Purans and the Qur'an are the same" and that

[20] *Cf.* Khazan Singh, II, pp. 565-580; cf. pp. 633, 697; Macauliffe, v, *in loco;* Malcolm's *Sketch*, pp. 148-197, etc.

both have missed the "secret" of Sat Nam. And he reminds Moslems that Allah's names as they use them, for example, ar-Razzak, "the provider," al-Karim, "the generous," and ar-Rahim, "the merciful," actually refer to the One God, Sat Nam.

As for himself and his own role in the emergency, there may be some difference of opinion. Gobind's work on *The Twenty-Four Avataras* is not included in the *Granth Sahib* proper. He assumed for himself no character or quality not inherent in the guruship and in the several gurus who had filled it. Unlike the former gurus, however, he did write his own biography, an apologia for his own career, and he couched it in terms familiar to the bhagat and to the Vishnuite. He had been very much impressed as he studied Hindu scriptures with the role of Rama and Krishna, especially, and may have realized that these were once mere men who played their part at a time of special need. He observed in bhakta theology that God became uneasy when "his saints were in distress" and was ever ready to succor them beyond what even the occasion might require. He could well believe himself called to such an opportunity, as one born in a time of stress, tracing his "birth" from divinity much in the fashion expounded by teachers of the Upanishadic doctrines, or in the manner of "descent" of the Puranic heroes,[21] or—if he had only known the Christian gospel, also—somewhat in the manner of the disciple Luke's account of the genealogy of Jesus. Gobind was aware that he came of providential stock and had a special mission to perform—he counted much, for instance, on his Sodhi lineage, even as Jesus counted on descent from David.

This is, in the main, his own account of his career and his mission in the line of gurus:

[21] *Cf. Vishnu Purana,* bks. IV, V, especially. On the existence around A.D. 1700 of Hindu disciples of Moslem saints (*pirs*), see M. T. Titus, *Indian Islam,* pp. 154f.

In the beginning God . . . extended himself, created the world and peopled it. He created demigods and powers and a dynasty of celestial kings, of which Raghu was born. From Raghu's line came Aj, the archer-charioteer, and Dasarath, father of Ram, Bharat, Lakshman and Shatrughan, and Sita whose sons married daughters of another earthly house of kings which had previously by divine decree been established in the Panjab.

The Panjabi line built the cities of Lahur [Lahore] and Kasur [twenty-five miles below Lahore]. Its descendants migrated to the Sanaudh [Sodhi] region of Banaras where they intermarried with the local stocks and produced distinguished sons, gained wealth, "raised umbrellas" [ruled] over many kings and "enforced religion everywhere."

Then came an era of worldly pride, of lust and wrath, whose progress no holy man could check, and the Sodhi clan returned up-country to their ancestral home. There they displaced some distant kinsmen of their own, the line of Kushu, who migrated to Banaras, where they became Bedis, readers of the Vedas and attendants on religious offices. The devotion of these Bedis [vedis] was reported to the Sodhis up in the Panjab, whose king recalled them and gave over his throne to them, himself retiring as a rikhi [rishi, "seer"] to the forest where he became "absorbed in the love of God."

The Bedi king, now ruler of the Panjab, gave his blessing to the Sodhi king-recluse and promised him that when he [the Sodhi saint] came back to birth again "in the Kaliyuga," he would bear "the name of Nanak" and would make the Sodhi line distinguished "throughout the world," and by repeated births would retain religious leadership for the good of all.

Nanak, born of the line of Bedis to make the Sodhi line distinguished, established true religion in the Kaliyuga and disclosed the path to holy men, a way devoid of suffering and sin, or pain and hunger, or death, to those who under God's guidance followed in his steps. Then Nanak disappeared, assuming immediately the body of Angad "as one lamp is lighted from another." Amar Das succeeded him and when the time was ripe for "the fulfilment of the blessing" [the barkat], there came to office Ram Das *Sodhi*. All these four, from Nanak to Ram Das, were one, although "fools considered them distinct" and all were of a blend with God. And by repeated birth and blending came Arjun . . . and Har Gobind . . . and Har Rai . . . and Har Kishan . . . and Teg Bahadur . . . and Gobind Singh!

Gobind Singh came to birth[22] while his father on an expedition in Assam beside the Brahmaputra was doing penance amidst the seven horns of Himakuta [a summit somewhere between the Himalayas and Mt. Meru where the Hindu gods of fable dwelt]. His father, the holy Teg Bahadur, worshiped Mahankal, "great death," with such devotion that he was at last blended with God through martyrdom. He had not really desired to come to earth, but God would have him born because men had become unruly and even the gods were arrogant, Brahma, Vishnu, Mahadeva each calling himself "supreme," and there was no one who recognized the Primal Essence, the Creator, God who truly was Supreme. And God intended also that Teg Bahadur should prepare the way for Gobind!

Gobind's account betrays, in spite of his general purpose, some consciousness of cleavage in the ranks of Sikhs. There were at least two strains in the guruship, regardless of the Bedi and the Sodhi blending. Gobind had every wish to reconcile them, may have wished to establish his own intimate descent from Nanak, also.

Gobind's arch-foe Aurangzib died in 1707, leaving him a brief opportunity to abandon his retreat. All Sikhs had not assembled at Bhatinda, many had carried on in various other parts, looking to Bhatinda for inspiration. Now their guru could venture out. When, upon the death of Aurangzib, two sons, Mu'azzim and 'Azam Shah, in the north, contested the succession to the throne of Delhi, and a third was ready for rebellion in the south, Gobind cast in his lot with Mu'azzim, and the latter's forces under Zulfikar Khan met and defeated 'Azam in a battle in which 'Azam fell pierced, says the Sikh tradition, by one of Gobind's arrows. When Mu'azzim ascended the Mughal throne under the name of Bahadur Shah (1707-1712), Gobind Singh took service under him! After the coronation (in Agra, as it happened), which Gobind attended, he accompanied Bahadur Shah into the south against the other brother claimant to the throne. Bahadur Shah was willing to conciliate the Sikhs,

[22] *Cf.* Khazan Singh, II, pp. 353ff.

rather than to antagonize them as his father Aurangzib had done, and Gobind may have seen a chance to disarm any lingering suspicion that the Sikhs were essentially a hostile sect and bent upon any forceful conversions to their own order. Perhaps Gobind was still in Mughal service when at last he died. Muhammad Hashim (Khafi Khan) says in his *Muntakhabu'l-Lubab*, "one of the best and most impartial histories of modern India," that "at the time that Bahadur Shah marched against Hydarabad, Gobind the chief Guru of the Sikh sect came to join him with two or three hundred horsemen bearing spears, and some footmen," and that "after two or three months he died from wounds of a dagger, and his murderer was not discovered."[23] There is some evidence, not necessarily contradictory, however, that Gobind was not actually engaged with Bahadur Shah at the time of death, but had withdrawn and gone to Nader, a village on the Godavari river in Hydarabad (Deccan, of course), where he was holding partisan conference with many of his followers, including a certain Banda (*q.v.*, below). If this latter version is authentic, the allegation likewise holds that the conference discussed some disagreement with the Mughals and reached a decision to wage war against them. Whatever the exact situation and Gobind's status, his death occurred. He may indeed have been slain, as one rumor had it, by Gul Khan, a grandson of a man, Painda Khan, whom a former guru, Har Gobind, had killed.

Not the least significant item of the so-called "conference" was the presence there of Banda, who upon the death of Gobind laid claim to the guruship. The active leadership of the Sikhs, of the Singhs in particular, doubtless fell to him, but he did not become the guru. The conference may have raised the question of the guruship. Gobind's sons had all been slain and there were no blood-claimants in the line.

[23] *Cf.* Elliot, *History*, VII, pp. 413-426, 456f.

But there was the Khalsa, not to be forgotten, with its governing panchayat. Banda[24] may have been made leader by the Khalsa, but the line of *personal* gurus had reached an end, as may be seen in subsequent events.

Some reconstruction must be undertaken of the transition from Gobind Singh to Banda and of subsequent Sikh history in the absence of contemporary records of the Sikhs themselves—except for scattered bits of ecclesiastical tradition. Moslem officials and historians of the time have left abundant records, but may not always have known what was happening "inside" Sikhism. How the Sikhs' own consciousness resolved and expressed itself is for us the chief consideration, with particular reference to Gobind's heritage.

Gobind was, unquestionably, the ablest man the Sikhs had yet produced, probably the most learned of them all up to the time of his death and certainly the ablest administrator. He wrote an excellent Hindi in the Panjabi and Gurmukhi characters, disclosed in his writings some specific knowledge of Sunni, Shi'i, Shaykhi, Rafazi, Imami and Shafiite Moslems, and an opinion of certain other peoples—he once referred to Persians, English and "the two-faced men of France" as among the "misguided." He had traveled widely since his birth down Bengal-way, and had fallen in with many types of men. There was no man of similar experience and comparable ability among the Sikhs to take his place.

And the Khalsa was not destined to assert complete control, because all Sikhs had not accepted it. Only the Singhs, wearers of the kakkas, who acquired the name Keshdaris, or "hairy ones," were its adherents. There were other Sikhs, a group unorganized but loyal to the Sikh tradition in an easygoing way—in fact, they were known as Sahajdaris, "easygoers." All were loyal to the gurus, including Gobind Singh,

[24] The standard work on Banda Singh is Ganda Singh, *Banda Singh Bahadur*. Amritsar, 1935. See below, pp. 212f.

but with some difference in their esteem of them. All were committed to the *Adi Granth* and did not object to its enlargement—in fact, all welcomed the addition in 1734, twenty-six years after Gobind's death, of that portion of his writings known as the *Granth of the Tenth Guru*, the *Daswan Granth*. Singhs themselves, of course, gave special reverence to this latter work, but not to the exclusion of the former. The *Granth* as a whole or either portion, the *Adi* or the *Daswan*, actually became supremely influential in the Sikh community—above the prestige of the Khalsa.[25] And its essential gospel in a new interpretation assumed control. In particular, what it revealed of Hukm, or the divine "bidding," the heavenly Guru's own "command," assumed authority above any person, any order and even, in effect, any book—yet the *Granth* as a whole embodied exemplary personalities and administrative ideals. It may be said that Hukm-theology (or theory?) became expressive of the common consciousness, whereby the Sikh religion was perpetuated—for example:

> By his [God's] hukm are all things formed,
> Not one is blessed, save by his hukm, and by his hukm alone doth nature run her course,
> All serve beneath his hukm, and none may act without it,
> Under thy hukm, O God, hath all been done,
> And naught is of itself alone.

This is not to minimize the Khalsa, for it, too, exhibited the fellow-feeling of the Sikhs, but it was more or less invisible at Gobind's death and had to wait for ultimate success upon the passage of years of internal dissension and upon what survived an international war. And even though

[25] To Gobind Singh himself are attributed these words:

Agya bhai Akal ki tabhi chalayo panth
Sabh Sikhen ko Hukm hai Guru manyo Granth,

(The way was laid by the grace of the Timeless,
The Granth is by order the Guru of all Sikhs). Cf. Khazan Singh, I, p. 203; II, pp. 573f.

at the last the Khalsa was successful, it realized less than universality for the Sikh religion. Sikhism continued to be larger than the Khalsa.

The Moslem historian, Khafi Khan, who has been referred to above, who had been an official under Aurangzib and was later a *diwan* or "minister" under the first Nizam of Hydarabad in south India, has given some opinion of the Sikhs, although at the expense of some confusion of names and terminology. He wrote by years and periods—historical diary style—as was customary with historians at the time, and allows some data to get out of place. He refers, as of our year 1708-09, to "a sect of infidels called Guru, more commonly known as Sikhs." It is not surprising that he did not clearly understand the Sikhs' own use of "guru"—it had so many meanings for them. It was natural for him to call them "infidels" (mushriks, kafirs), although many non-Moslems in India had come to be officially recognized as dhimmis, or tolerated unbelievers. And he is somewhat uncertain about Sikhs' garb and their theology, but gives the impression that in his time Sikhism was a movement of considerable proportions.

> Their chief who dresses as a faqir has a fixed residence near Lahore. From old times he has built temples in all the towns and populous places and has appointed one of his followers to preside in each temple as his deputy. . . . The sects consist principally of Jats and Khatris of the Panjab, and of other tribes of infidels.

However aptly the term faqir may have applied to some gurus, it did not apply to Gobind Singh. He mentions Gobind[26] and says:

> When the news of his death reached the Panjab, where the bulk of the Sikhs were living, an obscure member of the sect, about whose name there are various statements, gave out that in the course of transmigration, which the Sikhs believe in and call avatar, he had taken the place of the murdered Gobind come to life again as a

[26] Elliot, VII, p. 413.

bearded man embodied for the sake of revenge. This worthless dog, having published this statement, stirred up disaffection in the sect and raised the standard of rebellion. By jugglery, charms and sorcery he pretended to perform miracles before credulous people, and gave himself the name of Sachcha Padashah, True King.

The "obscure member," of course, was Banda, known among the Sikhs as Banda Singh Bahadur. He had been associated with Gobind, perhaps in the Dakkani campaign and in the Nader conference, and did become nominally the leader at the death of Gobind and until June 1715. He is held in high regard by many of the Singhs, although they do not call him guru. Khafi Khan has left a realistic, although sometimes uncomplimentary, account of him and of the years' events—but the Moslem was inhibited by temperament and politics, at least, from giving an *im*partial narrative. Here is a digest of what the Moslem says about him:

Banda set about plundering, having gathered around him pony riders and motley footmen, eighteen or nineteen thousand men in all, with arms. These accursed wretches carried on a cruel and predatory warfare [winning a number of engagements], shouting "Sachcha Padashah" and "Fath Daras" ["true king" and "victory to the doctrine"]. Many Musalmans found martyrdom and many infidels went to the sink of perdition. At the siege of Sirhind [south of Anandpur, where two sons of Gobind had been slain] the evil dogs fell to murdering the men, making prisoners of the children and the women of the high and low, carrying on atrocities for many days with such violence that they tore open the wombs of pregnant women, dashed every living child upon the ground, set fire to the houses, involving all in common ruin. Wherever they found a mosque or a tomb or the gravestone of a respected Musalman, they demolished the building, dug up the body, and made it no sin to scatter the bones of the dead. When they had done with the pillage of Sirhind [Khafi Khan, however, says that they set up an orderly administration in the district!], they went off to Delhi, where the Musalmans made against the villainous foe a manly resistance and sent many of the enemy to hell.

After the defeat at Delhi, the infidels suffered two or three discomfitures, but persevered and at Jalalabad began its investment with seventy or eighty thousand men who had swarmed together from all parts like ants and locusts, having siege engines, also. They strove in the most daring ways for twenty days and nights before they finally withdrew.

Shams Khan, the governor of Sultanpur, went forth against them with more than a hundred thousand men. The infidels, after many fruitless engagements, were finally put to flight, taking refuge in the fort at Rahun.

Having evacuated Rahun in the night, they ravaged the environs of Lahore. For eight or nine months, from Delhi to Lahore, all the towns and places of note were pillaged by these unclean wretches. In one place one or two hundred Hindu and Musalmani prisoners were slaughtered. These infidels had set up a new rule, and had forbidden the shaving of the hair of the head and the beard. Many ill-disposed, low-caste Hindus had joined themselves to them, and, placing their lives at the disposal of these evil-minded people, found their own advantage in professing belief and obedience, and they were very active in persecuting and killing other castes of Hindus.

The reference to the ban on the cutting of the hair identifies these Sikhs as mainly keshdari Singhs, with hosts of nondescript "Hindus" cooperating. Banda is evidently their active leader.

The Mughal emperor, Bahadur Shah, sent his general, Muhammad Amin Khan, against the Sikhs in 1710 and encountered them near Delhi, with this result ensuing—as condensed from Khafi Khan:

The enemy in their faqir clothing struck terror into the royal host. Rain fell for four or five days and the weather became very cold. Thousands of the soldiers, Dekkanis, especially, fell ill from the witchcraft and sorcery of the enemy. But the infidels were defeated, Banda escaping, leaving a false Guru in his place to deceive the Mughals.

The warfare continued, nevertheless, and not until February 1712 (1714?), was Sikh activity suppressed—after the death of Bahadur Shah. Khafi Khan has this also to say:

Sikh violence passed all bounds, indignities were freely inflicted on Musalmans by Sikhs who looked upon their acts as religiously meritorious. But at last in grave extremity the Sikhs offered to surrender. The chief Guru with his young son, his diwan, and three or four thousand persons became prisoners and received the predestined recompense for their foul deeds.[27]

In spite of what may have been legitimate "surrender," most of the prisoners were put to the sword immediately, their heads cut off and stuffed with hay and stuck upon spears for display in public. According to a letter of March 1716, from an East India Company agent in Delhi, seven hundred and eighty of the captives were put to death on refusal to accept Islam. Other captives, including Banda, Banda's son, and the Khalsa minister, were sent in chains to Delhi, where they were confined under orders in the fort. Khafi Khan observes that certain "khatris" offered money for their release, that it was refused, and that after a while, "The Guru was made to kill his own son in requital of his cruelty to the sons of others. Afterward he himself was killed."

The Moslem account indicates activities on an extensive scale. If Banda could rally "seventy or eighty thousand men" at Jalalabad in one campaign, there may have been upwards of half a million members, men, women and children, in the entire Sikh community, most of whom were in the Khalsa, actually or nominally. There may have been many sahajdaris in addition, making about seven hundred thousand all together. Apparently a force of a "hundred thousand" Musalmans were required to overcome the Sikhs. Gobind, on his part, must have laid his plans with great care, and left after him a well-trained nucleus for continued warfare. There was momentum, in other words, with which Banda Singh could carry on. Khafi Khan testifies to the great devotion with which all Singhs carried on. He cites an incident of which he was himself a witness: one of Banda's soldiers had been captured, tried and sentenced to death, and was in prison awaiting execution. His mother,

[27] Cf. Elliot, VII, pp. 456f.

without his knowledge, appealed directly to the emperor and secured a reprieve on the ground that her son had been forcibly converted and impressed into the service. When she brought the pardon to the prison and explained the circumstances, the son bitterly accused her of misrepresentation, renewed his pledge of loyalty to the Khalsa and took his sentence.

Khafi Khan's account may be taken as, in the main, authentic, but there was far more in the situation than was known to him. At least, there were elements within it which stand in need of a more sympathetic explanation. And Banda's own career in relation to the Khalsa was essentially what it has since come to be in Sikh tradition. A research student and historian of the Sikhs, Ganda Singh, of the Khalsa College in Amritsar, has published recently (1935) a life of Banda Singh Bahadur,[28] which gives an altogether sympathetic estimate, a sketch of which is offered here:

Banda was born of khatri stock in Kashmir, where learning was, in those days, "the exclusive monopoly of brahmans." He became a disciple of a bairagi, or adherent of the Hindu Ramanujist fraternity, acquired a new name (he had been known as Lachman Dev and Madho Das) and journeyed to Bengal. There he attached himself for a while to a yogi skilled in Tantric science, until he had himself gained some mastery of Tantric Yoga, a form of shakti exercise in the name of the goddess Durga. Thereupon he settled in Nander (Nader) in a math, or "monastery," of his own, maintaining the Tantric yoga discipline and gathering about him chelas (pupils) to share the training. It was in Nader that he met Gobind who had drawn aside from the campaign in Hydarabad, and where he soon declared himself the Guru's "slave" or banda—his designation ever afterward, it becoming a title equivalent among Sikhs to the Moslem abd or to the Hindu das, although Sikhs did not

[28] Cf. p. 208 above.

resort to any wide use of, e.g., Gurbanda, the "slave of the Guru," which would have been equivalent to the common Abdallah and Ishwardas—"the slave of Allah" and "the slave of God," respectively. In becoming "Banda," says Ganda Singh, "the dross of the Bairagi was at once transformed into the gold" of the Sikh order. Gobind himself initiated him by pahul and a draft of amrit into the Khalsa, making him "a full-fledged Singh."

Upon the death of Gobind, Banda Singh returned to the Panjab, bearing all the essential tokens of Sikh leadership, including five arrows from Gobind's own quiver, a flag (nishan), a drum (nagara), five duly appointed aides (pyaras—who constituted a panchayat?) and a guard of twenty other Singhs. He had also, as tradition holds, hukmnamahs, "warrants," from Gobind, bidding all Sikhs support him. But, it seems, he proposed on his own initiative some things unwarranted, in which the Sikhs did not support him. He offered the Khalsa a new battle-cry, "Fatah Darshan" (victory to the revelation),[29] intending that it accompany (or, perhaps, displace!) Gobind's "Wah Guruji ka Khalsa, Wah Guruji ki Fatah." Some essential of Sikh theory was thus apparently at stake. There was, for instance, no "Guru" in Banda's cry. Was he by this omission intent on emphasizing "revelation" above an earthly guru and beyond the Khalsa? There was use, however, for the battle-cry with an appropriate connotation, although in itself it seemed to be sectarian. Moslems had watch-words and war-cries of their own, as early Christian sectarians, also, had. Hindus, however, have never used such party cries. The Sikhs themselves adhered to those which Gobind himself had invented.

On his arrival in the Panjab, Banda proclaimed himself with a pallu pherna, or "scarf-waving," to be the protector

[29] Khafi Khan reports it as "Fath Daras," merely a variant form.

of the poor and the weak against all tyrants and robbers, and promised all who cooperated in the Khalsa a share in the fruits of conquest. The common people flocked to him for food and blessing, but something of an inner crisis developed over the sharing of the spoil. There had been among the Sikhs a special class called chaudhris, or those who were entitled by custom to a chauth, or "one-fourth" of the loot of conquest, but Banda was promising a share to all! Some compromise, therefore, was made and the campaign got under way, whose military features were brought to our attention[30] by the Moslem Khafi Khan. One series of raids included the capture of "the hated town of Samana" (which is obviously the Sirhind of Khafi Khan's account), where the executioners of Teg Bahadur and the younger sons of Gobind lived, and yielded Rs. 20 million ($7,000,000?) in cash and kind.

Banda's men lacked elephants, artillery and horses, and only a few were armed with matchlocks. Elephants, of course, might have been a liability, on the whole, but might have had symbolic value. Hindu rulers employed them customarily, but they have never been of military value to the penetrating Moslems—except as they were usually embarrassing to their Hindu owners in their fights with hostile Moslems! The early Sikh successes under Banda were achieved, in fact, principally on foot, with arrows, spears and swords for arms. Nor did their equipment improve considerably, or become sufficient to meet really formidable Mughal opposition. "Three classes of men" engaged in the campaign, says Ganda Singh, namely, "true Sikhs" serving in a spirit of devotion and self-sacrifice and not for love of "booty," "paid soldiers" supplied by neighboring chieftains (e.g., the Phul rajas who many years afterward joined the "Sikh Confederacy") and "irregulars" who were none other than reckless robbers or impoverished and greedy peasants.

[30] P. 212, above.

Indeed there were still others, also. Certain Gujjars who joined the ranks in the neighborhood of Saharanpur and Jalalabad, declared themselves to be "followers of Guru Nanak" styled "Nanakprasht," or worshipers of Nanak. These, of course, were actually Nanakpanthis, "the party of Nanak's way," such as may still be found in various parts of India from the United Provinces to the Central Provinces and Bengal. And there were still other "Sikhs," the Ramrais, or party of Ram Rai, for example, who were at least passive resisters of the campaign, and against whom Banda was obliged to take some action.

Banda made Sadhaura, a town in the Ambala district, his headquarters, reconditioned a fort nearby "among the steeps of the Himalayas," adopted a royal seal with the legend, "Kettle, sword, victory, enduring favor of Nanak and Guru Gobind Singh." He struck coins inscribed with the names of Nanak and Gobind, and bearing on the reverse the legend, "Lohgarh, model city, ornament of the happy throne, and refuge of the world." He proclaimed a "new era" with the abolition of the zamindari land system and the substitution for it of a system of tithes. And he made arrangements for the payment of monthly salaries to officials. It was all short-lived, however, as we have learned already. For a while the emperor, Bahadur Shah, had lived outside the Delhi neighborhood and in the south at his capital, Daulatabad, in the western Ghats, until he had effected an understanding with the warlike Rajputs of Rajputana, of whom he stood in awe. Then he returned to the north and began his campaign against the Sikhs, which for many Moslems was a "holy war" (jihad). Some mullas, for example, who were Shi'i Moslems, planted near the 'Idgah mosque in Lahore their green banner, the "hydari flag," and summoned the faithful to jihad. Khafi Khan has told us that the Sikhs themselves regarded their "hostile" acts against the Moslems as "religiously meritorious."

Banda was to all Moslems, of course, an "unbeliever," was a "dog" to Sunnis, an "impostor" to Shi'i mullas, an "untouchable" to Hindu brahmans, a "rebel" to the Mughal government itself, and he was to many disaffected Sikhs, mostly sahajdaris, only a "false guru." But to Khalsa Sikhs, the Singhs, especially, he is now remembered as a man of valor, cool in the face of death, a champion of the cause of sweepers and pariahs but one who found favor with the well-born, also, a leader who would himself have chosen to propagate the faith by persuasion rather than by force of arms, a Sikh who "led a pure life, true to the rahit" or "code," of the Khalsa, who never cut his hair,[31] never used tobacco or ate halal (unlawful meat), who was never guilty of immoral intercourse with women (although he may have wanted, at one time, a second wife while the first still lived), and whose defeat at last in warfare was not due to any defect in himself or in the cause he led, but to overwhelming odds against him.

Banda's death, nevertheless, left the Sikhs without a generally recognized leader and the question of the guruship still somewhat indeterminate—although, as we have seen already, this question was answering itself by a gradual but sure process. Meanwhile the unshepherded people scattered for their lives when danger threatened them, but retained allegiance to the general cause, cherished the memory of their gurus, of the line of ten, especially—Banda's status, however, had not been finally determined—observed the appointed times of prayer, nourished an inner devotion to truths they held as revelation, and kept kindled the fires of hope—and of vengeance, also, for they looked to their rehabilitation at the further cost of war. The Mughals took a

[31] The claim may plausibly be made that Nanak held it man's religious duty to preserve his hair.

frightful toll of them. Meanwhile, through executions, some of the weaker Sikhs themselves lost heart and there were some backsliders, too, but the purged remnant itself persevered with courage, refusing to give up swords for staves, drums for alms-bowls, and trumpets for the rebeck.

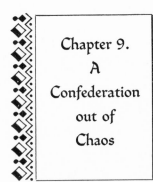

## Chapter 9. A Confederation out of Chaos

The Khalsa had actually been caught between the upper and the nether millstones. The lower stone was Hinduism, for the most part static, resting on the basic earth, and the upper stone that turned and ground was in the hands of Moslems. The figure holds not only for comparisons of theory, but for mere geographical location, also. Sikhism had sprung up in a middle region between Hinduism and Islam—or was it born in a sort of no-man's-land? At any rate, the form it had most conspicuously assumed, that of the Khalsa, was being ground to fragments in the first decades of the eighteenth century, fragments with, nevertheless, some political significance which fell in their turn amidst other elements more exclusively religious. Sikhism became a conglomerate of sects and parties—but sects sometimes have saved a faith, and parties now and then have preserved an order against a better day. It was to be so among the Sikhs, and their tragic century reproduced in miniature that fragmentation and diversity which have often seemed inevitable and not without some final value in the progressive process of religion in the life of man. Major faiths have had so many "sects that brawl," Christianity perhaps more than any other, but they have also had divisions through whose sincere devotion the total life has been renewed. Sikhs had their "differences" (firqa) and their different panths or "paths."[1] Perhaps these have not always been sects in the strictest sense, that is, with the connotation

[1] Details of these many "parties" have been gathered from many sources, including Ganda Singh, Cunningham, Macauliffe, Khazan Singh, and at first hand, altogether too numerous for specific mention.

of a "cutting or tearing" that *hurts* someone, notably those themselves who are cut off or excommunicated; but Sikhs have had divisions which have suffered in disunion. These have been matters not so much of distinction in creed and revelation as they have had to do with men, with influential and distinguished leaders.

Consider the Bandeis, for example, "the party of Banda," known also as the Bandapanth, or "those of the Banda-way." This is not the first party in point of time, or one of unusual importance, but is a group formed out of the emergency attending Banda—the simplest sort of partisanship which sheer emergency produces. The Bandeis emphasized their difference not only from ordinary Sikhs, but from many members of the Khalsa, also. There may have been some question of expediency in their conduct. For a while, as we know already, there was a price on the head of every Sikh, on members of the Khalsa, in particular. An "imperial edict" was for a brief time in force calling for the extirpation of the Sikhs. They especially were marked men who wore beards and topknots and distinctive party symbols. Ordinary Sikhs were allowed from about 1718 on to resume their normal life in their several villages, but long after that the Mughals carried on a campaign of suppression, making martyrs of all they slew—in the estimation, at least, of the Sikhs themselves. Where many of the Sikhs were executed in Lahore in 1745 has been known to their fellows as Shahid Ganj, the "place of witness" (*i.e.*, of martyrdom). Some Bandeis now and then were martyrs. But the "Banda men" had other causes of complaint besides the Mughal persecution, such issues, for example, as the legitimacy of the guruship, the regularity of administration, the personal habits and marks of Sikhs, and temple and gurdwara management. Bandeis had complaints beyond the mere rejection of their once proposed battle-cry of "Fatah Darshan"! They were not committed completely to the kakkas. They objected to the eating of meat and confined themselves to vegetables—except onions. They even counted fish as meat, and preserved a taboo on meat and fish and onions. Regular Sikhs have eaten meat, fish and any vegetable. Bandeis fell into the habit of arranging marriages within their own ranks exclusively. Although they did not repudiate the authority of the ten gurus and of the *Adi Granth*, they came to insist on living under their own mahant or spiritual superior; and the great issue which ultimately brought them into clear relief as a party with a "difference" was that of temple management, the administration of the central shrine, the Darbar Sahib, in Amritsar; and their failure to secure control of this central sanctuary was more decisive in their fortunes than any idiosyncrasies of garb or diet or domestic management.

Those Sikhs were uncommonly conspicuous who controlled the Darbar Sahib, so great was its prestige, and Amritsar was all the more the central city of the Sikhs with the waning of the glory of Anandpur which did not recover from the damage done it by the Mughals in 1704, although the Sodhi Sikhs themselves had partially rebuilt it. The Bandeis made a bid for Darbar Sahib sovereignty and precipitated a crisis in 1721 during the Baisakhi festival by laying claim to a proportion of the funds of the temple and the kitchen. The various gurus had had charge of these funds and had relied on them for their own expenses and for the maintenance of the public kitchen whence guru ka langar, or "guru's victuals," were dispensed, and after the virtual termination of the guru-line the funds had been administered by a committee of the Khalsa. And now the Bandeis contested this arrangement, assembling on one occasion at the Darshani gateway under their own chief, Mahant Singh, and making their demands known to the Khalsa party. Fortunately the dispute was arbitrated by Mani Singh, of the committee of temple-management, in consultation with Mahant Singh, with only a minority of the Bandeis finally dissenting. The dissenting few were themselves expelled from the temple precincts, but were never fully excommunicated. They took up residence in Jammu State, south of Kashmir, in a village beside the Chenab river, to which they gave the name of Dera Baba Banda Singh. Long afterward they were recognized officially as loyal Sikhs by the great Sikh maharaja Ranjit Singh who made them certain grants-in-aid, their partisan activities had long since ceased, although they had preserved among themselves some sense of "difference."

Many other parties actually antedated the Bandeis, and some of these survived them. They varied in importance and effectiveness, even as they varied in their emphases on things religious and political. Several minor groups seem to have been more intent on politics, if not on matters personal, among whom we may cite, for example, the Handalis, the Ramraiyas, the Mine of Pirthi Chand, the Dhirmaliye and the Masandis.

The Handalis, as they came to be known, were dissenters from the uncertain days of the third guru, Amar Das (d. 1574), who were at last, about 1640, completely ostracized by reason of a free-love alliance between Bidhi Chand, their chief, who was an official of the Jandyala gurdwara, and a Moslem woman. He retaliated by proclaiming forthwith a party of his own and by the formation of yet another cult, for which he compiled his own edition of the *Granth* and a janamsakhi, or "life" of Nanak, in which he portrayed Nanak's own free-love with a Moslem mistress! And he recorded in this "life" a journey Nanak made, supposedly, to the "true land" of the "bright god" Niranjan where he became aware of the pre-eminence of Kabir the humble weaver, and where he learned of the coming of God's special messenger "Handal." Bidhi Chand subscribed to these revelations and instituted at Jandyala with himself as the expected messenger the worship of Niranjan. He gained a desultory and disreputable following and was succeeded as head of the cult by a son of his born to a Moslem mistress. The party became more and more Islamic, took part with Moslems sometimes in the destruction of Sikh documents and properties, and were finally penalized and dispossessed by Ranjit Singh.

The Ramraiyas (Ramrais) sprang from Ram Rai, son of guru Har Rai by a concubine, and maintained themselves in dissent in the vicinity of Dehra Dun[2] with no peculiar doctrines of their own apart from Ram Rai's own pretension to the guruship. Guru Gobind Singh had some reason to think they were responsible for some of his father Teg Bahadur's difficulties and had acquiesced in his execution, and, consequently, he once dealt severely with them. Banda Singh, also, held them in contempt and once expelled some of them from evening prayers for what he deemed an insult to the memory of Gobind Singh.

The "mine" or "contemptibles" of Pirthi Chand were designated thus by guru Arjun, his brother, who denounced them for their attempt to poison him in the interest of Pirthi Chand's own claim to the guruship. Mi-ne, etymologically, described primarily an ox made unsightly by drooping horns that curved over its face. These contemptibles settled south of Firuzpur in the neighborhood of Kot Har along the Sutlej river, maintaining opposition to guru Arjun. Perhaps they and the Dhirmaliye, also Arjun's opponents, were actually one and the same group, for Dhir Mal was a name sometimes applied to Pirthi Chand.

The Masandis were at first personal agents or deputy revenue officers of Arjun selected from the Masand clan of khatris. Their special task was the collection of the offerings preparatory to the annual assembly, but they came to think of themselves as a body of hereditary stewards to the guru

[2] Macauliffe, I, p. lii, mentions a temple of theirs there.

and to arrogate to themselves something of the guru's personal prestige in their intimate relations with his household. They actually resisted later on the authority of guru Gobind Singh and he, in turn, denounced them—and dismissed them, all but two or three in whom he had some confidence.

These preceding four or five lesser groups were by no means comparable with such major groups as, for example, the Nanakpanthis, the Udasis, the Akalis or Nihangs or Shahidis (known by all three names), the Nirmalas and the Sewapanthis.

The Nanakpanthis have been on the whole fairly numerous, although never closely organized. They may indeed be the very oldest "sikhs," if, as they claim, they stem from immediate connection with guru Nanak. They have followed vaguely the panth or path of Nanak, without the establishment of any maths or monasteries. The majority of them have professed no blood connection with the guru, although some others who call themselves Nanakputras, or "sons of Nanak," and some, also, called Sahibzadas, or "sons of the master," have claimed blood-kinship with him. Some Nanakpanthis, found among the predatory Gujjars of Nanauta, styled themselves Nanakprashts, or "worshipers of Nanak," and still others, among the Sidh Sain of Mandi, called themselves Nanakgharana, "Nanak's household." Adherents of the group, in general, were enlisted in central India, Bihar and Bengal, mostly, and all together made up an indefinite allegiance whose object was only slightly less vague than that of a later people of those parts called Satnamis. They make use of Nanak's name, employ some technical Sikh terms and a few of the Sikh prayer formulae, but are in no other way at last related to the Sikhs.

The Udasis, whose acquaintance we have made already by pilgrim visitation, are the oldest specific subdivision of the Sikh religion in actual *operation* still as a clear-cut group. Representing a certain state of mind, cherishing an intimate

THE ARJUN DEVA MELA, LAHORE, LOOKING TOWARD THE RIVER RAVI

THE ARJUN DEVA MELA, LOOKING TOWARD THE WHITE GURDWARA AND THE IMPOSING TOMB OF RANJIT SINGH OUTSIDE THE FORT, LAHORE

connection with Nanak through his son Sri Chand, they developed some objectivity and set up an *elective* guruship whose incumbents would exemplify, they said, Nanak's own indifference to the world. They emphasized udas or a "sorrowful" condition of lonely isolation from the world—or was it in token of separation from a sorrowful *world?* Nanak's own teaching and example gave some occasion, as we have seen, for their point of view, but the third guru, Amar Das, questioned specifically such interpretation, and tended to refuse to recognize them as true Sikhs. There was no separation, however, in his day, nor did Udasis become numerous. Their principles failed to find much favor among the various active classes who composed the growing Sikh community, and the Singhs, especially, to whom the welfare of the Khalsa was of more concern than life itself held isolation to be futile. Udasis, of course, had no political ambition, nor did they exert influence in affairs of state. Gobind Singh resented their inaction and classed them with various "quietists," for example, with the siggum, or "head-plucked" Jains (who plucked out their hair lest it harbor insects which might perish there) and with kan-kata, or "ear-cropped" yogis, an ascetic, ear-marked type of world-renouncers.

The Udasis, in the end, became virtually a monkish order of those who had given up their families (cf. the latter ashramas[3] of the Hindu way) and would not remarry. They wore their hat uncut, or cropped it, or shaved it off, as they themselves might choose. They wore caps (unless, as a few did, they wore their hair in tufts) and reddish dhotis[4] in the Hindu manner, dyed red ofttimes in contrast with the blue of the keshdari Singh. They rejected the *Granth* of Gobind Singh and confined themselves to the *Adi Granth.* The psalms and prayers of Nanak, in particular, were preserved

[3] In these two latter "stages" the Hindu has become definitely, irrevocably ascetic.

[4] The dhoti is the garment covering the middle body.

in their simple ritual of worship, but some of their rites reflected Hinduism, especially, and they did not object entirely to images. They used the tilak, wore the janeu, or sacred cord, and the mala, or rosary, like any Hindu, and they observed the Hindu rites of birth, marriage, death, cremation, and the postmortem ceremony of shraddh.[5] After the burning of the corpse, the ashes of it were deposited in a samadh or tomb, after the custom of the yogi and sannyasi. Some of the stricter members of the order actually allowed themselves to be castrated to avoid impurity of conduct.

There was another order, the Nirmalas, "those without blemish," who emphasized *as a group* the virtue of personal purity, but without recourse to physical disfigurement. These Nirmalas arose with one Bir Singh in the days of Gobind Singh, when such virtue was in peculiar need of emphasis, and they came to be known and very highly respected for their habits, being quite sincere and genuine, and unlike certain earlier sutre or "pure ones"—a sheer euphemism in this instance—whose habits were a stench and a byword among decent Sikhs. The Nirmalas at first wore white at all times in token of their worthy principles, were active in many Panjab villages, and maintained a large establishment about the temple itself in Amritsar. It was not long, however, until a change occurred within the order—without compromise of the ideal of purity, however. They organized under a mahant of their own, with a council which they designated the Akhara, because it "wrestled" with their order's problems. They took to wearing reddish ochre gowns similar to those worn by Udasis and Hindu sadhus—with whom, on that account, they were readily confused. And they assumed other Hindu ways: preferred, for example, to read the *Vedantasutras* and other Hindu books, practiced Hindu rites of birth and death—but with no Hindu mantras

[5] Literally, faith and a rite which testifies to the same.

at their weddings—and included Hindu shrines in their rounds of pilgrimage. As a matter of fact, their weddings were few, because generally the Nirmalas were celibates and lived in monasteries. But they did not beg as Hindu sadhus did, being more self-respecting, like the Jains, and they disregarded caste in the manner of all good Sikhs.

The Sewapanthis, "those of the service-way," were very circumstantial in their origin. During the Mughal siege of Anandpur a certain water-carrier by the name of Kanhaiya attempted to be neutral and to serve both sides impartially. On one occasion he came into the presence of Gobind, who administered to him a rebuke. At which Kanhaiya quoted some words of Gobind's own to the effect that sewa, "service," was something meritorious *in itself*, and that, anyway, all men were really equal in the sight of God. The guru thereupon commended him and gave him leave to go, and the humble servant gained, in consequence, a following among Sikhs, especially, with his theory of disinterested toil—and with his refusal of gifts or gratuities in return for service—as also with his theory of a non-partisan ministry both in war and peace. A rich money-lender, Adan Shah by name, once joined this group and subsidized it and the Sewapanthis were often called, accordingly, Adanshahis.

The Akalis-Nihangs-Shahidis are by all odds the most important group which began to function in the eighteenth century—with an importance, in fact, lasting well into the present century. Call them "immortals" (akalis), "reckless" (nihang), or "witnesses" (shahidis, martyrs), they were always *militant* ascetics. War and religion to them were by no means incompatible, they were all soldiers of Akal "the Timeless"—which is God's true name to them—as if he had said to them that sooner or later under certain circumstances his loyal subjects must resort to war. They first appeared about 1690 under one Man Singh, in the days of Gobind Singh, contemporary with Bir Singh's Nirmalas, and antecedent to the formation of the Khalsa; and they became the most ardent and able defenders of the Khalsa—against any innovations, for example. When Banda proposed the cry of "Fateh Darshan," they drowned it with their own cries. They were ever ready for a demonstration on the Khalsa's behalf, and readily associated politics, as well as warfare, with religion. They were zealous in Anandpur after its rebuilding, where memories of Gobind stirred them, where they might recall that Man Singh, their founder, had borne Gobind on his back through the very line of Mughal sentries to the house of Gulaba, when the guru's feet were themselves too sore to bear him, and that in the last extremity when the guru's final escape was necessary, Man Singh and other faithful singhs bore the ostensible "corpse" of Gobind on a litter toward the burning ghat, while Daya Singh walked beside it waving the chauri fan above it and reciting from the requiem ritual.

And they were zealous in Amritsar, were these Akalis, often assuming the leadership in worship. They convened there in 1764 the first Sikh gurumatta or diet, and were often truly feared not only by the common people but by the sirdars or "governors." In the days later on of the Sikh Confederacy they were virtually a misl or administrative unit in themselves. Their zeal frowned emphatically on Hinduism. Following Gobind's own example, they rejected the Hindu rites of birth, marriage, death, etc.; and, although they had in their own way foresworn the world, they were ever ready to fight in the open as khatris, or "soldiers," of Akal. It was then with "reckless" abandon that they could become shahidis, "witnesses." They were accustomed to discipline, could fight singly or in companies. They had their own distinctive uniform of blue (a Pathan or Turkish blue) —once resisting Banda's specific order to abandon it! The most distinctive devotee[6] among them has since worn a blue

[6] See illustration No. 5.

coat or tunic tied about the waist with an ochre-colored sash, a lofty, conical turban of blue cloth held together by a steel discus, steel bracelets on his wrist, an iron chain across one shoulder and an emblematic sword at his side (emblematic, but real enough for tragedy on occasion). But this of late has been the distinctive garb of the exclusively *religious* devotee, although at once reminiscent of the Khalsa uniform in action. The headquarters of the order has been the Akal Takht,[7] opposite the temple in Amritsar.

The Akalis served themselves the chosen heirs of the peculiarly Gobindi tradition and ultimately rallied many other Sikhs besides to build the Khalsa of Gobind's dream, whereby some active unity was forged at last out of the many parties which had gone their several ways. Therein politics comes to the fore, with special reference to the Moslems against whom the Sikhs contended then as a definite "third religion," to use their own expression. Sikhism as a religion would build itself, therefore, a house of state, all ties with Islam being at last severed and those with Hindus disregarded.

From the middle of the eighteenth century bands of Sikhs, representatives of various parties, were everywhere in the Manjha region of the Panjab and in the Doab region below the Sutlej river. They lived precariously, but with a steady access of prestige—sometimes adding to it even in defeat, when the victors deemed it wise to favor them with terms. Many members of these parties, even while a price was on their heads, boldly visited Amritsar for worship at the Darbar Sahib. Sikhs suffered, for example, with the rest of northern India during the six invasions, 1747-1767, of the Persian monarch Ahmad Shah, and were once defeated by him in 1762 near Ludhiana with a loss of twelve to twenty thousand men—the figures vary, but Sikh tradition calls the rout the *Ghulu Ghara*, the "great disaster." The Sikhs, however,

[7] See illustration No. 6.

recovered from this, their ranks filled up again and their spirits rose with ever new opportunities for war. They had likewise tested out their mettle meanwhile against other Indians in the Panjab proper. For two years, 1756-1758, during an interval between Ahmad Shah's incursions, the Khalsa leader, Jassa Singh, had seized and occupied Lahore, had officially proclaimed the Khalsa and had issued coins in its name. And soon after the "great disaster" they made their power further manifest in that very neighborhood by plundering Kasur, where the wife and two sons of Gobind had been slain, defying the Moslem rulers there, meanwhile—and distributing their loot widely and generously among the villagers below the Sutlej in token of their good will and their prowess.

There was indeed a gathering bitterness toward the Moslems—the hated "Turk," as they kept calling them.[8] So bitter was the Sikh reaction against their former masters, that sometimes when a mosque was included in a region captured, it was razed at once, and its former custodians were forced to wash its platform and foundation stones with the blood of *hogs*. And there was increasing strength as well as bitterness, and in 1764, on the very eve of Ahmad Shah's last raid, a committee of the Akalis undertook to call a gurumatta, or diet, in Amritsar, to proclaim the independence of the Sikh state and religion. This was a seal of larger and more inclusive unity among the Sikhs, a representative assembly sitting as a committee of the whole (sarbat) and

[8] Political adjustment by Sikhs was sometimes sought by a doctrine of two sovereignties, the spiritual rule of Nanak and the temporal rule of Babur the Turk, all men being creatures of God himself (cf. Khazan Singh, II, p. 494), but Gobind is once credited with saying that he had cause to keep himself aloof from both the Hindu and the Turk in their absurdity (*ibid.*, I, p. 179), and Nanak could be made to say "Hindu Turk din sabh kure" (Hindu and Turk religions are both false)—Rag Asa.

taking counsel (matta) in the name of *God* the Guru—this was indeed a gurumatta, a theocracy.

Not that unity was by this time actually and permanently achieved! It could not be achieved merely by a proclamation. However, there was an effective leadership by a party, rather than by a single individual, and God himself was Guru. Diversity remained: varieties of blood and blood-relationships, of official prerogatives and ranks, of vested interests in land-holdings—and the peculiar status and activities of converts to the order. Most Sikhs had once, of course, been Hindus, and many of them cherished feelings with respect to inter-dining (some of them continuing to be reluctant to join in the common meal, the ritual communion, at the diet in Amritsar). Some Sikhs were madhabis, or Moslem converts, *i.e.*, converts from Islam, and some had been "untouchables." Many were untutored—in fact, few were educated men, including even those who had come of the kayastha, or "writer," class, while some, like Nanak and Gobind, were indeed literate in several languages. The more literate would, naturally, fill the posts of granthis, or "readers," and take charge of the services of worship in the temples of Amritsar and Tarn Taran and in the gurdwaras in the villages, but there was no guarantee at all of uniformity of religious education. There were, in fact, two *Granths* on the very altar before which the gurumatta met, the "book" of Nanak and the "book" of Gobind Singh, and although all Sikhs recognized the former, the authority of the latter was limited to Singhs.

Sikh unity was at this time that of emergency and action, rather than that of theory and culture. There was theory, to be sure, in the movement as a faith, but there was yet no culture adequate to afford it a unified expression. Sikh culture was that mainly of the poor Jat cultivator and it had little to commend it in comparison with brahmanical and Islamic culture, whether that of learning or of art. In time some Sikhs became woodcarvers, for example, of extraordinary skill, whose doors and windows in several old Sikh towns are admirable examples of the handicraft, and others acquired skill in a certain imitative architecture and design, but Sikhs long remained chiefly men of action—the keshdari Khalsa type, especially, who took pride in stubborn courage. These held in high esteem men who could pierce a thick tree with a sharp shaft from a strong bow, and who could slay a tiger with one sure stroke of a swift blade. They relied on strength of arm to protect their fields and herds and families. Cattle-lifting was an honorable profession among them—and in their many raids, we should observe, they seldom violated womanhood or tortured captives.

Unity of action came at last by way of parties, bands and ranks called misls, "equals."[9] There was contest among them, to be sure, and they were not altogether *equal*, but rather something feudal, and yet, nevertheless, there was a merging finally productive of comparative stability. Political occasion and incentive combined with religious zeal into an ethical and social constitution. Each misl—there were about a dozen misls—bore its own distinctive title, and had its own sirdar or chieftain who gathered followers from local, nearby villages. The misls varied in importance with the ability and prowess of the sirdars, the numbers of their followers, their capacity for forage (perhaps we dare say pillage, too) and their contributions to the general funds.

The Phulkia misl belonged to the Malwa Doab region below the Sutlej river, and their Patiala branch acquired most distinction. The other misls belonged above the river in the Panjab and were composed, in general, of Sikhs of the Manjha region, the Bhangi misl being in the lead (see below). Each misl under its own earthly leader preserved some independence and often acted on its own initiative,

[9] *Cf.* the accounts of these in our many sources, including Cunningham, pp. 106-110; Khazan Singh, I, pp. 264-301.

and misls now and then opposed each other, but all were linked together in a loose confederation which called for common action against a common foe—against the Moslems, generally. Only one conspicuously religious panth, the Akali-Nihang-Shahidi, was in effect a misl, although it was not so styled, because it professed complete independence of any earthly leaders, except as they acted in devotion to Akal. The Akalis (to use the one designation only) were actually, after all, a cross-section of the Sikh community and were a sort of interdenominational constituency in an exceptional position to assume the lead among confederates. This character, together with inherent strength, placed them in the presidency of the general diet. They more than any others conserved the memory of the martyrs and exemplified the role of martyrdom. As recently as 1921-1925 they engaged in ominous political demonstrations against British rule and had figured previously in the "massacre" in the Jallianwala Bagh.[10]

The ten more exclusively separate, political misls under earthly leadership were these:

AHLUWALIA. Its sirdar was a Jat distiller who rallied about him his own "people" (ahl, an Arabic word much in use by Moslems, often with a religious connotation: there were, for example, ahlu'l-lah, "people of God," saints, faqirs, and there were walis, friends of God and saints. Ahluwalia may indeed connote some fervor).

From these "people" came later on the house of Kapurthala, a leading ruling family of the Panjab.

BHANGI. Its chief was a Jat peasant who was himself a hemp-addict, as some of his people, also, were. Such is the very meaning of the name—bhang is "hemp" and a hemp-concoction has been very widely drunk, although with the Sikhs it was not a ritual act, as it was, for instance, with the hashishin, hemp-infuriated "assassins" of Crusader times among the Syrian mountains.

DALIWALA. A band gathered about a khatri shop-keeper whose principal commodity was dal, or "rice" in commercial form, or other

[10] *Cf.* pp. 32f. above.

kinds of "split" foods, such as peas and lentils. A dal-wala was a dealer in pulse, and there may have been such an interest among most of the members of this misl.

FYZALPURIA. Its sirdar was a Jat land-owner who assumed the title of nawab, a "nabob" or governor. He boasted that he had slain with his own hand five hundred Moslems. His people, needless to say, were Singhs! The name may be merely that of faisalpur, a "settlement" or a "division" in a particular location.

KANHAIYA. The name is that of a Jat peasant—merely a proper name, except that otherwise it was sometimes among Hindus a name applied to Krishna.

NAKKAI. A group under a Jat peasant of Nakka, a village southwest of Lahore.

NISHANWALA. Its leader, whatever his given name, had been a nishan, or "standard," bearer in a previous Khalsa army, and this group may have rallied under this nishan.

PHULKIA. Its sirdar was a Bhatti Rajput whose holdings lay below the Sutlej. He was in a position to assemble an imposing following. From his line have come the "Phulkian chieftains," Patiala, Nabha and Jhind, who have figured prominently among the Indian aristocracy, Patiala being pre-eminent among the Sikhs.

RAMGARHIA. This group dwelt in the Amritsar neighborhood and derived their name from a garh, or "fort," which they built and called Ram-garh, which, somewhat enlarged subsequently, still stands outside the city's western wall.

SUKHARCHAKIA. Who indeed was he whose name this misl bore? He may have been a Jat, or a Bhatti Rajput, or even a Sansi gypsy—it doesn't matter much, for the name is best remembered in connection with Maharaja Ranjit Singh, a scion of this house, the most successful of all the misl leaders.[11]

To an outside observer before the close of the eighteenth century Sikhism was a loose collection of misls and sirdars, of panths and mahants, and the Sikhs all together were a small minority of the total population. Politics among them were more apparent than religion; in fact, politics and warfare had, it seemed, preserved religion, which otherwise might not have lasted in the abstract. But the close observer

[11] See below, pp. 238f.

would have seen that this loose confederacy was, nonetheless, dominated by an ideal, a most compelling factor, none other than the ideal of the Khalsa—and religion was one, perhaps the chief, of its ingredients. And within the province of religion there were considerations of human character and conduct. The men of action who were meeting the emergency moved in a field so large and varied that no less than a three-fold standard should be applied to its appraisal, namely, politics, religion and morality.

Politics, perhaps, is pre-eminently man's affair, while morality is, doubtless, God's, for good is good and right is right, whatever men may strive to make of them. Right never can be wrong, nor goodness evil, in the providence of God who must himself be good and right, no matter to what variant degree men may misrepresent him. Politics may be good or bad, according to men's standards—there is no divine standard of the state as such. Morality, as God's affair, is morality or—nothing; and although men's conduct may be weighed in part by men's own standards, the final judge is God. Religion, on the other hand, has to do with both God and man. It may be good, it may be bad, although true religion in the end is good, because it leads to God who intends to be discovered in and through it. Man too often has made religion his own affair, even constructing God in man's own image, while professing to have had it all by revelation—that is, from an objective source, he says. It is not at all surprising that sincere men have often tried to get out of politics, and away from religion and come somehow face to face with goodness, truth and right. Other sincere men have tried to integrate politics and religion with morality—and the worth of statecraft, creed and ritual has varied as men have more or less succeeded in this very integration.

Sikhs faced these very issues, but had yet realized no one of them sufficiently to understand fully their mission as a people in the world. Nor had their demonstration yet convinced their neighbors, who insisted on applying to their movement the three-fold test of value.

Sikhism had yet to be a state, whatever its religion and its morals; and its leader in the venture was Maharaja Ranjit Singh—in whom still another earthly leader was to play his part.

Ranjit Singh[12] became in 1791 at eleven years of age the chieftain of the Sukharchakia misl in succession to his father, who had himself succeeded his own father, the founder of the misl and its first sirdar. Ranjit's father, actually, had died when the lad was eight years old, and the misl had been governed for three years by his mother and a minister (diwan), while Ranjit himself was cared for by his mother-in-law-to-be, a woman of the Kanhaiya misl whose daughter had already been betrothed to him. Ranjit owed to his mother-in-law his early induction into the office of sirdar of his own misl, and he soon thereafter had ample opportunity to demonstrate his powers, proving that Ranjit and peculiar fortune were well met.

During Ranjit's earlier years Zaman Shah, the king of Afghanistan, gained sufficient control of the Panjab to count it a province of his kingdom. The Sikh misls offered him no telling opposition. When Ranjit became sirdar of the Sukharchakias, he, in fact, put himself and his misl at Zaman Shah's disposal, and in 1797 he was made governor of the province, with Lahore his capital. In 1799, in Ranjit's twentieth year, the king made Lahore over to him as a royal grant. What was the meaning of it all? To a large extent it was the game of politics—international diplomacy in miniature. Lahore was actually within the sphere of influence of the

[12] *Cf.* L. H. Griffin, *Ranjit Singh* (Oxford, 1911); N. K. Sinha, *Rise of Sikh Power* (Calcutta, 1936); Capt. Murray's *Ranjit Singh* (ed. Prinsep, 1834), and especially Cunningham-Garrett's *History*, pp. 125-168.

Bhangi misl who ruled Amritsar, and Ranjit's "governorship" and "grant" were, therefore, only nominal. To make them more effectual, having Afghanistan's good will already, an alliance was arranged between the Sukharchakia and Kanhaiya misls through which pressure was exerted on the Bhangis, enabling Ranjit thus to assume control over both Amritsar and Lahore—thirty miles apart. Thus far successful, he soon thereafter commenced negotiations with Ahluwalia, within whose jurisdiction lay Tarn Taran, once the home of guru Arjun, and the second city of the Sikhs. He visited the shrine for worship and exchanged turbans with the Ahluwalia sirdar there in token of alliance. Then he linked the Nakkai misl closely to himself by marrying—as a *second* wife—a daughter of the sirdar of the Nakkais. By 1805, at the age of twenty-five, he had "arrived," was the most conspicuous leader of the Sikhs. That year, he celebrated in Lahore, his capital, the great annual festival of Hola (the Holi of the Hindus), making of it an affair of state as well as of religion.

He had no fear of Hindus. Several rajas of the lower hills of the Himalayas had challenged him as early as 1803 and 1804, and he had easily repulsed them. He could ignore the Moslems; they made no serious trouble for him. He may very well have been—and maybe *was*—more concerned about the English of whose warlike prowess he had learned by 1805 from a certain Maratha, Jaswant Rao, a fugitive from Bombay. He had learned that by the treaty of Bassein on December 31, 1802, English influence had been established at the very heart of the previously formidable Maratha confederacy. Jaswant Rao, now in flight and seeking refuge with the Sikhs, had thought to teach the English just exactly what a Maratha war was like—and for his pains had been chased by the English General Lake up to and across the Sutlej into Ranjit Singh's dominions! Not only in distant Bombay were the English settled, they had been yet longer in Calcutta and Madras, and now they were within effective reach of the thin border of the Sutlej. But had not guru Teg Bahadur himself seen them coming![13]

Ranjit yet had time, however, to imitate them, having somehow learned of their accomplishments—including a dramatic lesson at his very doorstep (see below). And in this he had the good will of his people, with prestige, also, among his own. He must have seemed to them a kind of messianic figure for their present need. In his earlier years he was robust, a skilful and untiring horseman and a good tactician, altogether an able, fascinating person, in spite of shortness of stature and—in time—in spite of features that were pock-marked and imperfect eyes—his left eye was weak and his right eye disproportionately large and capable of a piercing, fiery glance. In these earlier years he was alert, quick of apperception, and knew how to bear himself with dignity. He was appreciative of the opportunity he had for learning, acquired command of Panjabi and Hindustani for public purposes and learned a great deal about Indian history and affairs.

This was the dramatic lesson: a British ambassador came from Delhi to Amritsar to discuss boundaries with the Sikhs, and brought with him a guard five hundred strong, mostly Moslem sipahis under several English officers. He stayed two months, during which the annual Shi'i Moslem ceremonial of Muharram came due.

(Muharram, we may explain, is an elaborate "sacred" season extending through the first ten days of the Moslem year. For the Sunnis the new year has some significance as such, but for the Shiites these first days commemorate the martyrdom of Husayn, son of Mohammed's daughter Fatimah by his cousin 'Ali to whom she was married in Madinah. For the Sunnis the season includes a day in which

[13] *Cf.* Khazan Singh, I, pp. 161f.

they celebrate the birth of Adam, the creation of Eve, and the origin of heaven, hell, the pen and fate. For Shiites it calls for lamentation which culminates in special, spectacular exercises of devotion which may clash with their Sunni kinsmen of the faith, since Husayn lost his life at the hands of Sunnis. Taziahs (this is a Persian word for "consolation") are built and carried in procession, representing the tombs of Husayn and of his brother Hasan at Karbala, not far from Baghdad. Tabuts or arks, also, are made and carried to represent the litter with its body of the slain Husayn.)

The ambassador's guard, therefore, would celebrate Muharram, both the Shiites and the Sunnis oblivious of any hostile meaning in the act. But the Sikhs in those parts registered objection. They objected especially to the "tombs" and arks, although not to the mere element of martyrdom. This gave an opportunity for crisis, for Moslems merely in the presence of the Darbar Sahib had already generated tension. The Akalis, in particular, objected—and Sikhs in the neighborhood numbered several thousand. A clash occurred, but was soon over—to the Sikhs' dismay, we may observe. The several hundred sipahis put the several thousand Sikhs readily to rout! It was enough of a lesson to the alert Ranjit to prompt him immediately to undertake a reorganization of all his military forces. He had employed cavalry almost altogether, his one respected arm of service; his infantry were little better than camp-followers, and his guns were negligible. He organized, therefore, artillery and infantry. He welcomed khatri Hindus and Moslems to his ranks, established them in separate units, providing Sikh predominance in every branch of service, and engaged European officers to drill them all. He made himself the supreme commander, the European officers themselves being subordinated to his own authority.

He never, however, was at war with England, both parties

being content to treat with one another, and Ranjit willing to recognize the British "paramountcy." It was by that principle that Britain then kept herself in virtual control of Indian states. Ranjit tested out the matter, nonetheless, by way, at least, of organizing his own misls—for the "Phulkian chieftains," it may be remembered, lived below the Sutlej which was tacitly the boundary line between British influence and the Sikhs. In his campaigning—and in his negotiations—among the misls, he, indeed, sometimes crossed the Sutlej. This came to the attention of the English, and negotiations with *them* ensued, whereby in 1809 an understanding was arrived at, the Sikhs to retain their holdings below the river, but to confine their military operations henceforth to their domain above the river. And in accordance with this understanding, Ranjit proceeded to extend his holdings northward to Kashmir, westward to Multan and northwestward to Peshawar, all of which regions had previously been subject to Islam. Altogether, by conquest and by treaty, by means of an efficient national army and by diplomacy, he established the Khalsa in actual operation and in such strength that it flourished until his death in 1839. Only then was the balance so disturbed that further war ensued.

What, however, in more detail was the situation of the Khalsa under Ranjit? What of morals and religion, in particular? Ranjit's own religion was scarcely more than form; it was what he made it, political and diplomatic, an affair of man and not of God. A contemporary doubted if actually he had any "fixed religion," and thought he may have supported Sikhism as something expedient to do, without ever making it the "state" religion. This same observer, however, remarked that his support was given "in the most munificent manner." Ranjit was punctilious in worship, was not only present regularly at public prayers, but listened daily to readings from the *Adi Granth* rendered by "well-attired granthis." He was careful, whatever his basic motive, to honor Sat Nam and to regard the Khalsa above himself. In his official signature he styled himself Akal Sahai, "God-helper." He completed the temples of Amritsar and Tarn Taran substantially as they are today, and erected religious buildings in Lahore and elsewhere, as we have learned already (p. 35, above).

Nevertheless, his "Sikhism" had something of a Hindu odor, perhaps more pronounced with him than the Hindu features of any former leader. He celebrated Hindu festivals, for example, Holi, but favored a Sikh appropriation and revision of them. He visited and gave financial aid to many Hindu holy places. He countenanced sati among the Sikhs in general, and at his own funeral women of his household were burned, as if by his intention. The sati of four wives and seven concubines is commemorated by symbols on his samadh, or "tomb," beside the fort and the gurdwara in Lahore. In all these respects he yielded to the quiet temper of the times. He may indeed have felt no greater personal responsibility for the Sikh religion. He the Maharaja was but a glorified sirdar, sirdars were men of state, and at the most mere patrons of religion. In this they differed from the ten gurus who were primarily leaders in religion. Before the time when governors, in fact, assumed office, religious leadership had been otherwise provided for—there was the *Granth*, for instance, and it was in itself the token of Sat Nam. And, in addition, there were mahants[14] among the panths who had assumed something of the priestly office among people otherwise indifferent to a priesthood.

Maharaja Ranjit Singh may not, however, escape personal responsibility for morality. He must have taken undue liberty in office, for his acts were not expressive of the

[14] Mahants, "superiors," or dini sardars, "religious headmen"; and the panths were the "sects" as distinguishable from the misls, or political divisions.

habits of the common people. That is, to be specific, his sexual license was largely personal and not in the manner of the Khalsa. The families of the simpler peasants had every reason to preserve their purity. Household and misl ties had themselves peculiar social and economic value. Titles to property and the inheritance of it were strictly guarded—and so highly esteemed that there may have been an economic reason for a certain peculiar marriage rite among the Sikhs which ran conspicuously counter to the Hindu custom, and which aimed at conserving family holdings: a widow might marry the brother of her deceased husband, or she might stay single and administer her own property; and she might even as a woman or a widow head a misl and administer its affairs. Marriage rites, it must be said, were normally observed, whether they were those of the regular vyah or shadi ("marriage" in the higher sense), or that of chadar dalna, "the throwing of a sheet" over the intended bride, a survival, doubtless, of the more primitive marriage by "capture." License was by no means common with the peasantry, although among the Sikhs there was neither pardah (the "veil") as among the upper classes of the Hindus nor harim (seclusion) as observed by Moslems—unless, as with some "proper" women of the Sikhs, there has been some voluntary practice of seclusion. In the open fields and on the threshing floor many sturdy, unveiled women, usually of Jat descent, worked beside their men and kept their chastity.

The Maharaja was himself promiscuous in sex affairs. His mother had been dissolute and he had license, therefore, in his blood—and *rulers* of the day, in fact, were under no restraint. Sometimes he observed the marriage ritual, taking nine wives by formal shadi and another nine by the more vulgar rite of chadar dalna. And, as bazaar gossip had it, his clandestine affairs were legion. He maintained several households, including the famous "summer palace" in the town of

Wanieke.[15] But only one son was *officially* born to him, he the simple-minded Kharak Singh who succeeded him, and in whose hands the headship itself of the Sikh confederacy was sadly impotent. There were, on the other hand, many births attributed to Ranjit, many claims on his paternity, and on two occasions he generously "adopted" babies smuggled into his apartments.

In other ways, also, Ranjit was immoral. He was addicted both to liquor and to bhang. He came, of course, of a hard-drinking race, but his own favorite beverage, they say, was "a fierce compound of distilled corn-brandy, mixed with hemp or opium, herbs, musk and the juice of meat." He drank frequently and long with jovial companions. Many of the sirdars took liquor freely, and used bhang for special stimulation, being generally, in time, wretched men without it. Liquor and bhang were both common to the rank and file of Sikhs, also, the Akalis alone consistently abstaining from the former—and all Sikhs, of course, refrained from smoking. Ranjit did not use tobacco, but from his excesses he was a broken man at fifty years of age and a paralytic in his last five years of life.

Ranjit was at last a symbol of uncertain times, and Sikhism under him fell far short of realizing its ideal. The great omission was morality! Many Sikhs, especially the Singhs, were men of courage, but they often simulated bravery with bhang—and then they sometimes put their foes to flight through the very fear stirred in them, more than by their own enthusiastic, brave devotion to a high ideal. They exercised some restraint by refraining from tobacco, quite unaware even then that confidence and self-control came, if at all, by some higher, sounder method. Indulgence in drugs and drink offset the virtue of ascetic abstinence in another quarter. If there was any sense of opposition to

[15] Cf. above, pp. 34f.

abstemious Islam in their own indulgence in intoxicants,[16] if they were inclined to renounce smoking because it was a Hindu habit, the matter was in each instance scarcely moral, but rather religious. Nor was sati for the women a moral demonstration of devotion. Sikhism had gained much, but at the disregard of morals—men had really disregarded a moral God.

Even the Khalsa had not been realized in terms commensurate with the larger plan of Gobind, which held in delicate balance considerations of politics, morals and religion. Ranjit had himself achieved in miniature something, we might say, antecedent and analogous to Mussolini's fascism and Hitler's nazism, all of them playing fast and loose with morals, and according never more than formal recognition to religion. There is some weighty evidence for all of us in what he did, that politics alone spells ruin. A merely political state contemplates no proper bounds, and operates, accordingly, toward expansive self-destruction. Ranjit, in his turn, really sealed the Khalsa's doom! If he ever expressed—as he sometimes did—an interest in education, medicine and commerce, for example, it was an interest incidental to political ambition. We sometimes wonder why he did not lay more stress even on religion as an aid to political preferment? His disregard of morals may be the answer. Or was he disinclined to be a "prophet"?—a question not entirely irrelevant.

There was, in fact, a man in Ranjit's day by the name of "Ahmad Shah"[17]—the name itself is common—who was active as a "prophet" and who cloaked adventure in the guise of holy war. He is indeed a symbol of several things: what a designing "prophet" *can* do among untutored people,

[16] Too little regard was paid to words attributed to Nanak that "He who drinks the [non-inebriating] juice of Hari is sufficiently intoxicated" and that "All other juices are contemptible" (Trumpp, *Adi Granth*, p. 532).

[17] *Cf.* Cunningham-Garrett, pp. 186ff.

what the times were which made his particular adventure possible, and what the end always is of such a movement. This Ahmad Shah was a Moslem of Bareilly, a town two hundred miles east of Delhi and northeast of Agra in a section which the English East India Company soon controlled. He was a sayyid Moslem, one, that is, who claimed descent from Mohammed, thus belonging in the Indian setting of Islam to the uppermost of the four castes into which most Indian Moslems resolved themselves—there were, for instance, sayyids, shayks, mughals and pathans. He had been a mercenary trooper in early campaigns against the English, and had gone to Delhi about 1820, a little while before the English got control. There he came under the influence of a Moslem preacher and embraced religion. His emphasis was scriptural, like that of a simple "Bible" advocate, and he quoted Koranic precepts only, without reference to any commentary and canonical opinion. He gained a hearing, as one of his kind has always been somehow able to do, and attracted several pirs or chelas, "pupils," to himself, one of whom brought out a written "basis of the faith," an *Urdu* pamphlet in which he argued that the Koran as God's word could be understood by the simple folk and not only by the learned, and that God had sent a prophet from among the "ignorant" for all mankind's instruction—maybe the pamphleteer was playing upon the common but erroneous idea that Mohammed was actually an "illiterate." He presented as the cardinal belief the Unity of God, and as the fundamental practice the exclusive worship of the One God and obedience to God's Law through devotion to the Prophet. Incidentally, he deprecated angels, saints, monks, friars, priests and others who somehow interfered, as he insisted, with man's supreme regard for God; and he, of course, denounced idolatry. In all of which there was, to be sure, nothing new, unless its only novelty was an oversimplification of religion in terms of the Koran alone—

and that through the medium of an Urdu exposition as if there were no textual or critical problems involved even in a translation of Koranic verses into an artificial "camp" (that's what Urdu means) vernacular.

Ahmad and his group actually operated awhile in central India and in 1822 found passage from Calcutta into the Red Sea to Jiddah, and thence to Mecca and Madinah, making the Moslem hajj, or pilgrimage. They returned to Delhi somehow in 1826, the city and region by that time having become an English province. Without objection from the English authorities, he proclaimed jihad, or "holy war," against those he called the "unbelievers" (mushriks, kafirs), creating the impression that he meant the Sikhs, primarily. He organized, in fact, a campaign, enrolled perhaps five hundred ghazis or crusaders, and proceeded westward to Khairpur on the Indus River in northern Sindh, gathering additional support in men and money as he went. From Khairpur he journeyed to Kandahar inside Afghanistan and thence to the neighborhood of Peshawar along the Khaibar Pass, where he aroused the warlike tribesmen of the Usufzai hills to join him. At last, with his ghazis and his Usufzais he descended into the plains of the Panjab against the Sikhs and their Panjabi allies! There was frequent desultory fighting, with fortune favoring first one side and then the other, until after several years Ahmad actually won Peshawar itself and held it for a twelvemonth, proclaiming himself khalifah and "defender of the faith" of Islam. But the Usufzais themselves grew restless and withdrew. Ahmad was slain in May 1831, in a skirmish, and the miscellaneous ghazis slunk back home again. It had been a great adventure, and nothing more, for Ahmad, at least, although he had altogether a stirring day before he ceased to be. He had caused Ranjit and the Sikhs some slight anxiety, but when the finally helpless Ranjit died in 1839, there were still other sorts of Ahmads to stir the Sikhs to grave concern and to engage them in bitter conflict. England, for example, entered the lists in earnest and thus another great religion came upon the scene, penetrating the very environs of the Khalsa and becoming itself the religion of a conquering *state.*[18]

[18] It may be recalled that Ranjit himself had not declared a national religion. And it may be added that the presumptive bearing of political ascendancy upon morals and religion may not wisely be ignored.

# Chapter 10. A British Two-edged Sword in Upper India

Christians came upon the scene as Sikhism, after Maharaja Ranjit's death, passed into yet another stage of its career, and there were thus *four* powers in the Panjab to vie with one another. Sikhism had reached some understanding with the previous powers, Hinduism and Islam or, rather, had determined its essential attitude with reference to them. Toward Hinduism it was a somewhat noncommittal attitude, often one of compromise, but one, nevertheless, of essential differentiation. With Islam an armed truce was established, with a hostile mind prevailing on either side. Sikhs had known Christianity only in the abstract—at least, there were no churches and congregations yet in northern India—and only *as religion*. They had known of England at a distance, but knew her chiefly as a trading nation bent on empire backed by arms. They were to learn, however, of a long, strong blade with a *double* cutting edge, and to be aware of ample opportunity and need for comparative appraisal—or did they actually enter the new stage of experience for themselves with self-preservation their supreme concern? There was at any rate no vestige left among the Sikhs of their former consciousness of mission as a reconciling faith! And they were aware that four religions would now contest the field.

Three aspects of Sikh power, let us be reminded, were manifest upon the death of Ranjit Singh: the political *state* —call it still the Khalsa—with civil authority centered in Lahore, the capital, where Ranjit's son, the Maharaja Kharak Singh, presided; the *faith* as such, its ritual centering in Amritsar, with a certain waning prestige lingering at Anandpur, and with some bands of Sikhs accustomed to separate paths across what we may call the commons; and, third, the *army*, possibly 125,000 strong, the best equipped and most efficient soldiery above the Sutlej, which shortly found itself to be most potent and most expressive of the Sikh ideal.

An uneasy balance of the three elements of power was soon further, inordinately disturbed, beginning with the army. With the great man gone and none to take his place, the soldiery grew more and more unruly and a want of discipline was soon distressfully apparent which dissolved the army's unity. A bisection of authority occurred: panchayats, those "five-man committees" of Indian tradition, were instituted by the common soldiers who sought thus to provide themselves, in contrast with the supreme command, a more immediate authority than that of their former superiors. This placed the intermediate officers in a difficult and dubious position somewhere between the administrative authorities of the Khalsa and the army personnel; and they suffered, in consequence, a distinct loss of power. The panchayats themselves did not assume by rebellion supreme authority—anarchy was not the issue of their action—but loyalty was indeed undergoing transformation with reference to its true objective. The army, at least, was creating and responding to an ideal of its own, and that ideal was none other than the spirit of Gobind Singh, the very founder of the Khalsa and the organizer of its military forces! His spirit became actually more real and authoritative among the troops than the *Granth Sahib* itself; it became virtually their "Guru." He became the very incarnation of the Khalsa and the reincarnation of the whole of Sikh tradition from the time of Nanak onwards, himself subservient to Sat Nam and Akal alone. This army ideal, therefore, *could* unite again both officers and men.

In the name of guru Gobindsinghji, accordingly, a peculiar militancy developed, and its advocates, the keshdari Singhs themselves grew yet more prominent in comparison, for example, with the sahajdari, "easygoing," Sikhs. The keshdaris put within a single frame and side by side the likenesses of Nanakji and Gobindji, and linked the two men in one divine succession—representing Nanak now as *bearded*,[1] attended by a bearded minstrel and a bearded chauri-waver! In such a scene[2] Gobindji sits on a royal carpet in imposing state, his left leg drawn under him, his right knee upright; clad in a flowing gown of rich fabric held about the waist by a heavy, corded sash; garlanded with rosaries of precious gems; wearing on his head a feathered, jewel-studded crown; a sturdy bow slung over his left shoulder and a straight, sharp arrow in one hand. A hooded falcon, swift and powerful of wing and deadly in attack, sits on the forefinger of his right horizontal hand, and a heavy scimitar in its jeweled scabbard is suspended at his hip. Nor are the "hill-forts" omitted from the scene, which represent his refuge in the mountains when Mughals hunted him. In such a scene Gobindji is no longer the faqir of Khafi Khan's report; his dress, rather, has greatly altered, and there is no more, perhaps, to add to the bazaar print, unless a matchlock and a fieldpiece, to make complete the army's new ideal, himself in his new role the devotee of the "timeless" god of War. Here, then, is the patron saint of the bearded trooper, not to be mistaken, even in a picture, for either a Moslem or a Hindu, for example—Gobind's beard is both uncut and undyed, whereas the Hindu has always trimmed his beard and the Moslem has cut his own below the lower lip and underneath his chin; and the Moslem has dyed his beard a reddish or a bluish black. Within the meaning of this newer symbolism the army of the Khalsa, by means of its panchayats, assumed control in a militant democracy.

Of course, the army and the state were soon at war with

[1] Cf. the tradition that Nanak himself forbade the cutting of the hair.

[2] That of a bazaar print, for example.

one another. The soldiers demanded that the state increase their pay, while the state, by reason of its dwindling resources, was actually allowing the army's wage to fall into arrears! While restlessness increased among the army, two civil factions in the state were in competition for control, and the stage was set for an army demonstration. One of the two civil factions was led by Maharaja Kharak Singh's wazir, Dhyan Singh, who was not a Sikh at all, but a Dogra[3] of Jammu State, who on the death of Kharak Singh, installed, with the aid of the sirdars of several misls, one Shir Singh, a reputed son of Maharaja Ranjit. Jealousy, intrigue and even assassination interfered at once with this arrangement, and in 1844 still another reputed son of Ranjit, Dalip Singh, was installed against the will of the Dogra wazir Dhyan Singh, with Dalip's mother as queen-regent and his own brother as wazir. And when these new civil rulers took stock of the army, they decided to disband it. At which the regimental panchayats acted with becoming promptitude, forbidding a single company to disband, unless on their own specific order, and renewing their demand upon the state for an increase of pay, threatening at the same time to plunder Lahore itself if necessary to make up their pay. The authorities at Lahore promptly avoided the issue by suggesting that there was richer booty to be had elsewhere, if the army chose to go and get it—in the not-too-distant provinces, that is, of Multan and Kashmir and in the lands below the Sutlej!

The army, of course, could not remain in idleness, soldiers must have opportunity to fight. The weak state of Lahore which chose to represent the Khalsa tried to save itself by dispatching the restless army into foreign parts and thus strengthen its delicate position. This practice had often been

[3] Dogras, a primitive, migrant mixture of mountain folk, whose very name may be connected with the Persian dogla, meaning mongrel.

adopted by the petty states of India in response to some principle which seems active also in this case, namely, that a state cannot live within itself without party strife and degeneration, that self-preservation requires activity beyond itself, even the dominance of alien territories. War had been the method always used to such an end and the Sikhs had learned no other method—or had they already forgotten Nanak's way? The matter was not, however, weighed with care, circumstances may not have been auspicious, the times not ripe, for such procedure, and action was somewhat automatic. Neither the Sikh state as such nor Sikhism as religion would profit *ultimately* from following such a customary course of action. However, it is a problem for prolonged discussion: to what extent *can* a state maintain itself, renew its strength, through foreign conquest, and to what extent can a religion serve itself likewise by other than purely inoffensive propagation into foreign parts? A state may resort to war and a religion may be missionary, and both of them defy thus some sounder principle of action toward the common good. A religion may be militant while simply using the arrows of a legalistic creed and availing itself of the armed expansion of a friendly state. The history of India in the regions where the Sikhs were operating holds facts for many fruitful judgments on the international polity of state and church.

In September 1845, while the seasonal "monsoon"[4] was ending, the die was cast among the Sikhs for plunder and for war. A darbar had been called in the city of Lahore, whether by the Maharaja or by the army does not matter, and the army assembled about the open square in anticipation of an audience with the court for whose presence a gaddi, "throne," had been erected in the center of the square. Young Maharaja Dalip Singh, the queen-mother, the

[4] This word comes from the Arabic "mausim" (season), whereas "barsat" is the native word for rains.

wazir and their attendants all came and took their places as the army cheered them, but it was soon apparent that the army itself was master of the situation. The army council had already decreed the death of the wazir for his various crimes and misdemeanors, and accordingly steps at once were taken to carry out its will. The queen-regent and the little maharaja were conducted respectfully to a tent made ready for them where they might not see the execution, and the wazir was seized, compelled to hear the judgment and dispatched in the sight of all the army. This demonstration of the army's power in affairs of state seemed to satisfy the soldiers at the moment, and they were willing to accept the state's suggestion that they do their further fighting somewhere else. This was actually the plan of the queen-mother, whose fundamental motive is by no means clear. That she feared the army is clear enough. She may have feared the English, also, and even more, and may have expected inevitable war between the English and the Sikhs to accrue somehow to her advantage.

A British envoy to Afghanistan had written in 1841 to the English East India Company's governor-general in Calcutta advocating the crushing of the Sikhs and suggesting that roads throughout the Panjab be macadamized. The company did annex Sindh in February 1843—proclaiming the acquisition by the famous message, "We have Sind," which some interpreted as "We have sinned." The Sikhs thus knew what surely was in store for them, if they, too, declined to accede to the English policy of "protection" which was then expanding—unless, indeed, they could beat the British (some Sikhs thought they could) and themselves inherited the government of India! In any event the Sikhs were ready and eager for the fight, to test their merits with a Christian nation—although there is no evidence of "holy war" on either side—and in December, two months after the darbar, the army of the Khalsa, thirty to sixty thousand strong, with a hundred to a hundred and fifty guns, crossed the Sutlej under its commander-in-chief, Teja Singh.[5] This was a breach of the boundary agreed upon in 1809.

The Sikhs had at least some ground for thought that their task was not impossible. They knew that the British *could* be whipped. In January 1842, a contingent of four thousand fighting men and twelve thousand followers returning from Afghanistan, where it had been to thwart a move by Russia, had completely perished, except for a single surgeon by the name of Brydon, wiped out by the snows, privation and the deadly volleys of hostile mountaineers. The Gurkha ruler of Nipal waxed bold over this disaster and gave puppet shows in Khatmandu, his capital, in which despicable, low-caste natives were garbed as Englishmen and dragged ignominiously through the city streets. And the Sikhs had known that the peoples of the Doab had not been altogether well-disposed toward their English "protectors" there, although no attempts at *armed* resistance had been made. They counted also on the good will of many who had suffered at the hands of Englishmen or under English rule. The memory still lingered of the appalling famine of 1837-1838 which had taken a toll of about eight hundred thousand lives from Allahabad to Delhi, in spite of certain measures of relief by the Government and by several Christian missionary agencies. And Britain's speedy reprisal for the Khaibar Pass disaster of January 1842 was accompanied by such wanton destruction, barbarity and bombast, that her good name had suffered sadly. The crossing of the Sutlej was accompanied by high hopes. The Sikhs at least anticipated loot, if not a martial victory in the end.

Their numbers and equipment were impressive, but their

[5] The Cunningham-Garrett *History*, pp. 224-273, tells fully the story of events 1839-1845, and the war with the English is fully told in pp. 274-329.

discipline was weak. The authority of the two commanders, Teja Singh and Lal Singh, was seriously impeded by the regimental panchayats' more immediate control, and the panchayats themselves did not thoroughly cooperate. The very first encampment of the forces and their intrenchment at Firuzpur, ten miles below the river, was desultory, and when on the approach of the English army, they advanced ten miles to Mudki to meet it, there was no coordination of attack—and they met with quick disaster. They were put to flight with a loss of many men and many guns, and retreated to the river to Firuzshah. Both sides lost heavily in the ensuing two days' battle, but the British won. A month later, the British won again at Aliwal, and two weeks thereafter concluded the campaign by the battle of Sobraon in which Sikh resistance vanished and the roads were left wide open through the Panjab to Lahore. On the 20th of February 1846, fifteen months after the Sikhs had undertaken war, the British army occupied Lahore, and three weeks afterward the Khalsa submitted to a final treaty.

By the provisions of this treaty between England and the Sikhs, the latter renounced any and all claim to lands below the Sutlej, surrendered their holdings between the Rupar-Sutlej and the Beas, and reduced their forces to 12,000 cavalry, 20,000 infantry and a modest battery of guns (they had lost ninety guns in action and had surrendered thirty-six). The British on their part confirmed the independence of the Khalsa and recognized thirteen-year-old Dalip Singh as Maharaja. But they went still further toward the adjustment of affairs in northwest India beyond the Sikhs. They seized Kashmir from its Dogra raja, Gulab Singh, brother of the wazir whom the Khalsa army had executed in Lahore—two brothers who had been named to office by Ranjit—and then made a treaty with him by which they allowed him to "buy" his kingdom back again for seventy-five lakhs of rupees (Rs. 75,00,000, or about $2,500,000).

By another treaty with the Sikhs it was provided: that a British "resident" should be stationed in Lahore, that internal reformation be accomplished, that arrearages be paid up to the Khalsa army, and that the jagirs or land-estates be redistributed. This treaty was signed by thirteen Sikhs representing "the chiefs and sirdars of the state" and it called for the virtual administration of the state by the British of "all matters in every department" until the Maharaja attained his majority in 1854. The British thus extended over all the Sikhs their "protection" policy. A Christian power had at last gained the ascendancy above the Sutlej and even up to the northwest frontier of India.

The respite was very brief, however, and many things persisted to make it so. The British acquisition of the Panjab afforded new occasion for a conflict of older issues much debated elsewhere and never fully settled—not yet settled in 1945. In politics it was the perpetuation of a form of "dual government" which caused disturbance. The Resident, Henry Lawrence, whom the British settled in Lahore, was one of the most Christian men and ablest administrators ever in the India service, and some historians have said that he and the British government were disposed toward "justice and moderation . . . in accordance with the customs, feelings and prejudices of the people," a profoundly sympathetic policy; but, after all, it was, in theory, a dual government. The Sikh queen-regent and her wazir had been removed, Maharaja Dalip Singh had not attained majority and the English Resident was, therefore, meanwhile in absolute control.

Dual government had failed before in India, not only in Bengal under its Nawab and the East India Company's Governor-General Clive, but elsewhere, also. It represented the company's method under the British charter of acquiring actually, but not in name, various new territories which were thus kept out of any direct control by the British

Crown. It was a plan by which everything administrative was done by and for the company but in the name of some powerless, dependent prince. It was not a method, even if anyone thought it was, of effectually concealing foreign domination, or of ministering to Indian pride and conciliating Indian resentment. The common people, of course, cared little then *who* governed them, if only the taxes which they had to pay were not too heavy, but the Indian leaders well knew who really ruled—and *they* greatly cared. The leaders of the Khalsa, for example, chafed under "residential" rule, in spite of any prospect of legal, economic or general melioration in the state, including a regulation of the taxes.

There was, to be sure, another cogent phase of the administrative problem, and that was the quality of Indian officers themselves—officers not merely of the army, but rajas and sirdars, also—in spite of any consideration of whose problem it was. Maybe it was India's own problem even at that time. Indian administrators, however, had not made too good a record among themselves nor on behalf of their own people. They were usually bred in the traditional methods of squeeze and graft, and were by tradition and their own nature prone to partiality and patronage, and, although these methods were sometimes modified and even nullified by tribal, caste, sectarian or some other form of communal consciousness, the interruption was not for long, as the history of Sikhism itself shows, and sometimes this very communal consciousness has itself approved the traditional methods of squeeze, graft, partiality and patronage. Indeed, the corruption in Sikhism under its non-Sikh Dogra rulers may have been the leading factor in the break-down of the Sikh confederacy. Many Sikhs had come to distrust their own officials, and some thought they might do better under British rule, but neither the poorest quality of native rule nor the highest quality of alien rule seems to be just warrant for the dual scheme of government—at least, neither makes the dual scheme efficient and commendable. An independent nation, on the other hand, is not free to be unjust, nor may corruption be established, legalized, within it by an international arrangement.

Religious factors, also, were at stake—*four* now, instead of three, as formerly, if they be designated by general terms alone: Hindu, Moslem, Sikh and Christian. Whatever adjustment had been achieved amidst Hindus, Sikhs and Moslems, these three communities with increasing sensitivity looked anxiously upon the fourth which made it clear to them and to all the world that the Panjab was its own latest proper field of missions—or, in other words, according to the times, a field for conquest and conversion. The British Resident in the Panjab or any of his aides did not, of course, officially interfere in matters of religion, but the situation, nevertheless, changed somewhat after 1849. In that year, after the bloody, costly and indecisive battle with the Sikhs at Chilianwala, near the Jhelum above Lahore, and after the finally decisive victory over the Sikhs and their Afghan allies along the Chenab at Gujrat, the Panjab became by annexation a British province.[6] Thereupon followed a large influx of European and Indian Christians, mostly soldiers. In 1850 there were eight thousand Catholics alone under the care of the Capuchins, although some of these had been long already in the Panjab, perhaps from the earlier activity of Jesuits who had "blessed" in 1597 the first Roman Catholic church in Lahore, and from missions of the Carmelites of Agra who occasionally ventured into northern India. North India, however, had been practically impervious to Christianity until the time of British annexation.

Protestants—and, of course, Catholics, also—had extended their mission work from the south up to the boundary of the

[6] *Cf. Cambridge Shorter History of India*, p. 677, or George Dunbar's *History of India*, pp. 502-503.

Sutlej, had occupied Ludhiana, for example, since 1836, biding their time until they could go yet further under the "protection" of the state. A biographer[7] of an early Panjab missionary, Robert Clark, says that they "prepared themselves for the work their faith anticipated when the set-time of favor dawned" and that "the long-watched-for day came in 1849 with the triumph of the British arms." "Christian men had been victors alike in tortuous diplomacy and on bloody fields" and the mission which was soon established in the Panjab "was intended to be a thank-offering to Almighty God for victory granted over a terrible foe." Substantial sums for the new enterprise were collected in the army camps.

Sikhs themselves, as well as Moslems and Hindus, who might read such words, would surely judge that the Christian campaign was a "holy war," or, at least, that Christian missions awaited hopefully and at last approved the Christian army's conquest, whereby missionary effort might continue under the new governmental auspices. To be sure, no state religion was proclaimed—nor had the Khalsa of the Sikhs proclaimed a state religion—but obvious prestige would be enjoyed by Christianity, and although the English military campaign may not appropriately be likened to what the Moslem himself may call jihad, or a "striving" on the faith's behalf, Christianity stood to gain advantage and was free to exercise a certain moral suasion, with the promise of incidental benefits to converts.

There were likewise other aspects of the religious situation which accrued to conquest. There was, for instance, around 1800, the debatable issue of a Christian government's connection with non-Christian practices. In Bengal, in particular, the government had been accused by church folk at home of encouraging "idolatry." Certain restorations of

[7] Martyn Clark, *Robert Clark of the Panjab*, New York, 1907.

temple properties and subsidies-in-aid had sometimes been granted. A historian of Indian Christianity, John W. Kaye, said in 1859 that "the English in India, not very keenly alive to the beauty and holiness of their own blessed religion, and considerably ignorant of the real character of Hindooism, had been rather attracted by the 'excellent moralities of the Hindoos,' than repulsed by their abominations, and had seen in many of the barbarities which we now most deplore and condemn, only the courage of the hero and the patience of the martyr."[8] The case of Jagannath[9] and his shrine at Puri in Orissa had served to test the general situation, and Kaye records that "the Christian Government of India . . . was openly and authoritatively aiding and abetting the worst forms of devil-worship, taking all the hideous indecencies and revolting cruelties of Hindooism under its especial patronage, sending their own masters-of-the-ceremonies to preside over the hellish orgies, and with paternal tenderness managing the property of the idol temples, pampering the priests, cherishing the dancing girls, and doing such honor to heathenism generally as was best calculated to maintain it in a high state of exultant obesity." He complains that "the State became Juggernauth's churchwarden" at the time, although that was, he says, "half a century ago, when the question of political supremacy was yet unsettled, and our government, in its dealings with the people of the soil, thought it best for its own safety to be openly of no religion." What he virtually means, it seems, is that government thought it best to *favor* for political reasons the indigenous religions, chiefly Hinduism, and not that it had *no* religious interest.

As political control was gradually extended, governmental policy with reference to Indian religions was radically

[8] *Christianity in India*, London, 1859. *Cf.* pp. 475-506, especially.
[9] *ibid.*, pp. 366-392.

altered. The government announced a severance of any official connection with these religions and issued orders intended to prevent *any interference* with them by any government official. Incidental to the establishment of this procedure, the attempt was made to distinguish clearly between the Christian servant of the Government and the missionary servant of the Church, and even to distinguish, in the case of any given servant, between his status as an officer of government and his activity as a missionary—an effort that would have been amusing, had it not involved some serious, undifferentiable relations. It was in April 1847 that the official action was announced by the Directors of the East India Company, calling " 'immediate and particular attention' to the necessity of Government servants, civil and military, abstaining from all interference with the religion of the natives of India."[10] It had been observed that "soldiers and civilians were usurping the functions of the missionary," and that "some indiscretions had been committed." The alteration was at best a superficial action based on a want of understanding. The principle of "non-interference," for example, was left altogether vague, for the foreigner had not yet discovered how closely interwoven with religion among the Hindus, Musalmans and Sikhs were such civil questions as the inheritance of property, marriage and funeral ceremonies, and the very status of the Christian convert. Although neutrality and toleration were explicitly established as the policy of government, religious tensions were inherent in administrative action, and were bound to be disruptive and to lead to blows.

In the Panjab in 1849 and following, the territory having been annexed to Britain, the natives had occasion to observe

[10] For the religious difficulties of the Company and the Crown as it took over from the Company, including the Company's relations with the Sikhs, an excellent source is Ramsay Muir's *The Making of British India*, London, 1915.

the working of the "machinery of conversion" set in operation by Catholics, Presbyterians and Episcopalians, in particular. By 1850 about two thousand converts had been added to the previous thousands, "mostly soldiers," of the earlier days, and among them were a few Moslems and some Sikhs. In February 1852 a Protestant local Church Mission Association was inaugurated in Lahore under the honorary presidency of the governor, the then Sir Henry Lawrence, and having certain missionaries active as its secretaries. In April of that year a Protestant mission station was opened in Amritsar, "the key to the wealth and genius of the Panjab," and there in July 1853 its "first convert" was baptized—a Sikh attendant of a gurdwara in a nearby village—the ceremony performed openly in the vicinity of the Darbar Sahib. His name was Daud Singh, he knew no English and "was lamentably deficient in the merest rudiments of education" but, as the record goes,[11] "a flowing beard was not the least of his qualifications" and he was ordained as minister in Amritsar by the Anglican Bishop of Calcutta in October 1854. These and other events advertised throughout the Panjab the presence of Christianity as a two-edged sword, and while outward peace prevailed for several years in interfaith relations, the restlessness was growing which brought on in 1857 the "Great Rebellion" with its curious and significant effects on all concerned, whether Sikhs, Hindus, Musalmans or Christians.

The Great Rebellion—Ghadr ka Waqt, "season of rebellion"—which has been often merely called "The Mutiny" was not simply a military demonstration. The mutiny was incidental, a sign of something more comprehensive and influential going on in India—and, perhaps, beyond her bounds. The Panjab itself was less affected than other parts as a field of actual battle, but was no less concerned with

[11] Martyn Clark, *op. cit.*, p. 101, etc.

what in general was altering the total scene, and the Sikhs themselves played a most peculiar part in the actual rebellion.[12]

The malcontents were numerous in the middle years of the India of the nineteenth century, but it is easier to count them than to understand and clarify their grievances. Only a comparatively small proportion of the total population may have been affected with unrest, but it was a scattered few and among them were many Indian rulers. The restless rulers, in particular, seem to have been reacting most of all against what in reality was an increasing efficiency of government. The British Company under various pressures and incentives, not the least of which was "home" opinion, was demanding, exercising and accomplishing efficiency, and not only was efficiency in general distasteful to the native ruler—unless it was merely the method of the autocrat—but that of the alien was intolerable. The alien's own motives for improved administration may not themselves have been unselfish. The British had discovered how indispensable peace and order were to trade and commerce, and, although their Raj, or "rule," was not orderly everywhere in India, it was more widely effective and more generally just and impartial than any government had been which India had known for many, many centuries. Several of its virtues were themselves defective in the Indian situation—two, at least, namely, its constitutional prejudice and its religious intransigency. The Raj acted in conformity with a constitutional ideal, and the missionary, by government permission, acted also uncompromisingly amidst India's own religious institutions; and an impression gained momentum that Christianity intended to convert the whole of India. The government had intro-

[12] An adequate work of reference for the disturbances of those years is T. Rice Holmes, *A History of the Indian Mutiny*, London, 1913. Alexander Duff published in 1858 some interesting letters under the title, *The Indian Rebellion*.

duced European literature and science into India and had fostered English culture. In 1854 it made the English language the official medium of education in the schools it organized. In many of the higher mission schools, in which non-Christians usually preponderated, the pupils were given for their reading religious books in English. By instruction and example the schools aimed at reformation, but not always with the most appreciative understanding of all that was involved. It seemed wise, for example, to act as they did against the rite of sati, widow-burning, and to provide for the remarriage of Hindu widows, but, we may ask, were they too uncompromising in some other matters, for example, in defying the non-Christian laws of property-inheritance by preventing a convert from losing his estate by his change of faith, and by outlawing for the convert all non-Christian festivals? The Christian missionaries denounced in the schools and market-places the "heathen" scriptures, the Koran, the Shastras and the *Granth*, and condemned as false guides in morals and religion the bhagats, sufis, sadhus and mahants. Hindus, in particular, began to be alarmed for that socio-religious institution of theirs which we know as "caste." Moslems, perhaps, were less alarmed, because their system is more rigid, and the Sikhs, least of all, because no crucial test of caste had yet arisen—and, certainly, caste-reform would not disturb them!

The occasion—not the *cause*—of the Mutiny may have been the *greased cartridge* of the new Enfield rifle issued to the Indian Army—but was it *suet* or was it *lard* with which the bullet was rammed down the rifle barrel? and what bearing had it on pollution? We know now that the story of the grease was "all delusion." The truth of the matter seems to be that "the grease contained tallow of doubtful origin, but no cartridges greased with the fat of cows or swine were destined to be issued to the sepoys" (sipahis, Indian troopers). Alexander Duff, a Scotch missionary, wrote in 1858, that "orders were given at *three* of our military stations to prepare cartridges according to the English prescription, *i.e.*, with tallow which, of course, may be a mixture of hog's fat and cow's fat. The sepoys took the alarm. When this became known, orders were given to issue none of the greasy cartridges; and none were actually used." A recent history of India affirms that "the story of the cartridges . . . is probably a fable with the slenderest possible foundation in fact. Animal fat had doubtless been used at Woolwich, where the earliest Enfield rifles were made up. But all those issued to the sepoy troops had been prepared at Dum Dum, where Brahman workmen had handled the fat without question . . . mutton-fat and wax, etc."[13]

Whether the story of the grease is fact or fable, the Moslems and the Hindus in the army were much concerned and the *occasion* was provided for the army's reflection of a widespread discontent. The sipahis could readily believe that Government would destroy their faith by making them unclean—mayla, napak, as the vernacular might say, "dirty, untouchable and sinful." Indian troops predominated in all three Indian armies, those of Bengal, Bombay and Madras, since the British regiments were withdrawn in 1854 to serve in the Crimea. At Delhi there were no English troops at all. With all the Indians, ritual purity was indeed a serious concern. There was a saying (*hadith*) of Mohammed current that "the practice of religion [Islam] is founded upon cleanliness" and the Koran itself said—in Sura 4:46—"O ye faithful, assemble not for prayer while suffering from pollution." The Moslem had no doubt at all of the indelible stain of pork, which no wadu or ghusl, "washing," could wash out. Hindus were at least as careful with respect to cows—but on another ground, for cows themselves were sacred to them —and just as hesitant to "break caste" by certain unclean

[13] *Cf. The Cambridge Shorter History of India*, pp. 737-738.

acts. Their own Shastras provided elaborately for snan karna, "bathing, cleansing," and ordained minute prescriptions for keeping clean. The Sikh, too, had his rules of cleanness, but in no degree comparable with those of Hindus or of Moslems. Nanak himself had qualified the use of pork, but did not make all meat unclean, and he minimized the rite of cleansing, saying:

> When body, feet and hands are soiled,
> Let water wash the stain away, . . .
> But when the mind is soiled by sin
> The Name alone can make it clean.[14]

And Gobind, whose influence among the Khalsa troops was greater, possibly, than that of Nanak, had this to say in connection with the pahul ceremony:

> Men bathe at pilgrim centers . . . and perform their special ritual . . .
> Some performing millions of ablutions . . . even bathing in the seven seas . . .
> Of what avail is such devotion? . . .
> The world entangled in false ritual hath not yet found the secret of Akal![15]

The Mutiny began below the Sutlej, and the Jamna-Ganges plain of the Doab from Bengal to Delhi was the scene of the chief uprising. This was a region under Bengal guard, and there the mutineers of the Bengal Army gained by sudden action, pillaging and massacre temporary possession in May and June of 1857 of Meerut, Delhi, Lucknow, Cawnpore and other Doab stations. Those mutineers who were Moslem called their movement holy war (jihad) and raised in Delhi, the seat of their former Indian empire, above the Jama Masjid, or mosque of general assembly, the black, triangular standard of jihad. This, as it happened, was very indiscreet on their part, offending both Hindu and Sikh

[14] *Japji* 20. *Cf. ibid.*, 21.
[15] *Cf.* Macauliffe, v, pp. 261-266, 283, etc.

sipahis, who had vivid recollections of what Moslem holy war had meant previously to their households of faith. But the mutiny, although it was intense and tragic while it lasted, was short-lived. After eighty-seven days of blood and tears —there were women and children among the besieged—Outram and Havelock broke "their way through the fell mutineers" at Lucknow, above whose Residency a banner of confidence was "rear'd on high" . . . "Flying at top of the roofs in the ghastly siege of Lucknow." What was left of those tortured by cholera, scurvy, fever and wounds was, "Saved by the valor of Havelock, saved by the blessing of Heaven!"[16] All the English records of the various disasters of those months account for the final outcome as something providential.

In the whole of the Panjab itself there were only 10,500 English troops and 58,000 Indian at the time, but the latter were quickly and quietly disarmed in Lahore, Peshawar and Multan, and within three days the government was in complete control. Some observers have said that this promptitude not only saved the Panjab but the whole of India. It was indeed a brilliant achievement for the Army, but other factors, also, must be kept in mind—the Sikhs themselves may have saved the situation! There were nowhere any actual mutineers among the Sikhs, even among those in the Bengal Army, and on the contrary they and Sikhs outside the army, also, gave their aid against the mutineers. At the very outset the Sikh chieftains below the Sutlej under the leadership of the Maharaja of Patiala offered the government their resources. This, too, was the reaction of the Panjabi Sikhs, prompted, in the main, perhaps, by two considerations: one, there was among the peasants a common mood of satisfaction over a succession of good harvests and a just administration, and, two, the misl chiefs enjoyed a measure of independence and saw their own welfare linked imme-

[16] From Tennyson's poem, *The Defence of Lucknow.*

diately with the government's success—recalcitrant remnants of the Khalsa forces had previously been expelled at the time of annexation. And there may have been a potent third consideration! The British Commissioner of the province followed somewhat the example of Maharaja Ranjit Singh who counted on the keshdari love of war. The commissioner, in a letter to them, summoned the chiefs "to retrieve their character and come at once with their retainers," intimating, at least, that there would be good fighting. They came, were organized and were sent at once to attack the mutineers at Delhi and elsewhere in the Doab. One governor gave them and other loyal soldiers permission to kill mutineers at sight and to take their equipment without question. The Sikh chieftains of the Doab may themselves have been lured to loyalty by some prospect of indemnity for any damage done their states, or they may still have remembered with gratitude the protection against Ranjit Singh himself which the British had guaranteed them by the proclamation of 1809.[17]

Sikhs took special satisfaction in Delhi's fall—its recapture by the British—and the capture of the Mughal king, seeing in this a measure of revenge for the death of their guru, Teg Bahadur, at Mughal hands. The Sikh ruler of Jind himself cleared the way for the advance of one British contingent against Delhi, and Nabha with eight hundred of his men escorted the siege-train. Patiala supplied five thousand men and held one hundred and twenty miles of communication from Delhi to the Panjab. Kapurthala led two thousand of his men into the British ranks to replace the mutineers and fight in Oudh. Sikhs of Oudh and of Bengal fought in the British ranks side by side with Scotch Highlanders. When, after the mutiny was over, the ranks of the Panjab Army were refilled, and additional units were organized from new

[17] *Cf.* Sir John J. H. Gordon, *The Sikhs* (London, 1904), pp. 221-236.

enlistments, the Sikhs alone contributed one-third of the grand total of seventy thousand men, most of whom had already had experience in war. A corps of mazhabis, or converts to Sikhism, twelve hundred strong, had previously been raised for the siege of Delhi from among the workers along the Panjab irrigation canals. Even the deposed Maharaja Dalip Singh enlisted in the English army.

Sikhs had thus survived another momentous change of circumstance! During all these troubled years a singular spirit had characterized the members of the Khalsa, in particular—a spirit to some degree of "good sportsmanship" and partly, also, a lingering, if subconscious, sense of mission. An English political officer[18] who knew them intimately from 1837 until his death in 1851, who was present at the battles of Buddawal and Aliwal, and served at the battle of Sobraon as an aide-de-camp to the Governor-General, said of the Sikh soldiers who came to Lahore after their final defeat at Gujrat in the second Sikh War that they

> . . . showed neither the despondency of mutinous rebels nor the effrontery and indifference of mercenaries, and their manly deportment added lustre to that valour which the victors had dearly felt [at Chilianwala, for instance] and generously extolled. The men talked of their defeat as the chance of war . . . they inwardly dwelt upon their future destiny with unabated confidence . . . and would sometimes say that the Khalsa itself was yet a child, and that as the commonwealth of Sikhs grew in stature, Gobind would clothe his disciples with irresistible might and guide them with unequalled skill.[19]

This observer expressed unusually sober and just sentiments with reference to the total scene of which the Sikhs were part, although he wrote in the florid style so common in his day:

[18] J. D. Cunningham, whose *History* is invaluable, especially as edited by H. L. O. Garrett in 1915.

[19] *op. cit.*, p. 321.

> The Hindus made the country wholly their own . . . Muhammadans entered the country to destroy, but remained to colonize, modifying the language and ideas of the vanquished and becoming themselves altered by the contact. . . .
>
> The rise to power of contemned Shudra tribes, in the persons of Marathas, Gurkhas and Sikhs, has brought about a further mixture of the rural population and of the lower orders in towns and cities. . . . The religious creed of the people seems to be even more indeterminate than their spoken dialects. . . .
>
> England rules, but the thin superficies of her dominion rests tremblingly upon the convulsed ocean of social change and mental revolution. . . . Her rule has hitherto mainly tended to the benefit of the trading community. The merchant alone sits partly happy that the path to wealth has been made smooth and its enjoyment rendered secure. The peasants are oppressed and impoverished by a well-meant but cumbrous and inefficient law.
>
> England has carefully to watch the progress of that change in social relations and religious feelings of which Sikhism is the most marked exponent. The extension of Sikh arms would speedily lead to the recognition of Nanak and Gobind as the long-looked-for Comforters. The Sikhs have now been struck by the petrific hand of material power, and the ascendancy of the English has everywhere infused new ideas and modified the aspirations of the people. The confusion has thus been increased for the time . . . but England must hope that she can imbue the mental agitation with new qualities of beneficent fertility.[20]

These sentiments, as in the third paragraph, for example, were displeasing to this officer's superiors at the time and he was punished severely for expressing them, but he has since been amply vindicated by events in India, if not yet fully justified by general British judgment.

The Mutiny subsequent to these observations, and its accompaniments and issues, did not materially affect Sikh confidence in "their future destiny," although it permanently confirmed the subordinate status of the Khalsa which the annexation of the Panjab has originally established. When, on November 1, 1858, Her Britannic Majesty Queen

[20] *op. cit.*, pp. 322f.

Victoria was proclaimed Empress of India, and the Crown had taken over India from the trading Company, the Sikhs were ready to share progressively in the new era which then began. For all India existing dignities, rights, usages and treaties were confirmed and all the people were assured that Government had no desire or intention to interfere in any matters of religion—or of caste. With the transfer of authority from the Company to the Crown the Sikhs came at last directly under the imperial rule, and politics for them as a communal instrument was eliminated for a season, but Government dealt with them—as with members of other faiths, also—as individuals and persons for whom ample opportunity yet remained for progress in social welfare, religion and in morals.

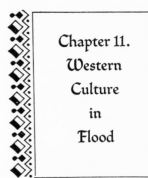

# Chapter 11. Western Culture in Flood

SIKHISM had accumulated many assets as it came through storm and stress to the middle of the nineteenth century. The net result of all was gain, and Sikhs had won a responsible position in north Indian affairs. Their history is peculiarly—almost non-politically—communal after 1858 and until the turn of another century, the twentieth, offered them newer times and fields for action. They had numbers and distribution meanwhile to depend upon. By the middle of the nineteenth century they may have numbered over one and one-half millions, perhaps two millions. There may have been a million Singhs alone, if there were in 1844 by official estimate, 125,000 warriors in the Khalsa army alone, all drawn from the keshdari clans; and there must have been another million of the less warlike or even non-warlike sahajdaris. The Sikh community was not as a whole compact, nor had it been compact of late. It constituted a comparatively small minority scattered unevenly throughout an area of at least a hundred thousand square miles, ranging two hundred and fifty miles northwest from Lahore to Peshawar, the Khaibar Pass and the Swat valley; one hundred and fifty miles southeast of Lahore into the Sikh states below the Sutlej; a hundred miles northeast of Lahore into the territories of Jammu and Kashmir; and two hundred and fifty miles westward from Lahore to the Sulaiman hills and the edge of Sindh. Sikhs were known and respected for their prowess throughout this area, although the bulk of the community continued to reside within a triangular space whose points were near Lahore, Kangra and Patiala, respectively, and whose area was less than ten thousand square miles.

There was the community-in-general made up of the many kinds of Sikhs with whom we have already made acquaintance, who cherished variations in the religious heritage; and there were within it the bulky fragments of what had been the Khalsa, which must now survive not as a political but as a spiritual fellowship—Sikhs were still disciples "with irresistible might" which the Mutiny had virtually augmented, although it had deprived them of any immediate prospect of "an extension of Sikh arms." Sikhs as a whole continued to derive "comfort" from Nanak and from Gobind, and for want of war to stimulate cohesion among the followers of Gobind, in particular, there was prospect of the leavening at last of the whole community by a common consciousness of one continuing tradition.

At the center of Sikh life was now the *Adi Granth* as the companion and the guide of all—it was now the Guru, especially to the simpler-minded Sikhs, and these made up the great majority. The gurdwaras had acquired additional importance as the repositories of copies of the *Granth* and as local centers of assembly, with no detraction from the prestige of the older, larger centers—Amritsar, in particular. In some gurdwaras, even in the Panjab, the *Granth* was really worshiped as if it were divine. In a gurdwara in southern India, at Conjeeveram, for example, a fire-sacrifice was offered to it, somewhat in the manner of the ancient Hindu homa-sacrifice, or with some such intent, perhaps, as that of the contemporary theistic Hindu cult of the Brahma Samaj which adored fire in such a ceremony. Some Sikhs felt inclined to enrich, if possible, the mystic eucharistic rite of pahul. The local centers were destined to assume increased importance from the wide distribution of the Sikhs, if for no other reason. Their development in relation to the larger, central shrines was somewhat analogous to that of the synagogues in Judaism in relation to the Temple on Mt. Zion—including some similarity in the occasional effect of politics. Control of the gurdwaras came to be an issue in somewhat the manner of the contest formerly waged for control of the temple in Amritsar.

The gurdwaras had sprung up locally and had often been, together with their endowments, in the control of local patrons, if not under the management of their immediate custodians, the mahants, for example. Although orderly and uniform control was not established until after World War I (see pp. 296 f., below), the Government made a move in 1863 by which all gurdwaras were placed directly under Sikh control, many of them having passed meanwhile, curiously enough, into non-Sikh hands. Some gurdwaras, in fact, had passed virtually into Moslem hands! —or so it was thought by many Sikhs. That is, the custodians were converts from Islam, whom original Sikhs called madhabis to distinguish them from themselves, the pakka, or "true," Sikhs. And some gurdwaras of the Udasis, for example, who were celibates, were subject to uncertain and questionable succession, which prompted Udasis now and then to abandon celibacy and to marry for the sake of a retention of property control within their own families. By the action of the government, even though it was somewhat inconclusive, the gurdwaras became on the whole more appropriately Sikh in character and in management. And the question of stratification within the ranks of Sikhs remained merely social.

The various strains should now be reviewed which entered then into the social fabric of the Sikh community,[1] if the strength of the communal consciousness be rightly

[1] The many sources for such a survey include D. Ibbetson, *Tribes and Castes of the Punjab*, Lahore, 1883, etc.; certain *District Gazetteers* (Panjab, especially), Panjab *Census Report*, 1881 (chap. on Religion); J. N. Bhattacharya, *Hindu Castes and Sects*, Calcutta, 1896; H. Edwardes, *A Year in the Punjab* (1848-49); Wm. Crooke, *Northern India*, London, 1907.

gauged. Sikhs had come in the first instance from the humbler levels of society, but their level became in turn the upper level of the new society into which low-caste peoples, including "sweepers," and miscellaneous tribesmen came. Some low-caste individuals had even come into Sikhism by way of prior conversion to Islam. These may indeed have been the madhabis, for Sikhs had been accustomed to calling Islam "that mazhab," or "that din," or, as we might say somewhat contemptuously, perhaps, "*that* religion!" And yet no stigma could justly have rested upon such converts, if, as certain records have it, Nanak's own minstrel, Mardana, was "a Musulman by birth"—indeed Mardana may even have been a sweeper! And the Khalsa gladly welcomed such recruits when it was in desperate straits. But when the Khalsa came to rule and when the prestige of the pakka Sikhs increased, some lines inevitably appeared, and genealogy, for example, came to be sometimes of tragic consequence, in fact.

Not only do the rules and regulations of religion bind or separate a people; a people may likewise be bound or segregated by tribal custom or by social theory. The Sikh had set out to modify the social theory predominant in his parts of the land, namely that socio-religious system known as "caste"—especially that type which emphasized hereditary occupation—but he had brought to bear upon the task no uniformity of agency save that of circumstance; and the result upon Sikhs themselves has been something hard to designate precisely—it is difficult to say if Sikhs are a race, a caste, a religion, or a community. Once they were, at least, the semblance of a *nation*. In the conflict with Islam, especially, Sikhs tended to develop a self-consciousness somewhat equivalent to caste within the Hindu background, and yet in the most exclusively Hindu portion of the original Sikh homeland, namely the Kangra hills, any systematic caste was not at all conspicuous. Could such an absence of caste from that region have been due to the fact that Islam itself had not yet entered there? This question may, however, be impertinent, for it is still an open question, What effect *has* Islam had on Hindu caste? It is clear, on the contrary, that Indian Moslems themselves have practiced caste, however strenuously they may repudiate it in theory. Even so, there were among the Kangra hills some low-caste folk who, when in time they joined the Sikhs, constituted a separate group known among the Sikhs as the Diwan Sadhs, "mad saints."

In the genealogical scheme some Sikhs actually claimed descent from brahman stock—for example, several bhats or bards. Some Sikhs came indeed of banya or merchant stock, whether Jain or Hindu, and continued as Sikhs in such hereditary occupation. Some others came of the Aroras and wanted to be considered khatri warrior stock, but found that genuine khatris would not recognize them. The majority of the Sikhs were in the first place Jats, but there were Jats *and* Jats, and the Sikh Jats counted themselves typical, superior. Perhaps they were, after all, typical as distinguished from the Rajputs around Amritsar and Lahore. Some Jats, of course, have claimed for themselves a Rajput origin in the distant past, but Jats-turned-Sikhs found such a claim to be sometimes of doubtful value, since *Hindu* Rajputs were not in high esteem with Sikhs. It was better to call themselves merely khatri (kshatriya, "warrior") and not Rajput, and this they were inclined to do, thus making the pakka Sikhs a "warrior" group on the kshatriya level (in 1880 they amounted actually to nine per cent of the total Panjabi kshatriya stock), while accounting for the lower-caste recruits as madhabis.

The madhabis were numerous and their low estate was much improved by their conversion—Sikhism actually was a godsend to them, even though their rating was never on a par with khatris. Mihtar, "scavengers," and chuhra, "sweepers," took to husbandry around Gujranwala and Lyallpur, and to tanning and leather-working elsewhere, counting themselves far removed from Hindu mihtars and chuhras. Chamars, "leather-workers," sometimes became kahars, "bearers," sometimes julahas, "weavers." Nor would a Sikh chamar who had changed his status stoop thereafter to taking water, for example, from the ordinary chamar—even if a Hindu chamar *would* give him drink! Ravi Das, "the slave of slaves" who, as he claimed, escaped hell by the "Guru's favor," who is quoted in the *Adi Granth*, was himself a chamar, and when chamars entered the Sikh fold, they made him—the "humble Ravidas, imbued with love to Ram"—their own patron saint. They made of him, in fact, the founder of *their* line, and often afterward called themselves Ramdasis either from Ravi Das's "love to Ram" or out of regard for the fourth guru, Ram Das, who may himself have been the first to admit leather-workers in Ravi Das's name. Some aheris (fowlers, hunters) of Bikaner, Jind and Patiala were converted, as were such other folk, also, as the sansi (who went by such a name) of Lahore, Amritsar, Ludhiana, Karnal and Gujrat. Nats (cf. natkhat, a knave), bazigar, lohar, kuṃhar, and others joined the convert-ranks—e.g., magicians, jugglers, iron-workers, potters, and the like. Some of the [Hindu] Kalal caste of distillers (kalal or kalar, "distiller") joined and took the name of Ahluwalia (cf. p. 235, above—ahl is Arabic for "people" of the same house or religion) and became the ruling family in Kapurthala, with no change in their hereditary occupation. They rather prospered under British regulation, and acquiring through wealth and political prestige social standing of great eminence, despite their humble origin. Other converts may not have fared so well, but all improved their standing.

There were indeed many dregs, much sheer social sediment, in early Sikh society. Consider further, for example, the sansis and other kindred stocks in the neighborhood of

Amritsar and Lahore, especially. They may have been aboriginals, may have been called "sansis" from their doubtful character or because they prompted fear ("sansi" is a term with some such meaning). They hunted and trapped wild animals and indulged in petty thieving. They were on every score outside the pale of Hinduism, and, for that matter, outside Islam, because they would not pronounce the kalima or "confession" or abjure forbidden foods, including pork. They carelessly ate *any* flesh, whether of pigs, cows, sheep, goats or deer, but relished most the flesh of the full-grown boar, especially if its meat was "kept" for several days, and the jackal's flesh when it was fat; and they have been known to eat even the flesh of an alligator carcass. They were fond of country liquor and of tobacco, a propensity which made them objectionable in the one instance to the Moslems and in the other instance to the Sikhs—to the Singhs and the Akalis, in particular. Nevertheless their conversion to Sikhism brought about in them some change of life and character. They often took to settled agriculture and a life of honest toil, although some of their personal habits were not in exceptionally bad odor religiously among the Sikhs. Their kind, in fact, have made up a large proportion of the total Sikh community, whatever peculiar problems their membership has posed. Many miscellaneous ingredients have contended for assimilation in the total order, while the order as a whole, under its own best leadership, has submitted in its turn to loftier incentives from without—to the pressure and inspiration of education, for example, as it has affected general culture, morals and religion.

Some woof of higher quality was all the while running through the many threads of warp, if we may so designate some purely genealogical strands, such as, for example, the Bedis who claimed descent from Nanak, the Tihans who said they came from Angad, and the Bhallas, the Sodhis and the Masandis who claimed descent, respectively, from Amar

Das, Ram Das and Gobind Singh. All these were at once both old and new. There was warp and woof in the total fabric, loosely woven though it may have been. Whatever ethnic warp and genealogical woof yielded to the weaving process, the cultural aspects of Sikhism loom ever larger during the latter half of the crucial nineteenth century.

Formal education[2] in any other than a traditionally religious sense was undertaken comparatively late among the Sikhs. In fact, Sikhs themselves had during their earlier years no specific educational tradition of their own beyond what was incidental to the transmission of their scriptures. They had shared somewhat in the common Indian tradition of the guru, but had made their own peculiar use of it. That is, whereas gurus were numerous among the Hindus, being the usual agents in the transmission of the simpler elements in the common culture, gurus among the Sikhs were very few, ideally only one—one at a time, that is—and his office was more religiously symbolical than secularly instructional; and the line of these personal gurus had ended in 1708 with the death of Gobind Singh.

When, in some instances, gurdwara schools were opened, their instruction dealt mainly with the reading of the strange Gurmukhi tongue in which the *Adi Granth* was written and with the merest rudiments of arithmetic. It was a beginning in imitation of Hindu and Moslem example, no Christian schools having yet appeared, but only tardily comparable with the pathshalas of the Hindus and the Moslem madrasas. The former gave such instruction in arithmetic as was required in accounting, taught the reading and inter-

[2] Cf. *A General Report on the Administration of the Punjab* for the years 1848-50 and 1850-51, *Educational Records*, pt. II (ed. J. A. Richey, Calcutta, 1922); Administration Reports (of the Panjab) of 1849-50, 1859-60; E. D. Lucas, *Economic Life of a Punjab Village*. For more recent details see M. L. Darling's *The Punjab Peasant* (London, 1925), *Rusticus loquitur* (New York, 1930) and *Wisdom and Waste* (New York, 1934).

pretation of vernacular literature (Hindi, Hindustani, or some other language) and the writing of the Londa or bhasha, "vernacular," script. The madrasas, also, gave instruction in reading, writing and arithmetic, and in the Koran and other Moslem literature, in particular. In none of these schools, however, was any physical or natural science taught. Their primary and almost sole concern was religious education, and any moral guidance, for example, was incidental to it. Hinduism itself had only an ill-defined branch literature of ethics, and among Moslems ethics was a department of canon law or proper custom with its prescriptions and its proscriptions. Among the Hindus and the Moslems were very few, if any, personal exemplars, moral patterns. At least, in neither religion could be found a line of persons such as the Sikhs now had in their line of gurus to whom they attributed not only reverence, ritual purity and immortality, but virtue also as expressed in brotherhood and loyalty. Every faithful Sikh shared in what came to be established as the essence of the Guruship from Nanak through the line to Gobind Singh, then by transposition to the *Granth* and finally with yet more spiritual precision in Akal Sat Nam. There was a lack, however, among the Sikhs of any instruction in the theory and practice of service among the brothers in the faith—not that it was present in the other households. The venture of the Sewapanthis (sewa, "service") in the days of Gobindji was accidental and its field too indiscriminate.

The Sikhs were noticed in the earliest program of education undertaken by the Government, and shared gradually more and more in the benefits of the policy pursued after the Mutiny was over. The first *Administration Report* of the Panjab province (1849-1850) mentions "schools of three descriptions, namely, those resorted to by Hindoos, Mussulman and Seikhs, respectively," and remarks that "at the Seikh school the *Granth* in Goormukhi, or the repository of

MAIN BUILDING ON THE 500-ACRE SITE OF THE KHALSA COLLEGE OF AMRITSAR, SEEN FROM THE GRAND TRUNK ROAD

INTERIOR OF THE NANAK NIRANKARI GURDWARA, JABALPUR, CENTRAL PROVINCES

the faith taught by Nanuck and Guroo Govind, is read." It refers, also, to a decision by the Government to found in "Umritsur a school partaking of a collegiate character"—something not soon accomplished, as may be gathered from a report in 1859-1860 that "there are no colleges or collegiate schools in the Punjab." The school which meanwhile was opened in Amritsar, together with three others elsewhere in the Panjab, was only a "district" (zillah, zil'a) school of lower than collegiate grade, one which merely taught "up to the university standard." Nor was a university (the Panjab University) established until 1882. This district school at Amritsar stood close to "the sacred Tank and Temple" of the Sikhs, but only "one-fifth of the whole number" of those enrolled were Sikhs, and these were mostly Jats in the "Goormukhee" department. The preponderance of its enrolment was probably Moslem, for Moslems at the time were "in possession of the field" (the Panjab) in matters educational. The general returns from the Panjab for 1857 showed "a very large preponderance of Muhammadan boys at school, with many Hindus attending some of the Moslem institutions, in order to learn Arabic or Persian."

Up to 1854 the Government of India's educational policy had exhibited great diversities of aim and method. The *Educational Despatch* of that year declared the need of "a properly articulated scheme of education from the primary school to the university." Previously, under Lord Macaulay's baneful influence[3] classical education through the medium of the English tongue had been in force, with unbalanced emphasis upon "university" training, and with the expectation that thereby useless and pernicious elements in Hindu and Islamic culture would be eliminated! Now vernacular and primary education were to be encouraged. Grants-in-aid would be made to schools, missionary or otherwise, and to

[3] Cf. R. Muir, *The Making of British India*, pp. 298-301.

volunteer bodies whose aim was education, and some provision would be made for schools among the villages and for scientific education—in the manner attempted in the Agra province from 1843-1853.

This "despatch" of 1854 was purely educational and wholly secular, and in no wise designed to further one religion and attack the others, although all religions might benefit therefrom—which led some Christians to observe that it was indeed ill-calculated to promote their faith. Its ideals, however, were in harmony with many social changes of the times: the slave trade had been suppressed in Britain, sati and thagi in India had been legally abolished. An act had been passed in 1850, valid for the whole of *British* India, which legally conserved for all those who broke caste or changed religions their peculiar rights in property, and in 1856 the passage of another act would legalize in British India the remarriage of Hindu widows. This "despatch," therefore, being in accord with such reform, was bound to have effects upon religion. Someone remarked, with reference to the total impact of imperial extension, that "the British government was by its nature, its ideas, its western outlook, bound to give a series of shocks to the world of India." In the Panjab these shocks were milder than elsewhere in India, and the educational department was able to supervise a swiftly, smoothly growing establishment. Its direction was first entrusted to "covenanted" and military servants, but after 1859 appointments were usually made to this department from among the educators. After 1882 the whole provincial program was in operation, and at its head was the Panjab University at Lahore to control and supervise the whole by means of a stated course of study with centrally devised examinations usually taken at affiliated local colleges with which lower schools were themselves affiliated. Sikhs, for example, soon found it possible to have certain accredited institutions of their own affiliated with the total plan, whereby their own men could be trained for their own leadership and for government positions.

Sikhs were well placed also in relation to female education, when this provision under government auspices was made in 1854. There had been previously Hindu, Moslem and Sikh schools for females "in all parts of the Panjab," according to the *Report* of 1849-1850, but they were not recognized as a part of the Indian educational system, nor did the government extend aid to any of them—or even to those which the Christian Church established. The first school for females under Panjab Government tuition was opened at Rawalpindi in December 1856. Female education had been even until then "almost unknown in other parts of India," that is, outside the Panjab. The Sikhs took unusual advantage of this new opportunity for the education of their women and contributed more pupils in proportion to their total numbers than any other faith. Women had in Sikhism from the time of Gobind Singh, at least, a status comparable with that of men. Gobind's own wife, it may be recalled, took part in the formation of the Khalsa and threw patase, "sweets," into the baptismal bowl of amrit, at the first initiation ceremony, in order that the Khalsa and its orders might be sweetened. Women as well as men received baptism (pahul), nor did the faith prescribe different duties (dharma) for the different sexes. Women worshiped with the men in the temples and gurdwaras, nor ever wore the veil. The absence of the veil may have been in itself, however, some indication of the initially low level of culture of the Sikh recruits (neither Hindu nor Moslem women of the *lower* classes have worn the veil nor have observed seclusion), but its absence afforded Sikhs a speedier avenue to education, and in the central Panjab area their women were by the end of the nineteenth century as well educated as Christian women and both were better off than Hindu and Moslem women.

This freedom among the women of the Sikhs is exhibited in the very form of marriage, in which women's rights were publicly acknowledged. Women were not betrothed as infants nor married till maturity—among the Singhs, especially. In fact the Singhs observed since the early days a form of marriage which other Indians, the Hindus and the Moslems, in particular, thought irregular, but which expressed in its own way the genius of the new religion with its own communalism. This Anand form of marriage came to be recognized by the Panjab Government in 1909, not thereby becoming incumbent upon all Sikhs, but to that extent, at least, constituting an official recognition of the rites of a "third," distinct, indigenous religion, and providing some further "uplift" in women's social status. This Anand form included a previous "engagement" celebrated by the girl's own parents who invited kinsfolk of the bridegroom-to-be—but not himself—to gather at their home and in the presence of a copy of the *Adi Granth* (with a granthi present, if convenient) to share sweetmeats and plan the wedding.

The Government in no sense prescribed the rite—such prescription would have been counted interference with religion—but the recognition dignified the rite whose details the Sikhs themselves administered. Nor was there any uniform, official service for all Sikhs. They might vary the details as they saw fit and yet have it counted legal, if only it was performed as Anand marriage in the manner of the Sikhs' own custom. A granthi has usually officiated, although any Sikh may serve as chairman of the ceremony, the central item of which is the use of the Anand hymn which seeks and confers blessing on the bridal pair. All types of Sikhs employ the rite, including rajas, sirdars, jagirdars, military officers, peasants, members of the professions, descendants of the gurus and members of the several panths—it may be a simple, inexpensive exercise in strict accord with any fundamental tenets of the faith. Sikhs are still at liberty, however, to practice other legal forms of marriage, if they choose.

The marriage question played of itself an extraordinarily effective part in the operation of the common consciousness, and the recognition of the Anand rite in 1909 modified considerably the previously prevailing official ruling that Sikhs as a people came generally for all legal purposes within the operation of the common Hindu law. Sikhs thus became in the eyes of the law either Hindus or non-Hindus—or, perhaps *both* Hindus and non-Hindus! Yet their legal status, even so, was scarcely different from that of a certain man who by the ruling of a British court in India in 1909 was judged to have married his "deceased wife's sister" contrary to the church's law, thereby becoming at one and the same time both a Christian and a non-Christian! In fact, Sikhs were Sikhs as much as ever, although marriage among them had ceased to be a matter of Panjabi law alone or of Hindu precedent. The Anand rite was current below the Sutlej and elsewhere among Sikhs throughout the world.

This essentially distinct community, as it had actually come to be, numbered by 1901 a remarkable total of four and one-quarter millions. There were then in the Panjab alone at least two millions and the rest lived mostly in the British United Provinces (of Oudh and Rohilkhand) and Bihar, in the independent states of Patiala, Kapurthala, Hydarabad-Deccan, and Kashmir, and in the Northwest Frontier. The total for 1901 should have been still larger, had all Sikhs then been accurately classified as such. Some had been carelessly returned as "Hindus," whether on the ground of lack of ethnical distinction, or because their social and religious practices were mixed, or yet because some enumerators were merely arbitrary. Some Udasis, for example, may actually have claimed to be Hindus. And some Sikhs were classified as "animists" for want of more specific data. With all their common consciousness, there was, nevertheless, among some of them a marked indifference. No great leader had moved recently among them, nor had any occasions of unusual importance prompted a communal demonstration, thus making them conscious of distinction from other groups, nor had any major party arisen among them to challenge the attention of the whole. Such factors, however, were destined to appear in the present century.

Meanwhile there appeared in the Sikhs' own neighborhood a *fifth* religion in the form of Ahmadiyyat, or "the true Islam"! The Sikhs had come in the first instance with a message to Hindus and Moslems, and now at last, with its headquarters at Qadian, not far eastward from Amritsar, had come an order, a qualified Islamic movement, with a special message *to the Sikhs*, as the founder himself said. The founder of the Ahmadiyyat was a certain Ghulam Ahmad Khan who took the title Mirza, "gentleman or lord," who devoted himself after 1860 to reformation in religion. The Mirza testified that Nanak the Sikh was "an embodiment of divine mercy for the Hindus, the last avatara, as it were, of the Hindu religion, who tried hard to purge the hearts of Hindus of the great hatred which they entertained against Islam," that whereas Nanak had come to bring about a union between Hindus and Moslems, neither of these religions had given him a satisfactory hearing, and Hindus had finally rejected him because "he admitted the truth of the religion of Islam." The Mirza Ahmad, himself a Moslem, thus made Nanak out a Moslem!

Ahmad claimed to know about Nanak and Nanak's mission through immediate, divine revelation, which was confirmed for him through his discovery of the very chola, "cloak," which Nanak wore and which was in turn worn by his immediate successors. It bore distinctive marks and letters, Ahmad said, in testimony of the final coming of the messianic "Ahmad" who would make Islam the dominant religion, and it had been preserved throughout the troubled, intervening years against the time of *his* own arrival—this on Ahmad's part a partisan, provincial and somewhat commonplace technique. But he, a "true" Moslem, would employ, said he, only peaceful methods to make Islam triumphant; he was the promised mahdi in whom the whole world, in fact, would be spiritually blessed. He notified the Sikhs, accordingly, that he had "discovered" by revelation this relic of Guru Nanak hidden under many cloths at a spot in the village of Dera Baba Nanak, where it would be found, if they would go and search with him (cf. Joseph Smith, the Mormon, and his peep-stones in Hill Cumorah, in New York State). They made their visit on a day in 1895 and found the garment—with Koranic verses inscribed on it which bore testimony to the divine Unity and refuted all false, non-Islamic doctrines! Had Ahmad really known of the Sikh's own tradition of a "mango-colored jacket" or "the blue garb of a Moslem" which Nanak wore on his pilgrimage to Mecca? It required more than that, however, for Ahmad to affect the Sikhs, for there were in their tradition such other items, also, as the tilak-mark on Nanak's forehead and his rosary of bones!

Nevertheless, the Ahmadiyyat made some headway and still persists. Ahmad came originally from Qadian, a village in the Gurdaspur district, in a tract once assigned by the Mughal emperor Babur to its occupants, and he claimed descent from Babur, whence his Mughal title, Mirza. He actually had scant personal regard for Sikhs, his family's fortunes having varied at their hands, and he was accustomed to declare that Sikh rule had been marked by "complete anarchy and bloodshed," and that the people ruled had been "plunged into unspeakable misery." He doubtless thought he saw in time a peculiar opportunity in his area for a new religion, although he was only eight or ten years old during the Sikh wars with Britain.

Security and credit were at their lowest ebb in the Panjab

in 1849. The Sikhs had collected taxes before the crops were harvested, and this threw the zamindar, "proprietor and cultivator," into the money-lenders' hands, from whom he had to borrow to pay the state. The land itself had little value as security, and to the zamindar's embarrassment he was compelled to be personally liable. The cultivator and his dependents were usually in penury, while "the fruits of the earth were almost entirely absorbed in maintaining the state and its officers in plenty." Ahmad used to say that the British brought "peace and tranquillity, but above all, religious liberty" and checked "the plundering career of those marauders"—meaning Sikhs. He may not have noticed that *after* the British came indebtedness assumed another form and actually increased—because the land came to have value as security for loans! Mortgages, such as were almost unheard of in the Khalsa days, appeared in every village; the twenty-three mortgages, for example, in Amritsar in 1865 increased to seven hundred and ninety-eight in 1880, debt following fast upon the heels of credit!

Mirza Ahmad's motive, however, was itself neither economic nor political. He would devote himself to the purification of Islam and to the conversion to Islam of all non-Moslems! His father had been loyal to the British in the Mutiny and Ahmad himself once served awhile under the British deputy-commissioner at Sialkot. In his missionary effort with the Sikhs he included in his propaganda a bi-monthly periodical called *Nur*, or "Light." He and his successors made almost no impression on the Sikhs, least of all upon the Singhs who were as ready to resist Islam in peace as they had been when fighting Moslems. Ahmad's "proofs" (barahin) of his mission began to appear in 1880 and by 1890 his movement, in its turn, had assumed distinctive form, when he announced himself the expected mahdi, the medium of final revelation to those of all religions, including especially Moslem, Christian, Sikh, Parsi, Jain and Hindu. Thus came a fifth religion upon the northern scene.

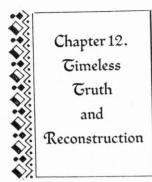

# Chapter 12. Timeless Truth and Reconstruction

WHO are the Sikhs within the present century, we may now begin to ask, and what at last has Sikhism come to be? What is it and what are its adherents in relation to the whole of India? And what, if anything, beyond this is Sikhism in the reconstruction of the Eastern world? Continued education by multiplying agencies, unusual political contingencies with their international codes, effectual alterations in the socio-religious attitudes of Indians, internal ecclesiastical adjustments with certain moral implications and world-disturbances in which the Sikhs have had a share—all these things have lately greatly modified the lives of Sikhs.

It is too soon to pass a final judgment on what precisely education is accomplishing among the Sikhs, how it is affecting the essence of the Sikh's religion and his fundamental morals, but changes have occurred and are occurring, as educational advantages have multiplied. The Sikh peasant, for example, has a fundamental interest in his daily bread, and as a result of scientific rural education has sometimes come to think that crops and religion are not causally connected—that fertility and a bumper crop are not to be induced by magic rites alone. It was discovered in 1930 that in a certain central Panjab village where two hundred and seventy-eight adult Sikhs then lived, only eleven of them prayed each day, and *they* prayed while at their work and not in the gurdwara. Ten others, also, said they prayed occasionally, for example, on Anwas, the "first" day of the month, and at Puranmashi, the time of the "full moon." Only a very few observed any formal "morning" or "evening" prayers.

Perhaps industry and thrift are themselves counted part of their religion by the better Sikhs. The stock whence come the pakka Sikhs has always been industrious and frugal. They have had good soil to work in, for the Panjab is the richest part of India. The Amritsar Sikh, for instance, is unsurpassed at cultivation, he eats well and works accordingly, in the manner of his proverb,

> Khawe ser kamave sher, khawe pa kamave sawah,

or

> "He who eats two pounds daily works like a lion,
> Who eats eight ounces works like ashes."

Nor have the Sikhs abandoned their religion—it has rather benefited from their thrift. The temples and the gurdwaras are amply subsidized, and often hold expensive copies of the *Adi Granth*. Sikhs have insisted that "hunger does not make the devotee" and have been ready to affirm that a full stomach does not itself prevent devotion. They may be willing, therefore, to receive instruction and still retain their faith.

Some Sikhs have indeed been critical of education, perhaps because it seems to indicate an unwholesome transition from former ways and an unwelcome contrast. An alumnus of the Khalsa College in Amritsar, the Sikhs' premier higher institution, who was living in 1934 in the village of Nowshera, himself using a modern Meston plow and raising high-grade cotton, cane and wheat, remarked that school made a boy "weak" where the army made him strong, that education up to "Middle Pass" might be good, but beyond that it tended to alienate him from his village. He had noticed that boys who went away to high school and college seldom came back home to stay. Another Khalsa College man, the proprietor of a village near Amritsar, said to the author in 1937 that although education might make a boy "weak" at first, agriculture would restore him, if he would resume it afterward. This kind of criticism can be readily appraised. It may be judged in the light of the comparative educational backwardness of the community as a whole, and may be weighed as a natural increment of a period of transition.

Education is not compulsory, but Government provides primary technical instruction, free to all villagers, and there are many gurdwara and Christian mission schools among the villages. Some indisposition toward their use must yet be overcome. For example, a primary school has run for fifty years in the village of Bakna Kalan, nine miles from Amritsar, and never more than sixty per cent of the boys have attended it, nor has literacy been achieved by more than one-third of the village males. The general trend among the Sikhs is, however, favorable; they have taken at least as much advantage of the schools as Hindus have taken and vastly more than Moslems have. They have long had some middle and high schools of their own, and their Khalsa College is an accredited branch of the Panjab University. A second Khalsa College has been opened in Bombay. A strong and influential missionary college, conservative of Sikh tradition, has functioned in Amritsar, training students for the propagation of the faith.

The Khalsa College of Amritsar is itself a symbol of genuine educational advancement, affording liberal and scientific training, with keen regard for the still unfinished task of Sikh reform. It operates its own department of research into the history of the Sikhs and their relations with other groups in modern India.[1] It has conducted daily prayers in its own gurdwara, has recognized the principal events of the annual religious calendar and has admitted to its student-body men of other faiths. Its recent president,

[1] Reference has been made already to the office and work of Ganda Singh, Teja Singh and others; the former, however, belonging to the *missionary* college.

Bhai Jodh Singh, is probably the Sikhs' most eminent theologian. He is the author of *Gurmati Nirnay*, the best work in systematic theology which Sikhs have yet produced, exhibiting an acquaintance with western scientists and theologians as well as with Sikh leaders of thought and action (cf. pp. 311 f., below).

Not education alone, but political contingencies, also, together with the need of internal administrative changes, have virtually transformed the Sikh community. The question of gurdwara ownership and management gave rise to serious agitation following the First World War. It was a question mooted first among Akalis, among whom, in turn, the agitation was begun. The Government itself played the ultimately decisive role in the settlement and the entire Sikh community gratefully accepted the results. The Akalis, it may be recalled, first appeared in the days of Gobind Singh, but they ran a dubious race until the time of World War I. A century ago (in 1846) an alien observer[2] said this about them:

> Ukalees are a race of religious fanatics, Taruntara [*i.e.*, Tarn Taran] their chief city. The Ukalee is a wild-looking character, displaying in his countenance a mixture of cunning and cruelty; those two propensities accordingly are the leading impulses of his life.
>
> Ukalees are ostensibly beggars, but differ from this race as found in other parts of India, in their extreme insolence and independence. To the sight, even of an European, they have a strong antipathy, and never fail to load him with abuse.
>
> Ranjeet[3] has done much toward reducing this race to some degree of order; and though the task is a difficult one, they have even been trained as soldiers, retaining, however, their own peculiar arms and dress.

They were greatly stimulated by the war, having made little progress before its time. They were not then (1914) numerous, but they soon became an important factor in Panjabi

[2] W. L. McGregor in his *History of the Sikhs*, London, 1846.

[3] Maharaja Ranjit Singh (d. June 27, 1839).

life. They were still "fanatics" and furnished most of the Sikhs enlisting in the army. Being, unlike other Sikhs, opposed to drink, they provided a glaring contrast in the British forces, of whose European constituents a contemporary observed that "a mouthful of rum was sufficient to quench their thirst more effectually, perhaps, than a gallon of water." And the same observer noticed that the Sikh was "paralyzed when he could not procure water." So much, for the moment, for the character of the Akalis.

There were about three hundred gurdwaras in charge of their own various mahants, and some of these establishments were heavily endowed, bequests having been made by pious Sikhs who stipulated that the funds should be used in perpetuation of the faith and in gurdwara exercises, thus following the example of the gurus and of benefactors of the temples at Amritsar and Tarn Taran. There were public kitchens of the Sikhs in many villages, and residential quarters, also, including accommodation for the mahants. All these centers, including the various properties, belonged in theory and in the mind of Government to the Sikh community at large, their administration being delegated to the mahants as trustees, the mahants being recognized as secular officials, not necessarily as granthis or gyanis, who presumably had themselves adopted a religio-ascetic career. But some of the mahants were known to be immoral men, and many of them lived at ease, sharing the public funds freely with personally agreeable associates. Some of these officials had managed to acquire an actual legal title to their shrines, when Government introduced into the Panjab a provision for free-hold estates independent of religion, and some of those who thus acquired such possession passed on their estates to appointees of their own.

Gurdwara ritual was often carelessly performed, matching the frequent indifference of Sikh communicants. Here and there Hindu elements were introduced, including pictures with Hindu mythological scenes adorning the walls, and images of Hindu deities beside the *Granth* itself. If any conscientious Sikh objected to all or any of this carelessness and adulteration—or to other phases of actual gurdwara management—his sole recourse, if he so chose, was a civil suit at law, with every prospect that the courts themselves would give no satisfaction, because the law had given opportunity for vested interests, assuming that custom had sanctioned this semi-private management. Many intelligent and faithful Sikhs were resentful of these legal processes which they little understood, and the English were often unaware of the essential issues of procedure, thinking it expedient to apply their own law to the case, regardless of special tenets of the Sikhs or other Indians.

Sikhs finally undertook some action of their own, not entirely without reference to issues likewise troubling all of India. World War I was over and martial law had been suspended and any agitation on the part of the people was the civil law's concern. The Sikhs first organized a provisional panchayat—which failed to function. Then in 1920—perhaps on the advice of Mr. Gandhi[4]—the Shiromani Gurudwara Parbandhak, "Committee of Shrine Management," was established and undertook to "take over" all the shrines, including the central Darbar Sahib itself—sometimes, regrettably, acting in a rather autocratic manner. On one occasion the committee met serious opposition which forced the issues into wider notice. It called upon the mahant, a member of the order of Udasis, of the gurdwara at Nankana, Nanak's birthplace, to reform conditions at his shrine or else to hand it over to the "Shrine" committee. He declined

[4] *Cf.* M. K. Gandhi, *Young India* (New York, 1927) *in loco;* R. E. Parry, *The Sikhs of the Punjab* (London, 1923); *The Indian Social Reformer* (magazine); *Notes on Political India* (ed. Sir John Cumming, 1932), etc.

compliance and took measures to defend himself, employing, contrary to Udasi pacifism, certain mercenaries.

Nankana became the scene of tragedy and a name to be remembered not so much in connection with the birth of peaceful Nanak as with the play of jealous greed and kindred lower motives such as have often sullied the history of religious reformation. Back in the 1880's this shrine was in the jungle thirty miles from the nearest railway station and a place of pilgrimage once a year on Nanak's birthday for a mere handful of faithful pilgrims, several hundred at the most. The mahant there lived on pilgrim fees augmented by the variable produce of several thousand dry or jungly acres which Government had assigned him. By 1917, however, the dry region had become a fertile plain watered from a government canal and productive of abundant crops (the first Panjab canal had been opened near Amritsar in 1861 and an extensive irrigation system had been gradually installed). A new line of railway then ran through the former jungle, and pilgrims came in by the tens of thousands (the first rails in the Panjab were laid in 1861 between Amritsar and Lahore). A prosperous settlement had sprung up and the lonely shrine with its uncertain living was now a large and rich foundation—owning tax-free lands—whose occupancy and succession were the mahant's own prerogatives.

The Nankana episode[5] is hard to analyze. It is clear that the Shrine committee wisely desired reformation and a change of management, and certain legal implications are obscure. Also, what seems to be religious zeal may sometimes cover baser motives. The blame for what took place that day in February 1921 was never finally assessed. There was—under Gandhi's influence, for one reason—a common wish among the Sikhs for an amicable adjustment of the

[5] Cf. W. R. Smith, *Nationalism and Reform in India* (New Haven, 1938), pp. 321-330; S. Zimand, *Living India* (New York, 1928), pp. 230-243.

matter. Certain other shrines had been quietly acquired. Perhaps the Nankana mahant was himself the most to blame. A rumor was abroad that he was an evil-liver, that he had a Moslem mistress. It was, however, more than rumor that he defied the Shrine committee and took precautions to defend his shrine by force of arms—after he had made a vain appeal to Government to intercede, to grant police protection. He reinforced the gurdwara's outer walls and loopholed the inner walls, laid in a good supply of arms and ammunition and placed his mercenaries—Moslem Pathans and some ex-army Sikhs—strategically in waiting. Then on a given morning the Akali Sikhs appeared—with committee sanction, or merely on their own? And just what was their motive? They professed to come for worship, and perhaps they did actually come for a satyagraha (passive, "truth-compelling") demonstration. There may have been at the same time other than Akalis in the band—some jatha or "lawless" gang may have accompanied them, and the jathas, at least, were not at that time instruments of satyagraha!

The visitors were admitted to the sanctuary and upon their entrance they gave the customary shout, Satt Shri Akal, "truth, honor, God," when almost on the instant, on signal from the mahant, the outer gates were closed and the company faced the fire of the gunmen from their several points of vantage. Most of the band were killed or mortally wounded—within a brief half-hour one hundred and thirty-one in all were dead—and steps were taken right away to cremate with lime and fire the bodies heaped in a pile in the outer courtyard.

The episode appeared to be a ghastly outrage deserving not only Sikh, but public and government, attention. The Sikhs themselves responded first with bands of avengers bearing down on Nankana, until Government was forced to interfere by drafting and dispatching thither large contingents of soldiers and police. The mahant and his accomplices were arrested, prosecuted, and had judgment of death passed on them—a sentence afterward commuted on the ground of self-defense to transportation to the Andamans for life. In the end the Akalis occupied Nankana. And thereafter the work of the Committee gained momentum with community support. On November 17, 1922, the reformation was officially approved by Government by the passage of the "Gurdwara and Shrine Management Act," which provided, to the satisfaction of the Sikhs in general but not of all Akalis, a Sikh Board of Control patterned somewhat after, or at least coinciding with, the Khalsa Sikh ideal. The Akalis who dissented from this arrangement continued for a while a campaign of their own which became so obviously political that they were bound to clash at last with Government. It was a case of politics returning once again among the Sikhs—with Akalis as the agents—at a time when the whole of India had begun to feel politically uneasy, when anti-British and pro-Congress demonstrations multiplied. But the moral tone of things among the Sikhs was meanwhile much improved. Sikhism as religion had actually undergone reform and was better qualified to cope with a round of circumstances and with its own intention—which together were to test its solidarity yet further.

From the 1920's on, many Indians and the Sikhs themselves had numerous occasions to qualify and to explain just what is meant by "Sikh." Peculiar circumstances and their shifting combinations raised the question and confused the issue. The occasions included political events, governmental regulations and the administration of the laws of suffrage, marriage and electoral representation, and changes in communal consciousness itself—and included even the operation of the census. There had been occasions of complaint in the taking of the census, for example, and with even greater accuracy of method Sikhs were no longer to be enumerated and classified by merely counting heads at the gurdwaras or at their houses, or by compiling lists of members of the misls and the panths. There were shades of opinion among them and public acts of theirs to take account of which were less regular than mere figures on a dial. In the whole of India the very process of political development, not to mention social change, was working in its own peculiar way, and this alone was sufficient to make a stricter definition yet of "Sikhs" and "Sikhism" a grave issue, whether as items of internal consciousness or as relationships with Hindus, Moslems, Christians, Ahmadiyyas, or any other folk. "Contitutional reform" alone was creating new attitudes on the part of different groups, with the Sikhs as much concerned in it as any. Sectarianism and partisanship in religion are always interesting phenomena, but doubly so, when they become also political!

The Satyagraha movement which Gandhi and others were promoting, and which first and last has had so great an effect on politics in modern India, raised some questions of identity among the Sikhs as they participated in it. On the face of it there was something at once contradictory in satyagraha for Sikhs—for Singhs and Akali Sikhs, at least—yet many Sikhs shared in it as a political expediency. There were Sikhs in the "Vykom" episode,[6] for instance, which was largely social, but somewhat political. It was an incident in the campaign against "untouchability," which provided an impressive test. The depressed classes (so-called "out-castes" or panchamas, "fifth" castes) in South India (Vykom is in the independent Hindu state of Travancore) had organized a Justice Party in opposition to the brahmans and were seeking the legal right of access to wells, roads and temples from which custom and Hindu social ostracism had debarred

[6] *Cf.* Gandhi's *Young India, in loco; The Indian Social Reformer;* C. F. Andrews, *Mahatma Gandhi's Ideas* (New York, 1930), p. 177, etc.

them. They adopted the method of satyagraha and undertook passive resistance by picketing the proscribed roadway—a convenient way they dared not take from home to market—which passed the brahman temple, and although police arrested and displaced them, they kept the depleted ranks continuously refilled, even though it meant picketing in waters that rose waist-high—for the rains were on. The final outcome was a compromise whereby another convenient road at a safe distance from brahman homes and from the brahman temple was opened to the untouchables. A young Syrian Christian, by the way, had led the demonstration and all India had watched it, Gandhi, in particular; and although Sikhs had taken part, Gandhi's periodical *Young India* of May 1924, included them among merely the "non-Hindu friends of the Hindu reformers."

This was taken by some to mean that Gandhi had classified Sikhs with Moslems, Christians and other non-Hindus, and, accordingly, a Panjabi friend[7] of his wrote to him to say that the Akalis were "more or less enraged" at being thus classified with their enemies—that whereas one group of them would disclaim any Hindu connection, others among them would still conserve it, and that several prominent members of the Sikh Gurdwara Protection Committee were actually members of the Hindu Sabha, or Association, also. This "friend" added that if Sikhs were wanting control of their own gurdwaras, their objective was but similar to what the Aryas (Arya Samaj), Brahmos (Brahma Samaj) and other Hindu orders wanted which were not quite orthodox. To which Mr. Gandhi replied in the columns of *Young India*, disclaiming any intention of calling Sikhs "*non*-Hindus" and saying that they are "a part of the Hindu community, the *Granth Saheb* is filled with the Hindu spirit and the Hindu legends, and millions of Hindus believe in

[7] *Young India*, p. 829.

Guru Nanak." He acknowledged that he had met some Sikhs who held themselves distinct from Hindus, but intimated that he would be pleased "to find that the separatist tendency is confined to only a very few Sikhs and that the general body regard themselves as Hindus." Gandhi is not here entering into an analysis of the historical relation of Sikhism and Hinduism, although he might indeed have classed Sikhs with Jains and Buddhists who represented, he said, "mighty reforms in Hinduism." He is speaking more as a Hindu *politician.* He reminded Sikhs that by their share at Vykom they had recognized essentially Hindu satyagraha, a means of reform within the range of orthodoxy. When, however, Gandhi learned that the Sikhs had established a free kitchen of their own at Vykom, in which to test untouchability, he reproved them for this intrusion, for their want of consideration, as he put it, for "the self-respect" of people who were neither starving nor in want and could have been adequately cared for locally! Perhaps Gandhi did not understand, after all, the real significance of the free kitchen in Sikh history! But Vykom settled nothing, least of all for Sikhs, and when in 1926 Gandhi made a tour among the Sikhs in their native Panjabi habitat and perceived there their strength and solidarity, he "promised never again to refer to them as Hindus"! Did he then see something in Sikh communalism which he as a keen politician might approve as an aid to *his* program of reform?

In 1896 a Hindu scholar[8] of Bengal had practically predicted the disappearance of the Sikhs as such. He published a study of "Hindu Castes and Sects" in which he made some comments on them. At some distance from the Panjab, he thought the Sikh "looked more like a Moslem than a Hindu," the mark of distinction being "the iron ring" worn by the Sikh, and he judged Sikhism to be "a mixture of Hinduism and Mahommedanism," and even, "Mahommed-

[8] J. N. Bhattacharya, *Hindu Castes and Sects* (Calcutta, 1896).

anism minus circumcision and cow-killing, and plus faith in the Gurus." He had the impression that "under British rule it is fast losing its vitality and drifting toward amalgamation with the Hindu faith properly so-called"; and he prophesied that "in the course of a few more generations it is likely to be superseded by one of those forms of Vaishnavism which alone have the best chance of success among a subject nation in times of profound and undisturbed peace." These inept remarks merely tell us how little was really known of Sikhism in some parts of India as late as 1896. Only thirty years after the Bengali's book was published Gandhi and many more Hindus besides knew more intimately of Sikh strength and solidarity. The Bengali did not foresee the invigoration of the Sikhs rather than their drifting into dissolution.

Still another episode, that of Jaito, of 1924, the year of Vykom, must be analyzed with reference to communal consciousness among the Sikhs and their relations with other groups, notably with Government. "Jaito" occurred on February 21, 1924, in the Sikh state of Nabha, one of the "Panjab States" south of Ludhiana, on the very anniversary of "Nankana." A jatha, or "company," of Akalis about five hundred strong had set out from Amritsar bound for Jaito, gathering associates en route, for purposes of worship, as they said, at the local shrine where certain relics of Nanak were preserved. This pilgrimage disturbed the Nabha state officials who feared so large and vigorous a body, and they took the precaution of halting the jatha at the border of the town, where they gave the pilgrims permission to proceed in groups of fifty only and on condition that only one group at a time would be present at the shrine. The Akalis would not agree to this, for worship, it then appeared, was not their only object—and Jaito became symbolic of a complicated scene.

Some of the jatha had been active in the contest over the

control of the gurdwaras and had been personally connected, for example, with the disturbance over the mahant at Guru ka Bagh, outside Amritsar. They were among those who had continued—who *have* continued, we might say—the agitation after the passage in the autumn of 1922 of the first Gurdwara Act, and with whose motives other than gurdwara interests solely had commingled. The agitation came to connote satyagraha or civil disobedience, and even to allow at times for intimidation and sheer lawlessness. The descent upon Nabha connoted something *Sikh*, since Nabha, a protected native state, was itself within the Sikh tradition, and some of the jatha members, moreover, had been among the "eighty thousand" Sikhs who had seen service among the British forces in the First World War.

However, there was politics of some sort in the venture, whether a desire to rehabilitate the Khalsa, or to express opposition to all government less than Indian autonomy. An eye-witness[9] has given this account of the participants and of the episode as such:

> . . . They were in great part rustics, but many trades and professions were represented. About noon the jatha started, marching like a regiment to war—as the Sikhs had marched in the British campaigns in Asia and on the western front in Europe. They had flags, a band, a separate kitchen and a small ambulance corps, but they had no arms. Every face was lit with the fire of religious devotion, and their continual shouts of "Satt Shri Akal" were like the murmur of an approaching storm. Five flags were borne in front and *Guru Granth Sahib* was carried on a palaquin in the middle.
>
> . . . The British administrator explained that if the jatha did not comply with his order, he would be compelled to open fire. The jatha kept on toward the shrine. . . . The firing was in regular volley. The crowds rushed away, the jatha advanced. Ordered under arrest, they submitted cheerfully. With heads erect they marched to the local prison, while their wounded and dead were deposited in nearby places.

[9] S. Zimand, *Living India*, pp. 239f.

. . . During the firing only three Akalis left the ranks, after they were wounded. The rest stood their ground. They kept their vows of non-violence under fire.

Estimates of the number killed vary from seventeen to twenty-one, and of those wounded, from thirty-one to thirty-three. At Nankana the dead alone numbered a hundred and thirty-one, slain by the mahant's mercenary guard. At Jaito, soldiers of the British Army opened fire. And Jaito was otherwise, also, wholly different from Nankana—unless indeed both incidents were somehow on the part of Sikhs examples of devotion! Jaito was not merely an incident in the gurdwara conflict among the Sikhs, and it continued beyond the 21st of February. A second jatha was formed and bore down on Jaito—and submitted to arrest. Every two weeks a new band got under way jathewar, "in a body," and was arrested, until fourteen thousand participants in this pacific demonstration had been arrested and imprisoned up to May in 1925. It was an heroic, if not fanatical, performance which greatly aroused many of the Sikhs' fellow-countrymen. Gandhi[10] and many other Hindus saw fit to acclaim the demonstration as one of Sikh devotion, asserting that the jathas were in reality shahidi jathas, "bands of witnesses," of the faith who only wanted to exercise their right of worship. He claimed that they were intent on performing their akhand-path, or "endless lesson" (continuous, that is) —an opinion arrived at ex *post facto*, doubtless, from his observation of the repeated waves of demonstration. There is no evidence that a succeeding jatha carried on the reading from the *Granth* from the point at which its predecessor had arrived! We do know, however, that these Akalis were demanding for themselves (in contrast with Diwanis, for example) complete control of all gurdwaras and gurdwara property, while advocating ostensibly a "central body" of

[10] *Cf. Young India*, pp. 832-835, 352, etc.

control, and that they sought the right of every Sikh (again the Akali, in particular?) to wear a kirpan, sword, of any size.

It is difficult to say with certitude who made the most of such events, the Akalis (and other Sikhs, also) or the growing number of Indian swarajists, "self-rulers," throughout India. These latter called upon all reformers to give the Sikhs "their moral support" in this matter of "a deeply *religious* question" (the italics are the author's)[11] and the All-India Congress Committee (which was and has been mostly Hindu) commended the Sikhs for their "amazing self-sacrifice undergone in the prosecution of the defense of their religious rights."[12] The Government, at least, understood "religion" in this case to mean politics, being severely blamed by many non-Sikh, vernacular newspapers for allowing such demonstrations to take place, but appointed a commission to inquire into the whole matter. As one result of its report a second and final Gurdwara Act, the "Sikh Gurdwaras and Shrines Act," was passed by the Panjab Government, under whose provisions *all* the mahants were dispossessed, subject to proper financial compensation, and all religious properties were placed under Sikh community control, with the centrality and the primacy of the *Granth Sahib* duly and appropriately recognized.

Through a persistent change of circumstance, including experiments in constitutional reform, Sikhism was in process of becoming what might be termed a "constituency." Events themselves were defining it beyond the meaning of mere consciousness-of-kind which had heretofore prevailed, and the term may serve to represent the Sikhs hereafter on the wider stage of politics as such. It does not represent merely religious unity or a transformed ecclesiastical order, for Sikhism has continued to be varied and

[11] Perhaps "religion" was often, at least, some cloak for *politics*.
[12] *Young India*, p. 352.

inclusive of variety, even as other *constituent* communities of India—for example, the Islamic and the Christian. Nor does the term necessarily represent what Sikhism might have become amidst changing circumstances under its own initiative. Perhaps it is some compulsion from without which molded such compactness. And it does not mean that Sikhism always will be such, for India has yet to pass through further reformation which must affect every considerable community within her borders. But for purposes of *government* Sikh self-consciousness comes to be distinctly set apart from that of "Muslim," "Christian," "Hindu" and the other religious communities which acquire responsibility for the exercise of suffrage. It may readily be granted, therefore, that herein lies *peculiar* unity, religion and politics among the Sikhs coming to offer one another some visible and tangible support.

These immediately preceding observations have had in mind a final estimate of what the Sikhs have come to be while India is yet a "subject" nation within the British Commonwealth, a people not yet fully tempered or organized for independence. The Sikhs have not had one single view with reference to this outcome—nor has any other one "constituency" been thus united. Sikhs still have their parties no one of which, not even the Akalis, has displayed a consistent attitude toward Indian independence. Some individuals, as in the Jaito demonstration, have been opposed to current governmental regulation, whether of the native state or Britain. Some have worked in and for the Indian National Congress in one form or another of its varied anti-British agitation, and some have shared in the work of the Hindu Mahasabha, a more conservative association of substantial Indian progressives. Few, if any, have identified themselves, at any rate, with the theory and activities of Pakistan, the Moslem League's indefinite proposal of an independent state in northwest India, because Sikhs might be included in it; and they have no desire to be ruled again by Moslems. Nor is it probable that Sikhs may once again have a jurisdiction of their own, the administrative control of a section of the Panjab, although there is precedent in India for minority administration—in Hydarabad-Deccan, for example, with its Hindu population under Moslem dynastic minority control. There is, of course, a lingering hope with some that the Khalsa may be restored, but it should be remembered that the Khalsa was originally established by force of arms, an accomplishment scarcely desirable again. The only warrant for a restoration of the Khalsa would be superior cultural, intellectual and political ability on the part of Sikhs, a status still merely in prospect, except in a very few localities where educational advance is most pronounced. If some Sikhs have opposed the British raj itself in a few of its administrative measures, many other Sikhs have expressed the view that their community has benefited greatly under it.

Sikhs *are* Indians and will continue to be such. They will link their own estate with the welfare of the whole of India, and toward this larger end they will take account of their own peculiar assets, insisting on these values in any further transformation of their status, both in ecclesiastical and political affairs. This has come to be the prevailing state of mind among the nearly four millions of Sikhs in the Panjab alone, and this is reflected among their kinsmen of the faith elsewhere. The census of 1931 was more accurate and discriminating, as we learned above, than that of 1901, for instance, and showed a grand total of 4,335,000, including—outside the Panjab—46,000 in the United Provinces (Oudh and Rohilkhand), 42,500 in the Northwest Frontier Province, 21,000 in the Bombay Presidency, 11,000 in the Central Provinces, and smaller groups in southern India. The census of 1941 gives a record "by communities" (whatever this may mean), whereas "at the past censuses the distribution was by religions."[13] There is some recognition, therefore, of a certain transformation in the composition of the body politic. According to this new "communal" census there is now a grand total of 5,691,447 Sikhs, including—outside the Panjab—232,445 in the United Provinces, 58,000 in the Northwest Frontier Province, 8,000 in the Bombay Presidency (a marked decrease), 15,000 in the Central Provinces and 16,000 in Bengal—with 1,500,000 altogether in the various Indian States alone (e.g., Patiala, Nabha and Jind).

Sikhs have been considered since 1918, at least—in the Montagu-Chelmsford Report, whose reforms were instituted in 1919—a "responsible" community "resting on an effective sense of the common interest, a bond compounded of race, religion and language." Since 1921 they have had communal representation in the legislative assemblies. Sikhs of the Panjab, in accordance with the findings of the post-World War I Round Table Conference, were awarded 18.3 per cent of the seats in the Legislative Council, although they constituted only 13 per cent of the total provincial population. They themselves, however, claimed thirty per cent of the seats, because of their literacy, their activity in public life and their communal history! And on such grounds they claimed one-third of all the seats in the Panjab cabinet. In 1932, when there were altogether in the Panjab legislature 175 elective seats, the three million Sikhs had 32 of these seats assigned to them, in comparison with 68 assigned to the thirteen and one-third million Moslems and 57 to the six and one-third million Hindus. In the same year another sort of political recognition, also, was attained on merit—a distinguished Sikh sat in the Council, in Britain, of the Secretary of State for India. The prestige of the Sikhs has risen steadily of late, quite in contrast with any former prediction of their dissolution.

[13] i.e., religious *constituencies* (q.v.).

Three major phases of theory and practice have been emphasized by Sikhs themselves during the last three or four decades in their demonstrations of communal consciousness: 1) It has sometimes been said that Sikhism arose in the first instance as a protest against the socio-religious system of the Hindus and that such a need continues to exist among them; 2) It has been pointed out at times that Sikhism developed largely from the unforeseen need of self-defense against the Moslems; and 3) It is well known that Sikhs had recourse to arms in former, rougher times only when they were greatly outnumbered by their active enemies. Almost no mention has recently been made of any original or continuing motive of religious reconciliation! And Sikhs are themselves generally quite unwilling to loose themselves in such a consummation. Resistance has been a fairly constant mood, whether against Hindu forces which would bring about their re-absorption into Hinduism, or against British courts and policies which might endanger their communal rights, and even against measures of "home rule" which might subject them in effect to Moslem overlordship. All of this has augmented their "constituent" or "responsible" communalism.

It remains for Sikhs themselves to detect and to manifest in these days that *spirit* which may have been preserved among them, in whose strength and by whose leavening their cultural processes may continue. This spirit has survived four centuries already with benefit to others and profit to itself in its various relationships with other major faiths. One man once spoke in exposition of this spirit where nowadays six millions are, if they choose to be, its advocates, from among whom conspicuous men arise to speak for them or to plead with them, on behalf of their ideal. Nanak's own gift was almost altogether theological, with some incidental rules of conduct—as we have seen already in detail—to which additions have been made from time to time—

which also we have noticed—and this initial gift is valued still as something worthy in the present crisis. Consider, for example, its exposition in 1936 by Bhai Jodh Singh of the Khalsa College in Amritsar in his *Gurmati Nirnay*.[14] In this Gurmukhi volume he has expounded what he takes to be essential Sikh theology, whose details might seem to be a digest of antecedent sources for the purpose of special education among his people and for their confirmation in traditions of the faith.

In Jodh Singh's exposition God is real, he is the One—Ongkar, say the Sikhs—in whose unity all Sikhs share and in whom all divergencies of doctrine may meet in full accord. Sikhs, to be sure, *have* recognized, he has observed, immanent (?) "manifestations" of the One, even as Hindus have often done and as Christians sometimes do. But to all Sikhs the One is essentially Akal Purakh, the Immortal Absolute, of whose mind the world itself is constituted, men's own minds being portions of it. Feelings of reverence and exhibitions of devotion on the part of men are in themselves virtual glimpses of the divine reality which nonetheless transcends the utmost limits of men's own minds—men have only a working knowledge of the otherwise unknown. The one God may be known as Sat, the True, for he *is* the truth unaffected by the falsities of, for instance, fear and enmity, and unaffected also by particularities and partialities of time and space, and by the accidents of birth and caste. God is real, of course, and not abstract, and yet he may not be represented by an image, for after all he is Sat Nam, True Name, beyond anything concrete and more than any object

[14] Bhai Jodh Singh, *Gurmati Nirnay*, or Exposition of the Sikh Religion (Lahore, Feb. 1936), with an introduction by Bhai Vir Singh, 1932. This work is, in the main, a collection under special topics, chiefly theological and psychological, of scattered passages from Sikh Scriptures, with comparative use of extracts from Eddington's *Nature of the Physical World*, Tansley's *New Psychology*, and other works.

which may bear a name—and more than all objects put together which bear names. He is the symbol of one whole and universal Truth. He is Sat Guru, true teacher and true guide, with whom men commune, from whom they as Sikhs may "learn" of the life and conduct incumbent upon them.

Men are Sat Nam's creatures, says Jodh Singh. In fact, creation came about—the creation of all life and every form, that is,—by God's own hukm, "bidding," even as Guru Nanak himself has said, "The whole creation is strung on the thread of his bidding." Men live as particles of the whole creation, and although they die at last, they are immortal and will be judged for their careers, punished or rewarded in the everlasting future in accordance with their present *deeds* (and "deeds" is a very comprehensive term, including words and thoughts). God's hukm has established right and wrong, as also it has established men's means of knowing these. Yet men must hearken to some inner bidding, again God's own provision, and shun the evil and perform the good. There is some human freedom by God's order, and man is made responsible. He is a moral creature and in this life men's "state and rank depend upon their deeds" and not upon the accident of birth. Caste is accidental, of no consequence in itself, for "of the same clay is the whole creation molded." If men are "baptized" as disciples of Sat Nam they not only sit together on a common platform and eat and drink from common vessels; they actually put food into the mouths of others and take it from others into their own mouths and pass a common cup of drink from lip to lip. This is the real pahul of fraternity.

Then Jodh Singh passes to another note, the destruction of egoism as the ideal of human action. The true Sikh will realize that he acts not by his own independent will, but by the prompting of, and in accord with, the will of God, Sat Guru, who is one with his disciples, high or low. He will remember that the guru has said, "Forget yourself, for selfishness is the cause of misery." He will know that the goal of union with Akal Purakh is reached through self-sacrifice and love. He must lose his individuality (shakhsiat), but not his being—for there is no ultimate annihilation (annihilation would be an utterly intolerable theory to Sikhs!). Karma and "transmigration" operate (as indeed they do with all Indian indigenous religion), but karma becomes more and more inoperative as the disciple puts reliance on, finds shelter in, the Guru, and as his mind gains harmony with truth. Man's reliance is on God, and not on any prophet, apostle, messiah, avatar or incarnation. But what is the immortal end of mortal man? Sikh theology seems not to posit heaven, as Jodh Singh sees it. There is, at least, no heaven in a Semitic sense, but there is God and man is saved to God, even as, unable to save himself, he is saved *by* God. And there is something communal in the hereafter, for a man is not saved alone, indeed cannot be saved alone, but saved only with others.

The *Gurmati Nirnay* is not an exhaustive treatise, although it is something more than topical. Quotations in it from the sources are abundant, sometimes extensive, but they serve as illustration and confirmation of a sincere and competent attempt to provide a simple, systematic exposition. Perhaps there are inconsistencies, for his theology—as it reflects his own thought—is eastern, Indian, the product of the soil and of circumstance which generally are Hindu, but with no little emphasis on several real distinctions not only between Sikhs and Hindus, but even also between Sikhs and Sikhs. At least, there are distinctions between keshdari Khalsa Sikhs (Singhs) and Hindus. His thought tends toward an idealistic Absolute, but his One God is far more than mere *idea*. As with Nanak, so also with Jodh Singh, God is real, personal and the *only* One.

There are other items, also, in the *Gurmati Nirnay* "exposition." Not only is essential Sikhism monotheistic, the

Sikh himself is properly monogamous. Any seclusion on woman's part is relative and should conform with general custom and the dictates of propriety, altering as custom alters. There is little reason for the "veil" and none at all for sati. The true Sikh avoids the use of opium, hemp and all intoxicants, and eats no meat, whether beef or pork. The proscription of meat has not come by "revelation" or any divine ordinance, but only from a due regard for the Hindu and the Moslem! Jodh Singh would give assent to the injunction posted in the Sikh gurdwara in Mussoorie against "smoking, betel-chewing, drinking, shaving and the eating of meat or eggs" upon the premises. There is, of course, no place for "caste." War at times is necessary, if for the retention of just gains, and for the winning of legitimate objectives when peaceful measures fail. This reflects, we see, the spirit of Arjun and Gobind Singh against the remoter background of Guru Nanak. War is incidental, if resorted to at all, to the welfare of the constituent community. Politics likewise is incidental to this end and rightfully exists in a mutual condition of creative harmony with religion, in both of which morality is basic as an exhibition of the will of God. The state *can* give expression to essential Sikh theology and morals—and this in full accord with the ascetic ways of Nanak. All of which falls duly in the round of karma and transmigration which reconciles it all within one process. Jodh Singh himself has studied Islam and Christianity and has felt their influence, but not to the elimination of all Indian fundamentals—he remains an *Indian.* Converts themselves to Christianity or to Islam in India tend to retain the Indian theory of karma, in particular. It, together with its concomitant theory of transmigration, represents the best thoroughgoing explanation of human life and destiny, with its incidentals and its fruits, which India of and by herself throughout many centuries and millenniums could contemplate. Sikhism has not discovered of itself a better explanation.

As Guru Arjun's *Sukhmani*, or Psalm of Peace, itself recounts, man may be a monarch or a beggar, of high estate or low, a vocal scholar or a mute and ignorant ascetic, and yet *always*

> His soul wanders as directed through life's mazes,
> As man or moth, as worm or elephant;
> He plays the varied roles assigned him,
> And dances to the tune of God the Master.

Nevertheless, karma and transmigration may become inoperative ultimately, as Guru Arjun, echoing the bhagats, likewise contemplates, saying,

> There comes a moment in the life of man
> When he realizes union with the Holy,
> From whence there is no coming back for him;
> He lives thereafter in the company of God.[15]

These two principles of action and cessation occupy the very center of Jodh Singh's "exposition of theology"—and he may be allowed to speak for many thoughtful Sikhs, besides. The morals he expounds are often casual, as with so many other Indians, or else incidental to theology, with no other *philosophy* of their own—although many prohibitions of the Sikhs are plainly spoken by him. There is room and need among the Sikhs for a thorough exposition of the discipline of ethics as it bears upon the urgent problems facing them as members of a changing social order.

For purposes of comparison with Jodh Singh's exposition, as well as for the sake of another consistent point of view derived from a somewhat similar use of sources, we may profitably include, in spite of its uncritical and somewhat

[15] These two sets of lines are adapted from Teja Singh's *The Psalm of Peace* (Oxford, 1938), pp. 56-57. *Cf.* Santokh Singh, *The Jewel of Peace* (Amritsar, 1924).

naive quality, "the doctrine of the Sikh Gurus" as summarized previously by Khazan Singh:[16]

1. The fatherhood of God and the universal brotherhood of man.
2. No worship but of the Lord God.
3. The hair and body to be kept intact [although no judgment is given with reference to the paring of the nails]. No circumcision nor boring of the ear or nose to be allowed.
4. Complete surrender of self to God.
5. To work in good faith as a duty imposed by God, giving up fear for a bad result and abandoning hope of reward for a good result.

Khazan Singh goes on to say that "if the religion of the whole world consists of the following items, then all dissensions with reference to religion will cease:

> Belief in the one true God; rejection of idolatry; rejection of the worship of intermediary agency between God and man;[17] implicit surrender of one's will to God; the practice of righteousness and rectitude; fatherhood of God, and universal brotherhood between man and man.

He urges that "these principles alone can form a catholic religion," which "even the Arabian prophet also admits"; that "then there will be no circumcision and shaving of the hair," and that "subordinate and auxiliary rites" will prove to be of scant importance. He holds such religion to be "a grand catholic religion, intended and designed for the whole world, . . . and the essence of all the scriptures, whether revealed to the Hindus, Jews, Christians, Muhammadans, or others."

Before our present study ends some further reference should be made to the character and strength of Sikhs in competition with Christianity, in competition with Christian missionary effort, in particular, as distinguished from the general "Christian" penetration of the Panjab by polit-

[16] *History and Philosophy of the Sikh Religion* (Lahore, 1914), pt. II, pp. 518-520.

[17] A rejection, however, which many Christians and many bhakta Hindus would not agree to, probably.

ical and military agencies. Facts and figures are available in sufficient numbers to serve the purpose of a comparative view, including an estimate of certain prospects. In 1931 there were 415,000 Christians among the 23½ millions of Panjabis in comparison with 3¾ million Panjabi Sikhs. The Sikhs were 15 per cent of the total population and the Christians less than 2 per cent. The Sikhs were nearly ten times as numerous as Christians. It is difficult to calculate how many Christians *had been* Sikhs, but it is highly probable that less than five thousand Sikhs had been "converted" to Christianity up to 1931. The Protestant Christian community of the Panjab amounts to about 250,000 nowadays, of whom 85,000 are communicants, and there are Roman Catholics in equal numbers. There were 505,000 Christians in the Panjab in 1941 among the 28½ millions, the Christians still constituting less than 2 per cent of the grand total, while the proportion of the Sikhs is about 20 per cent and their total now is more than ten times that of Christians. Moslems make up approximately 50 per cent and Hindus 28 per cent, a proportion which in itself lends increased significance to the Sikh position.

Although Christian missions have not made much headway among the Sikhs, these two communities, nevertheless, have much in common in the matter of recruits. They both have attracted to themselves large numbers of "untouchables." These peoples, perhaps, make up the majority in both, and constitute the surest immediate source of their increase in numbers. Christian gains among the chamars, chuhras and other depressed classes may have prevented a still greater growth in Sikhism than the recent census showed. One British mission has recruited nearly 50,000 from among them, including about 7,000 communicants. Sikhism enjoyed "mass" returns of this sort earlier. Which suggests some query about educational advance in these communities. In 1921 only 68 of every thousand Sikhs in

India were literate and in 1931 there were 91—nine per cent, roughly, of the total. Although Christian literacy was three times greater than the Sikh in 1921, it made no gain within the decade. Sikhs are at least as literate as Hindus and far more literate than Moslems. In the Panjab they are more than holding their own both in numbers and in the quality of their culture. Between 1921 and 1931, for instance, the Sikhs in *all* India increased 34 per cent and the Christians 32.5 per cent. If the figures for the Panjab differ at all from these, they would tend to show *more* progress among the Sikhs than among the Christians, for Christian gains have been made mostly in other parts of India. The gain in both communities, of course, very greatly exceeds the modest 15 per cent increase in the total Indian population—but this is hardly a just comparison, considering the great bulk and density of the total, and the prospective tendency of any smaller body to reach a saturation point in such a total.[18]

Very few, indeed, of the Christian converts from among the Sikhs were keshdari Khalsa Singhs. There have been some of these, including some who have entered "orders." There was one, however, the well-known Sadhu Sundar Singh (now long since vanished out of sight—in remote Tibet?)[19] who consented to be baptized as a Christian, but insisted on adherence to the traditional Hindu sadhu ideal and to the Sikh ideal of martyrdom, and declared it to be his purpose "never to become involved in any outward organization of human service" nor ever to become "an ordained minister of any Christian Church." He was virtually a bhagat in the name of Christ and a protestant against all

[18] One of the most intriguing problems of comparative religion, as also of progress in religious reformation, is the tracing of this very saturation point—or at least the record of proportion between the general bulk and the special sect.

[19] His death long since may be presumed.

Christian ecclesiasticism.[20] Others, including, for example, Daud Singh and Kharak Singh, have done otherwise, taking ordination and service in the Church—while continuing very properly to be Sikhs at heart. There was the earlier case, also, of the Sikh Maharaja Dalip Singh, son of Maharaja Ranjit Singh, who applied for Christian baptism, only to be refused on the ground that his motives for becoming "Christian" were "merely political and patriotic." The simple fact is worth recording here to indicate the place of motive often in the estimate and action of conversion. His father had contributed in 1835 Rs. 2,185, or about $700, toward the work of the then new American Presbyterian mission in Lahore. The contribution was accepted, although it must have been quite obviously prudential, for Ranjit's own devotion even as a "Sikh" was consistently political, and such a motive governed all his public actions. It would be unfair, however, to make too much of "motive" in inter-faith relations. That is, what may prompt conversion from one faith to another may not be always something that is *purely* religious. And certainly there are times when conversion itself is not the answer to confusion nor the solution to the problem of adjustment. This is peculiarly true when the Sikhs involved are Singhs.

As we have viewed the Sikhs in their relations with several other major faiths, we have not failed to notice, surely, something genuine and persistent among them, and also something somewhat adventitious and elastic. Elasticity is provided for and really indicated in the very name they wear. A "Sikh," we may remind ourselves, is "one who is under instruction, or is being instructed" (shiksha, "instruction" is the ancient Sanskrit noun, whence the title Sikh by personalization). Sikh*ism* is thus a *learning* process. Nanak did not use the term—if strict regard for language be ob-

[20] See C. F. Andrews, *Sadhu Sundar Singh* (New York, 1934) and F. Heiler, *Sadhu Sundar Singh* (München, 1926).

served—and had he done so, he could scarcely have given it a single meaning. It would still have remained derivative, vague, adventitious and elastic. He used few terms at all which held concrete, specific and restricted meanings, and he employed no single term which can compare with "Sikh" in its capacity to include the total sweep of his religion in relation to all other faiths—unless it was the wholly abstract Sat, or satya, "truth."

Sikhism has a mission still by reason of inherent flexibility, even though it be to lose itself in any greater, more effective whole which will, nevertheless, inevitably preserve it. Jesus, for example, used no single term inclusive of the whole round of his own teachings, and, of course, he did not use the term "Christianity." There is something in this name, however difficult it is to give it concrete and comprehensive definition, and the content must be included in the final total. There is meaning in "Hindu" also, and in "Muslim," indefinite though these titles are. Although Mohammed himself used the term "Islam" and gave it a working definition, the "House of Islam" (Daru'l-Islam) is a subsequent construction whose furnishings have varied with new needs and opportunities. Even Ahmadiyya may have a share in what could come of mutual understanding among the several faiths. No devotee need now confess that his living faith has been in vain, and *names* need not conflict and keep men separate—and also hostile, maybe—if only what they signify is comprehended, utilized. It is not a mere matter of "all roads leading to the summit," for there may be *many* summits. At least, there is no single, concrete summit which all men would or could attain.

Sikhism must reappraise itself in the light of its own history, with due regard for the fruitful vagaries of speculation among its members, and with a just appreciation of their sincere devotion. It has known how to be communal in spite of inner variations and should know from this experience and by the sheer weight of its present numbers how to act in inter-faith relations, mindful of the very gospel which the founder Nanak advocated. Within the Sikh constituency, for instance, are the quietistic, innocuous Udasis, and the activistic, militant and even fanatical Akalis. The little pilgrim band, we may recall, whom we met by way of introduction to our study, included such extremes as these. The Udasi hostel stands in Amritsar in close proximity to the Akal Takht, and they both are neighbors of the Darbar Sahib itself! These extremes may meet, have often met, in spite of intermittent controversies, and many a Sikh has found some satisfaction in what they represent—reference has been made already to comfort which a militant Singh had found at the ascetic Udasi hostel.

Nirbanji Phalhari (whom the present writer came to know in 1937) was until his recent death beyond three-score-and-ten guru of the Udasis—a blind seer, kindly, simple, celibate. They say he knew the *Adi Granth* by heart, and the whole ritual of his order. He practiced various arts, including native Ayurvedic medicine and took no fees for his advice. The *Ayurveda* is Hindu, is an appendix to the classical *Atharva Veda,* and is India's oldest authority on medicine. Its lore has been to Hindus divine revelation instructive in the use of herbs and magic, with spells for the cure of fever, dropsy, baldness, snake-bite, mania and many other human ailments. It holds also charms for love and vengeance, for prosperity in trade, for keeping cattle safe, for thwarting demons and all enemies, and for the expiation of "offenses, failures, stains, transgressions" and whatever else is "sin" as Hinduism sees it. The guru cured colic in his practice, and one day a layman came to him for a charm against an evil spirit that was troubling his nephew—cures in absentia are possible. His niece had previously been cured of a similar delusion. The Sikh guru need not hesitate to use these Hindu assets. Nirbanji had use for them and for methods of his own, also, with many types of Sikhs, including some keshdari Singhs, and he was a thoroughgoing Sikh in his own ascetic atmosphere, with an ochre robe as garb and several sadhus in attendance. His shrine was a gurdwara, but it contained, in addition to the normal furnishings, an image of Sri Chand, Nanak's son and the founder of the Udasi order—a peaceful contrast with Gobind's sword that rests in the sanctuary of the nearby Akal Takht. But has not Christianity had its Quakers and also its Crusaders, and Islam its conquering Ghazis and its peaceful sufis and spiritual Ahmadiyyas! And Hinduism has its fighting Rajputs and its pacifistic satyagrahis.

A certain highly-educated Sikh (known to this author) has made explicit reference to the many values in the *varied* Sikh tradition, which are still of use in any further mission: Nanak's novelty (he denied that Nanak copied anyone), Amar Das's castelessness, Ram Das's service, Arjun's devotion (martyrdom), Har Gobind's politics and Gobind Singhji's "third religion" (tisra panth kino pardani, "we have established a third panth," said Gobind). The very gurdwara (in Mussoorie) where this account was given is a house of prayer where, although certain prohibitions are observed within the premises, those of *any* faith—and either sex—are welcome, including Moslems. And such, in theory at least, are the Sikh gurdwaras anywhere. There is a tacit implication that Hindus, Christians, Moslems all might *lose and find* themselves, as Sikhs might, also, if they should come to know and practice truth alone.

There is opportunity now to begin to summarize our study, remembering that we have in mind comparisons and some appraisal of respective values, and that the geographic field is *India* in which the values must be tested. Three faiths, the Christian, the Moslem (including Ahmadiyya) and the Sikh are "missionary," operating in a subtle, preponderantly *Hindu* habitat, each standing in dire need of overcoming many inner defects and all enduring under some compulsion to resist a certain *suction*, if we may call it such, of the quicksands—in a figure—which we give the name of Hinduism. All four of them have interacted somewhat freely, as due perspective shows. Sikhism has yielded a great deal to Hinduism, a little to Christianity and almost nothing to Islam, with a net result to itself of *gain*. Christianity with its present enrolment of eight millions came early into India—sixteen centuries ago—and often afterwards, and last of all in force.[21] Moslems brought Islam to India a thousand years ago and the faith there amounts to eighty-five or ninety millions of adherents—possessed of great momentum. Sikhs have six millions for their four centuries of history. But Hindus number still two hundred and sixty-five millions who represent an order with three or four millennia of history. If India is not Hindu in the end, neither will she be Moslem or Christian or yet Sikh. The activities of these faiths constitute convincing evidence that India in the end will not be any one of these, namely, Hindu, Moslem, Sikh or Christian, *as we have known them* heretofore. And there is something constant in the changing figures of these faiths that seems to prove that whatever India in the end may be, she will *not* be irreligious! There are two sources of the Ganges, the Hindu legend says, one is in the sky and one among the mountains. The distillation of the sky flows clear enough at high Himalayan Gangotri, and continues fairly clear throughout the mountains, but runs muddy through the plains and especially by the sacred city of Benares (Kashi)—and yet the faithful, nevertheless, can trace the river to its sources. So it is with all the theories and practices of men themselves, the Indian might say, and so it is, also, with all phenomena, with the forms and doctrines of religion as men have molded them—but the faithful can ultimately find the sources!

[21] In connection, that is, with European penetration in force.

Whatever the Sikh disciples of timeless truth may seek and do hereafter, they must reckon with the whole of India whose constituent elements are not only numerous but typical, so typical, in fact, that the future of religion can be adequately studied within her borders. Among the items which the Sikhs have first to reckon with are certain *writings*, for example, the *Adi Granth*, the *Granth* of Gobind, the Koran, the Shastras and the Bible. Their spiritual leaders, in particular, would profit greatly from a thorough study of the history of these scriptures and of their character as channels of the truth. The *Adi Granth* itself is sufficiently composite to provide for critical analysis, giving immediate occasion for comparative analyses of the most important scriptures of the other faiths. It took heavy toll of other sources, and Sikhs have thought on such account that it must be in itself complete—although they have not applied to it a theory of revelation. It would not be difficult, therefore, for them to learn that no sacred scripture *as such* has been verbally inspired, that God had never chosen to speak to all men through *one* and only one linguistic medium—Hebrew, Aramaic, Arabic, Vedic, Latin, Hindustani or Gurmukhi. Had God spoken finally in Hebrew, for example, one might logically contend that all peoples should learn Hebrew as the avenue to final truth. The practical handicap in this is readily apparent. It is better to understand that God has spoken in any language most appropriate to his hearers![22] If then it is apparent that men find difficulty in exchanging among themselves by many tongues the fruits of revelation, they may come to know at last that the words of *any* tongue are symbols and that fuller reality lies without them and be-

[22] The language of the heart or of the mind is often cited by ardent devotees of the great religions, e.g., al-Ghazali's doctrine of the heart (*qalb*), in which "heart" is, rather, the seat of the mind, that which perceives and knows.

yond them and must be sought and found by surer means also.

Hindus themselves have distinguished, for example, between revealed, or shruti, scripture and a larger mass which is merely the scripture of "remembrance" (shmriti), a mere body of tradition, and yet they have, nevertheless, made the freest use of commentary (bhashya) in their definition of the contents. The Moslems have counted their Koran revelation, the very "word of God" (kalam Allahi), expressed in Arabic, "the language of the angels," as they say. Nevertheless, there has developed among them a "science of Kalam" in connection with which the contents of their book are viewed in many ways according to the literalistic, rationalistic or mystical dispositions of their interpreters. Some Sikhs have been aware of this. And the Koran has been *translated*—even as also the Bible and the *Adi Granth* have been. Some Sikhs have come to know of different views of the Christian Bible. The Protestants who have worked among Panjabi Sikhs, especially, have held consistently to their denominational tradition that the Bible was revealed and is "the word of God"—meaning by implication, if not explicitly, the *only* revelation. And they have sought to displace with it the *Adi Granth*, the Koran and the Shastras, creating ultimately some extreme confusion in the minds of those in process of religious education. This confusion cannot readily, but must finally, be resolved, and the resolution should be fairly easy to the Sikhs, who have been disinclined to think that any one scripture as such may properly *displace* another.[23] Nanak said "The perfect shall obtain a

[23] A distinction, of course, should be made between scripture and religion, as also between religions and religion—*i.e.*, true religion (panth ka dharm, the religion of the Khalsa). Sikhs hold that Nanak came to "establish true religion, removing the false" (dharm chalavo sach da devo kur uthae), when religions were struggling with one another, with no advantage to any one, and that

sight of God," and Jesus said, "Blessed are the pure in heart, for they shall see God." Any or all scripture might be incidental to this end, by whatever name a devotee is known.

Personalities as well as writings are involved in the quest of truth. Sikhs have a succession of their own, as have Christians, Hindus, and Moslems, and all of them are channels in the process. Sikhs have been quite familiar with such human agencies as gurus, brahmans, sufis, sadhus, sannyasis, bhagats, mullas, clergy, saints and their own granthis. An assembly of them all might yield convincing lessons in morals and religion and indicate what, after all, is the *ideal* life of man. There would be opportunity not only to compare the modes of dress and personal appearance, but personal habits, also, with reference to hemp, liquor and tobacco,[24] for example, and essential attitudes toward social problems, the economic order, and war and peace. Is there

by his doctrine of "the word" ("kalma," from Arabic "kalam") Koran and Veda, for instance, are only different names for one perfect source, even as there is one God, True Name. Cf. Khazan Singh, II, pp. 352-353, 654f.

[24] Nanak, of course, did not include tobacco and smoking among the sins whose doers would meet with severe punishment at last from God, namely, drinking intoxicants (sharab, zahuri, hemp-ferment, etc.), eating hemp, opium, poppy, lust-exciting medicines, meats roasted on skewers, etc. It appears that tobacco was unknown in India in Nanak's time, and that it entered into use in India during the reign of King James I (who declared smoking to be "loathsome to the eye, hateful to the nose, harmful to the brain, dangerous to the lungs" and likened "the black, stinking fumes" to "the horrible Stygian smoke of the bottomless pit").

It was Guru Gobind Singh who put the ban on smoking among Sikhs (the Singhs) and considered abstinence from intoxicants to be in keeping with the true spirit of the Khalsa. For members of the Khalsa any use of tobacco was as offensive as cutting the hair, cohabiting with a Moslem woman, and eating the flesh of animals improperly slain (the flesh might be eaten only if the animal was slain with a single stroke given with the invocation, "Sat Shri Akal"; this is jhatka slaughter).

justly a Christian, a Hindu, a Moslem and a Sikh interpretation of the ideal life, all of which practically are mutually exclusive? The bare necessity of facing these issues thus is in itself enlightening, but a sober conference on them would be inevitably constructive. Sikhs have known also of items more highly theological, such as the Vishnuite Hindu avataras, the Koranic kalam and the Christian incarnation, and should have occasion to compare them through acquaintance with the long history of the Logos theory of the Christian with respect to Christ, the Moslem theory of Kalam with reference to the Koran, and the Hindu view that Rama and Krishna and other personalities have manifested God. They could with all the greater understanding fit their gurus and their *Granth* into the total proper view of things, whereby they might appreciate all the more the presence of the *Granth as Guru*.

And the comparative values of temples, gurdwaras, mosques and churches, together with the forms of worship in them, demand consideration. Each of these types has its own history and its peculiar meaning which should be examined once again as men's minds are bent upon a truer worship. No single type of building might be agreed upon and utilized, but some deeper insight into true devotion might be the lesson to the devotee as he worships henceforth at his own peculiar shrine. Rites and ceremonies might take on truer meaning, and scriptures and personalities be better understood, each in its own peculiar setting. Nanak, Mohammed and Jesus, for example, had in mind a very *minimum* of ritual observance, and not one of them had for his own use the sacred canon which his followers have used! Hindu ritual has been very various and never simply uniform. The followers of all these faiths might come to understand that forms and furnishings and buildings (which they may be intent on using) are, like the words of scripture, *symbols*—as also are the very *names* of God.[25] This is the way of conservation, continuity and progress by immediate and realistic means, instead of provincial competition against limited historic backgrounds and in the light of abstract theory and dogma.

Three salutary principles emerge when we take account of all the facts we know and put the Sikhs in just perspective, and these are what we might designate as *recognition, devotion* and *cooperation.* They are by no means mutually exclusive, but rather operate in constructive harmony—if *men,* that is, will use them so, for human brotherhood under God is the goal they move toward, and they recognize as "missionary" the other faiths they work with.

One household of faith and all its members may very

[25] Sikhs have made in theory, at least, a great deal of all this. They ascribe to Nanak such words as these,

> Kiti lakh paikambran kite lakh autar,
> Pir, Mashaiq, Aulie, Gaus, Qutb, Salar,
> Qazi, Mufti, Maulvi, Mullan, Sadr Ulmae,
> Pandhe, Missar, Jotki . . . ,

being a list of Hindu and Moslem "prophets, avataras, saints, experts, pure ones, almsmen, princes, captains, judges, lawyers, scholars (mulla in Persian is the Arabic maulawi, both meaning the learned), premiers, monitors, guides and astronomers"—if the terms be translated seriatim—who represent mere names and passing offices, back of all of whom is the One Lord of both Hindus and Musalmans, whose Name is over all. This list is given in much the same mood as that of *Japji* 35 (*q.v.*) with its apparent multiplicity where reality is One, and where all is really subject to God's own hukm, "ordinance."

There is in this something, also, of the pantheism of the sufi and other mystics of the day, whether the distant Ibnu'l-'Arabi (whom Nanak may not himself have known) whose heart, he said, was "capable of every form:

> A cloister for the monk, a fane for idols,
> A pasture for gazelles, the votary's Ka'ba,
> The tables of the Torah, the Koran." — R. A. Nicholson, *Eastern Poetry and Prose,* p. 148; or, possibly the nearer (and familiar?) Sa'di of Shiraz whose catholicity recognized the "bounteous Giver" who nourished all mankind.

wisely recognize the existence and the rights of others, if the others indulge also in compensatory recognition. This would not necessarily validate or make conclusive any one religion or even all religions. It would assume tolerant and tolerable activity on the part of each toward the highest use of its own resources, especially for the improvement of its own condition. Hinduism need not hesitate at this provision. It has been tolerant to the point of indifferent regard of other faiths, if doctrine only was at stake and if its own judgment operated. Even in its *socio*-religious character it has indulged within itself in a certain effective form of recognition, advocating that a man make the very best of the opportunity and status to which he was born—an actual condition of ultimate adjustment in the lengthy round of life. Hinduism has *not* recognized, however, during the last two thousand years those social elements which belonged to orders other than its own. Recognition, therefore, would bring about in Hinduism some greatly needed social reformation within its own sphere of influence in connection with its attitude toward other faiths. Its recognition would be both practical and also theoretical.

Islam has recognized from the beginning *three* other faiths, the Jewish, the Christian and the Sabian, although it has assigned to them inferiority to itself. Hindus and certain others, also, were not reckoned on and Sikhs, of course, had not come into existence, but there was a principle by which they, too, might be recognized by Moslems as occupying a similarly inferior position—by the principle, that is, of qiyas, "analogy." Islam likewise has given place to subdivisions of its own and its orthodox (Sunni) mosques have been open for worship to all kinds of Moslems. It has had no socio-religious problems hinging purely on a Moslem's birth. Although Christianity has a long history of intolerance toward all non-Christian faiths and even toward subdivisions of its own, a more liberal attitude prevails today which makes easier than ever the many Christian bodies' recognition of each other and their recognition to a marked degree of the other living faiths. This does not entail the acquiescence of any man in theories and practices of another faith than his. He is still free to make comparisons and to estimate the values they disclose, and free, also, to act with reference to his membership in any faith.

There is a peculiar phase of recognition which pertains in India to Christians and to Moslems, if they recall that there their faiths are alien. Whatever Christianity and Islam have become or are becoming in the Panjab, for example, they at first were foreign. In contrast, the Hindu and the Sikh religions are indigenous, and the contrast between the native and the alien represents a valid and a vital difference. The members of the Moslem and the Christian orders may be Indian, but the Moslem prays toward distant Mecca and his very house of prayer is alien; and the sanction for the Christian rests somewhere outside of India, while his faith is more foreign to the Panjab than is Islam. Perhaps these two can never be acclimated, and their alien status may be, nevertheless, to some extent a virtue. Each has professed to be a universal faith and its extension has taken it to foreign parts. Perhaps any universal faith must be at once, therefore, both indigenous and alien! It may not be good for any faith at last to be altogether naturalized—or nationalized. An indigenous order unaffected by alien elements suffers serious limitations and in the end may hasten to decay. Hindus and Sikhs may really see this and be all the readier in consequence thereof to think well of the alien faiths, and to welcome them as incentives to their own improvement. And through their presence in the Panjab the Indians may be constantly reminded of what these faiths may still be in Ispahan, Baghdad and Mecca, and in London, Rome and Washington.

Meanwhile a second principle, that of devotion, *i.e.*, loyalty, is imperative and is of simultaneous operation with the first. In fact, it was a just condition of the first, for recognition operates among the faithful. A man must first to himself be true, duly conservative of his own inheritance and his sane conviction, if he would make comparisons and lay claim to any good in other faiths. The Moslem sense of mission to the world rests upon a prior sense of his submission to his God. The Christian likewise knows that personal devotion is the prior warrant of his own mission to the world, and he and the sincere Moslem must reconcile somehow these loyalties. And they must grant the Sikh the privilege and need of his own loyalty and in this way come to know that they have, at least, a common heritage of pain —martyrs have been numerous among them and they have a priceless heritage of suffering in the way of faith. Such manifestations and fruits of loyalty as patience in affliction and missionary zeal may not wisely be ignored when they have bred substantial character. Even the unmissionary Hindu knows the worth of patience and submission, and he has gained in varied and prolonged experience immeasurable concomitants to faith.

Devotion of the proper kind becomes ready to criticize itself and should enjoy unlimited occasion for this. Allegiance becomes more and more intelligent and discriminating as opportunities arise for mutual intimacies. In this way loyalty becomes unselfish, the only kind of loyalty which is a virtue. It looks objectively at forms and institutions, even while it cherishes the inner life of man as something fundamental in the last analysis. Jesus, Mohammed, Nanak and, for a Hindu example, Ramanuja, all emphasized the primacy of the inner life of man, and their followers who best understand the "mission" of their faiths insist that all devotees act truly—enthusiastically, sensibly and reasonably, that is—in accord with the genius of their several faiths and with due regard also for the inner merit of others' forms and institutions. The most genuine devotion to religion knows its own inherent kind and will recognize the fellowship this knowledge prompts. Unselfish loyalties must find inevitably at last some means of combination.

Such laudable devotion will induce cooperation in the meantime, not the superficial syncretism of ideas, but a common effort for the general good. Therein the mutual recognition contingent on every man's devotion to his own ideal and his effort to improve his order will germinate a *social* consciousness from which an active program comes for the improvement of the total order. Many elements indeed can be combined in such a state of things, including not only religion, but also politics and morals. The common good, in fact, requires such a combination, and the members of all the faiths as such must learn this lesson. It would allow for sects and parties (*cf.* Sikh panths and misls), for provinces and states, as well as for separate households of religion, and it would reveal the fact that morality is somehow basic both in church and state. It would emphasize in these unprecedented days the fundamental worth of morals and would anticipate the rehabilitation of religion and the social order. Hinduism, possibly, has minimized morality, and Islam has interrupted it with creed. Christianity has sometimes dogmatized not only in theology but also on good and evil. Nanak himself laid too little stress on human conduct, and Sikhs have yet to formulate a code for its true guidance. All parties might well take Sa'di's counsel soberly that it pays no one to "wag a tongue thou canst not guide."

The most immediate cooperative enterprise to yield the best results in human welfare would be to practice brotherhood. All these religions have advocated this very ideal, it being most conspicuous, perhaps, among the early Sikhs, unless the fellowship among the early Christians is a yet more conspicuous example. Moslems have been brothers *within Islam*, but Sikhs and Christians have usually denied a local limit. Hindus, probably, have been least brotherly. Sikhism itself has said, "Regard all men as equal, since God's light is contained in the heart of each." There have been many "brotherhoods" (ikhwan) in the house of Islam and many unequal peoples "by Allah's favor have become brethren" (*Koran* 3:98). Christian tradition, in its turn, urges kindly affection and brotherly love without regard for race and clan. And Hinduism has provided fellowships of devotees beyond the bounds *at last* of caste. But the practice of brotherhood among the many faiths is yet to be consistently exhibited and its fruitage nicely realized, whatever this fraternal method of devotion will lead to in the end. It must not be made to wait indefinitely on dogma; true religion cannot suffer from its exercise, nor can any one participating faith be denied thereby the just returns of its own existence. A religion will not have lived in vain, if in the full economy of God. Sikhs in particular, by making increasing use of new facilities and instruments, economic, medical and educational, may justify the dream of Nanak of man's supreme welfare in Sat Nam and confirm the confidence of subsequent disciples in Akal, thus realizing elements of "timeless" truth that are always manifest in time, which are particulars through which in an insubstantial world men may learn the truth of the eternal.

The suggestion that these three principles operate—namely, recognition, devotion and cooperation—and that they be employed, may indeed amount so far to a counsel of perfection. There is, however, ample warrant for such counsel against the background of all the facts which have now in this present study passed us in review. There are also some conclusions even more verifiable which the comparative religionist may reach through his study of the Sikhs in the relations they have had with Hindus, Moslems, Christians and the Ahmadiyyas, conclusions which also bear further upon the quest of timeless truth and indicate particularly the attitudes and activities indispensable among members of contiguous religions. They are five in number, as are the rivers of the Panjabi homeland of the Sikhs, and as the centuries are thus far in which the fortunes of the Sikhs are manifest.

1. The problems of any one historic, religious movement cannot be solved, its fortunes secured and its objectives realized, by itself alone. These ends come only in relationship with other faiths, with those especially which are contemporary and contiguous, whence the one religion may draw to its own advantage conclusions warranted by common interest.

2. No religion has ever arisen of and by itself, unless in vague and general pre-historic times when early men were ignorantly experimenting with institutions in a primitive, spontaneous atmosphere. Hinduism may indeed have had something of this sort of spontaneous beginning, according to our theoretical or even anthropological reconstruction. The other faiths are more particular and definite, Islam, especially, and Hinduism itself had become historical before the others appeared in India. No religion in historic times has lived within and of itself, especially if it has been a "missionary" faith moving into foreign regions.

3. The historic impact of a missionary religion upon any other has been fragmentary, partial and sectarian. In fact, no religion has been able to move into new associations competitively until it has gathered experience and strength in its original habitat throughout a certain length of years. The passage of time, even so, has already taken toll of the faith's originality and unity, and its subsequent extension has been usually sectarian. Time alone had altered and will always alter the quality of any creed and its practical objectives. Moslems and Christians who entered the Panjab were themselves sectarian.

4. No one religion, nor any sect of one religion, has dis-

placed or has absorbed another faith or sect, nor does it seem that it ever could accomplish this.[26] "Conversions" have occurred in the sense of transfer of a member from one religion to another, but one faith cannot convert in such a sense another faith. That is, it cannot uproot and destroy what is indigenous, and if it has become indigenous it has lost its own "ecumenicity." There is a still sounder content to conversion, a process other than substitution or annihilation, one of general alteration and mutual adjustment.

5. The history of particular conversion, including a study of the individual converts, shows amply and convincingly that the convert in becoming such has not changed radically and fundamentally, whatever sudden shock was registered, and that the *primary*, enduring effect upon him has not been his committal to an alien doctrine, or even his adoption and practice of a foreign ritual. Such results as these are incidental in the long run to a yet more immediate, compelling and even personal inducement or incentive, such as, for example, some social benefit within his old, traditional environment. Particular conversion is, after all, something essentially natural and human, and the truth and validity of this finally appears in any developing *community* of converts—communal character conforms so largely to natural locality.

These five conclusions to which our present study seems to lead us are by no means separate streams, but tributary altogether to a combination, even as the five waters of the Panjab join to make the Indus—"The Avon to the Severn flows, the Severn to the sea . . ."—or as the five centuries already of Sikh history which represent a continuous flow of time, or, even further, as the five peoples, Hindus, Moslems, Christians, Sikhs and Ahmadiyyas are all together Indian

[26] Is such the implication, at least, of the saying attributed to Nanak that "one religion can prosper only if the other is entirely removed" (ik rahe ik jai uth tab hi chale rahi)?

within a widening horizon. Yes, these peoples are all *Indian*, are children of a culture which is a long tradition to which many devotees and imitators have made their contribution. Length of years for India has so often effectually overbalanced novelty and has determined alteration. And yet these five fellowships of faith, these separate communities, have been experimental, have moreover found advantage in experiment and have learned to trust it as an instrument of further good. Nanak, Sikhs and Sikhism, in particular, have themselves brought novelty to India, and yet they move with the general trend and find increasing worth in their own movement while the culture itself of all India prospers —a process which, as a whole, whatever its extent in space and time, is essentially, as in the Sikh conception, timeless. The greatest moral lesson of the process is also something Sikhism has itself defined, namely: the triumph over self is the conquest of the universe,[27] and, Truth prevails "with blessing to the righteous and by the unrighteous man's destruction."[28]

[27] "Mani jitai jaru jitu" (*q.v.* on the title page of Khazàn Singh).

[28] "Sikh ubar asikh sangharo" —quoted by Khazan Singh, p. 657(44).

# Glossary*

Abu, father

Adhan (azan), the Moslem call to public prayer uttered from the mosque by the "crier" (muadhdhin, muezzin)

Adi, original, first, primary

Aham Brahman [asmi], I am Brahman, meaning in Hindu theo-philosophical terms, I have realized identity with the Absolute

Ahimsa (a-himsa), non-injury to any living being; a principle of Hinduism and Jainism

Ahl, people of one family or religion (or scripture)

Ahlu'l-kitab, people who hold a "book" religion

Akal, timeless, eternal

'Ali (Aly), the name in particular of a cousin of Mohammed who became also his son-in-law and the father of Mohammed's only surviving grandsons, two of whom, Hasan and Husayn, were martyrs in the eyes of Alids and Shiis

Alid, of the family of Ali

Allah, a symbol, whatever its original roots, of the God Mohammed came to know by revelation; Mohammed may have coined the word

Allahu akbar, *lit.*, Allah is greater or very great; supremely great

Amrit (amrita, a-mrita), un-dying; nectar

Anand (ananda), pleasure, delight, ease; an epithet of Akal, Sat Nam, or supreme Spirit

'Aql (aqlu), mind, intellect, reason

Arati (arta), the light waved before an idol, or the act of waving lights ritually

Ashram (asram, a-shram), non-exertion; an abode, a hermitage; or one of four periods in a brahman's life

Astik, a believer, theist (opposite of nastik, *q.v.*, one who says "there is not" a God)

Avatar (avatara, autar), a descent of deity, an "incarnation," a theory of Hinduism, in particular

Ayurveda, wisdom or prescription for long life; a work on medicine

Baisakh (Vaishakh), the Hindu 2nd month (half April, half May) in which the moon is full near Vishakha (four stars in Libra and Scorpio)

* See the Index, also, for proper nouns especially.

Baisakhi (Vaishakhi), the day of the full moon in the Hindu month Vaishakha
Baqr'Id (Baqarah'Id), "cow festival"; see 'Id
Barkat (barakat), blessing
Barsat, rain, the rainy season
Bhagat, a provincial form of bhakta, *q.v.*
Bhakta, devoted, a devotee
Bhakti, worship, devotion, religion, faith
Bhang, an intoxicant made from hemp-leaves, if used as feminine (as a masculine, breach, destruction, etc.)
Black Stone (hajaru'l-aswad), a dozen stones or fragments of stone cemented as one irregular oval about 7 inches in diameter, set in the southeast corner of the Ka'bah in Mecca

Chadr (chaddar), sheet, cloth
Chadr dalna, or chaddar-andazi, a marriage ceremony, as when a man marries a widow a sheet is thrown over both
Chakr (chakra), wheel, circle, discus
Chamar, leather-worker
Chandal (chandaliya), a sweeper
Chhatar, umbrella
Chauri (chaunri), a fly-flapper
Chauth (chautha), fourth
Chela, pupil, disciple
Chuhra, sweeper

Dagoba, a shrine for sacred relics, a tope
Dar (darun), house, habitation, as in Daru'l-harb, the scene of war
Darbar, house, court, hall of audience
Deva, a god; devi, a goddess
Dharma (dharma), religion; see index
Dhikr (zikr), remembering, a religious ceremony or act of devotion
Dhimmi (zimmi), a non-Moslem subject of a Moslem government, one in covenant relation who pays a tax
Dhoti, a cloth worn about the middle
Din (pronounced as deen), religion, as in Din-i-Ilahi; see index
Doha, a couplet, distich
Dwija (dvija), twice-born, a man of one of the three upper castes of Hindus

Faqir, poor, a mendicant
Fiqh (fiqah), knowledge, with special reference to divine law

Gaddi, throne (takht)
Gayatri, a sacred Vedic verse; see index
Gopi, milk-maid
Ghadr, treachery, rebellion
Ghadr ka waqt, "time of perfidy"
Ghazi, warrior, plunderer
Ghusl, water for bathing, bath
Grahast, a house-keeper
Grahasti, a married man
Gurmukhi, the sacred "guru tongue" of the Sikhs
Guru, a religious teacher and guide
Gyan, religious knowledge
Gyani, one who expounds religious lore

Hadith (hadis), traditions, sayings of Mohammed
Hajj, pilgrimage, especially to Mecca
Hajji, one who has made in person or by proxy the Meccan pilgrimage
Haqq (al-Haqq), fact, true, he who is true
Harb, war, battle
Hari, green, a name of the god Vishnu
Holi (Hola), a festival bearing the name
Hukm, judgment, a judicial decision, command

Ibadat, worship
Ibadat-khana, house of worship
Ibn, son
'Id, festival, e.g., 'Idu'l-Fitr at the close of Ramadan, Baqar-id (baqr 'id), cow-festival; etc.
Ik (ek), one
Ikhwan, brotherhood
Imam, leader, guide, priest
Imamat, a priestly succession
Iman, faith

Janam, birth
Janamsakhi, birth-record, life-story
Janeu, the brahmanical thread
Jap, praise, telling one's beads, saying prayers
Japmala, rosary
Jatha, band, party

Jati, birth (caste)
Jhatka, slaughter
Jihad, holy war
Jizyah (jiziya), a tax levied on dhimmis (zimmis), *q.v.*
Julaha, weaver

Kakkas, the five k's of the Singh's equipment; see index
Kalam, word
Karma (karm), action; see index
Kashf, the mystical
Kayastha, writer
Khand, portion
Khatri (kshatriya), warrior
Khilafat, caliphate
Khojah, eunuch; one of an Ismailian order
Kitab, book
Kumhar, potter

Lohar, blacksmith
Lota, a water vessel

Madhabi (mazhabi), a sweeper turned Sikh
Madrasa, school
Mahant, great, an eminent person, religious superior
Mala, wreath, necklace
Marga, road, way
Mausim, "monsoon," seasonal rains
Maya, illusion; see index
Mela, a fair, a religious gathering
Mihtar, scavenger
Misl, like; a political jurisdiction or province; see index
Muharram, a Moslem festival or celebration
Mulla, learned man, judge
Mushrik, an unbeliever (non-Moslem)

Nastik, one who denies the existence of Deity
Nat, Nath, Natt, "lord," a yogi, or possibly a knave
Nishan, mark, sign, signal, flag

Om, Onkar, Ongkar, name of God

Pagal, mad
Pahul, communion; see index
Pakka, good, true
Panchamas, fifth caste folk, outcastes
Panchayat, council of "five"
Pandit, adviser, teacher
Panth, way, sect
Parkash, famous
Patase, sweets
Path (patha), road, path, lesson
Pathshala, school
Patti, slate, sweets (patase)
Pir, old man, saint, priest
Puja, worship

Qadi (kadi, qazi), judge
Qadr, power
Qalandar (qalandara), a kind of cloth
Qalb, heart, mind
Qiblah (kibla), prayer-direction (Mecca)
Qila, fort
Qiyas, comparing, analogy
Qur'an (Koran), see index

Rebeck, a stringed instrument of music

Sabha, assembly, company
Sadhu, pious, a devotee
Salat, public prayer
Samadh, a tomb
Samaj, assembly, association
Sannyasi, one who has abandoned all worldliness, a jogi (yogi)
Sat (Sach), see index
Sati (suttee), widow-burning
Sayyid (Said), lord
Sewa, service
Shadi, marriage
Shahid, martyrdom
Shakhsiat, individuality
Shakta, Shakti, powerful, strength
Shiksha, instruction
Shirk, "association" of other power with Allah

Shraddha, faithful, memorial ceremony
Sipahi (sepoy), soldier
Sirdar (sardar), headman, chairman
Sloka, stanza
Smriti (shmriti), remembrance
Sruti (shruti), revelation

Tabut, taziah, bier, model of the mausoleum of Husayn
Tashdid, witness
Tat tvam asi, "that thou art"
Tawhid, Unity
Thag (thug), robber
Tilak, a sectarian mark on the forehead

Ummah, people

Vaisakhi (Baisakhi), a festival; see index

Wadu (wazu), ablution

Yogi (jogi), an ascetic

Zamindar, land-owner, proprietor

# Index